This Year I Sing

366 women's stories from three generations

Jean Steiner · **Mary Steiner Whelan** · **Shawn Whelan**

a-ha! communications · Minneapolis, Minnesota

Edited by Beth Wallace
Book design by Cathy Spengler
Illustrations by Morgan Brooke
CD by Ann Reed

Published by:　a-ha! communications
　　　　　　　　3141 Dupont Ave. S.
　　　　　　　　Minneapolis, MN 55408
　　　　　　　　steinerwhelan@yahoo.com
　　　　　　　　651-642-5116

Distributed by: Biblio Distribution
　　　　　　　　4720 Boston Way
　　　　　　　　Lanham, MD 20706
　　　　　　　　301-459-3366
　　　　　　　　www.bibliodistribution.com

ISBN: 0-9679925-1-6

Steiner, Jean, 1923–
This Year I Sing/ by Jean Steiner, Mary Steiner Whelan, Shawn Whelan

1. Women—stories
2. Women's studies
3. Daily readings
4. Three generations

Printed in the United States of America

To Sarah,
    With love and respect

    To Priya,
        With love and hope for the next generation

    And to Sheila Wellstone &
    Marcia Wellstone Markuson
    With gratitude

Acknowledgements

We wish to gratefully and lovingly thank some of the strong and beautiful women who inspired, shared, and helped to shape the stories in this book:

Agnes, Alice, Alyna, Amake, Amelia, Amy, Andi, Andrea, Aneesa, Angel, Angelina, Angie, Ann, Annah, Annette, Anseth, Audrey, Aurie, Babe, Barb, Barbara, Beatrice, Bernie, Beth, Betsy, Beverly, Billy, Bonnie, Brianna, Bridget, Candra, Candy, Cara, Carly, Carmen, Carol, Carolyn, Carrie, Casey, Cassie, Catherine, Cathy, Cecelia, Ceci, Celia, Cheryl, Chris, Christina, Cindy, Clare, Claudia, Colleen, Connie, Corky, Cynthia, Dale, Danielle, Dawn, De, Deborah, Delores, Denise, Diane, Dolly, Donna, Dora, Doris, Dorothy, Earline, Edna, Eileen, Elaine, Eleanor, Elizabeth, Ellen, Elvia, Elyse, Emily, Emma, Erika, Esther, Ethel, Eunice, Faith, Farah, Feliciana, Fern, Florence, Fran, Frances, Frankie, Gabriel, Gail, Gayle, Gemma, George, Georgia, Geraldine, Gert, Ginger, Ginny, Glennys, Gloria, Grace, Gretchen, Guadalupe, Hanna, Harris, Heather, Helen, Hetal, Hillary, Iben, Ingrid, Irene, Jackie, Jacqueline, Jan, Jane, Janel, Janice, Jean, Jeanette, Jeannie, Jeannine, Jennifer, Jenny, Jessica, Jill, Joan, JoAnn, Joanna, Joanne, Jocylin, Jodie, Jody, JoLene, Joy, Joyce, Judith, Judy, Julia, June, Justine, Karen, Kari, Kate, Kathleen, Kathy, Katie, Kelly, Kerri, Kerry, Kim, Kris, Kristin, Kristina, Lacresha, Lanaya, Laurel, Lauren, Laurie, Lavonne, Leona, Leticia, Lil, Lilian, Linda, Lindsay, Lisa, Lizzie, Lois, Loretta, Lorraina, Lorraine, Louise, Lourdes, Lucy, Lupe, Lyn, Lynecia, Lynn, Madeline, Maggie, Marcie,

Margaret, Marge, Margie, Margo, Marguerite, Maria, Marian, Marianne, Marilyn, Marisela, Martha, Marti, Mary, Mary Ann, Mary Jo, Mary Pat, Mary Rose, Mary Sue, Maureen, Maya, Mee, Meg, Megan, Melinda, Melissa, Melody, Mhairi, Mia, Michele, Mildred, Minaxi, Mitch, Molly, Monica, Morgan, MyCresha, Nancy, Natalie, Natosha, Nicole, Noreen, Norma, Olivia, Opal, Oprah, Pam, Paris, Pat, Patricia, Patty, Paulette, Pauline, Peg, Peggie, Peggy, Phyllis, Polly, Prisca, Priya, Rachel, Rebecca, Rhonda, Rita, Robin, Robyn, Robyne, Rochelle, Ronna, Rosa, Rosalio, Rose, Rosemary, Rosie, Roxy, Roz, Ruby, Sally, Sandra, Sandy, Sara, Sarah, Shada, Shala, Shannon, Shawn, Sheila, Shelly, Sherry, Shirley, Sophie, Stacey, Stacy, Stephanie, Sue, Susan, Susie, Suzanne, Sylvia, Takii, Tammy, Terry, Tichelle, Tiffany, Tina, Toni, Tonya, Tracy, Trish, Trisha, Tyronia, Urvi, Valeri, Vanessa, Verona, Veronica, Vicki, Violet, Virginia, Wendy, Wilhahista, Yvette, Zoe

Introduction

What would happen if one woman told the truth about her life?
The world would be split open.

• • • Muriel Rukeyser

In *This Year We Sing,* the authors—grandmother, mother, and
daughter—bridge three generations to present women's lives
in stories they have lived and stories women have told them.
In these stories, women from a broad range of backgrounds
share the feelings, beliefs, and experiences that are often hidden.
Without the masks of public or private image, others' expectations, the nice or good girl, the perfect companion or mother
or superwoman, the stories offer you the opportunity to look
at the truth of your life. To think about the power you have,
to walk with yourself proudly, to be yourself and to know that
you are not alone.

Written by three generations of women, the stories have
been marked to show you which stage of life, or which era,
they spring from.

generation born before 1942.

generation born between 1943 and 1962.

generation born after 1963.

The stories belong to you. We hope you will take joy and strength from the life experiences of other women. Play the enclosed Ann Reed CD, "This Year I Sing," often and loudly— or softly, as you choose. Write your own story in the blank pages at the end of the book. Join other women in singing along with Ann: "I'm gonna bring my life to light. Give it wings: let it all take flight. This year I sing."

This year I walk. This year I sing. This year I promise, I devote, I plan to be me. This time the bruises of insincerity, prejudice, deceit, pain rinse off my body as I drench in the reality of my power. Power vested in change. Love anchored in trust. I will search for you, the other person who satisfies your hunger for a breathable life with nibbles from your ancestors, peers, and to-bes. I see you now filled with stories. We are interwoven through our connecting glances, glances filtered by eyelashes so long the history of she rides with every blink; the history of struggle sheds with every tear; the bright, piercing light of tomorrow is shaded allowing for growth, patience, a safe haven. This year I bring to you my unwritten stories, the ones they said were not about me, but because of me. This year I listen for your voice. Sister, oh sisters, this year of all years I am looking for you.

january...

Friends are family we choose for ourselves.

· · · Edna Buchanan

She likes fishing, real fishing—big fish, large hook, bloody blood-sucking leeches fishing. She wears jeans with makeup on fancy occasions, styles her hair, drives a truck, captains a fishing boat, wears no perfume and absolutely no high heels, drinks beer, eats burgers, plays softball, listens to Van Morrison, and reads on an as-needed basis or when something strikes her fancy. She is certainly practical. She plays the field safe?

Not all the time.

She travels to places people close to her would be frightened to look at on a map. She loves folks people close to her would be frightened to read about. She challenges authority people close to her admire. She finds love in places people close to her would never venture.

She is the person I call in the middle of the night because I know she will drive her truck, not style her hair, bring a veggie burger, herbal tea and a great book at 2 a.m. Why? Because she loves wholeheartedly, never stops to judge, and remains committed with or without my presence.

She is a silent warrior, an advocate, a confidant; she is my friend and I am privileged.

Age is mind over matter. If you don't mind, it doesn't matter.

• • • Anonymous

The elevator moves upward. Six pairs of eyes fasten on lighted numbers over the doors. A silver-haired couple good-humoredly chide each other about forgetting the number of the floor where they are to get off.

They decide on the tenth floor. A pair of college-age kids, near the door, press "10" for the couple and squeeze back so they can exit. As the two leave, the young woman asks her companion, "Weren't they cute?"

"Don't you hate it when young people label people our age 'cute'?" I ask my husband when we step out one floor later.

"No. They could say worse," he answers.

"You don't really mind getting old, do you?" I say.

"Nope," he replies. "I like old."

Since you are like no other being ever created since the beginning of time, you are incomparable.

• • • Elizabeth Cady Stanton

I have the sound of her voice. Her persistence. The older I get the less doubt there is that she is my mother.

She has her grandmother's height. My exuberance. The older she gets the more she resembles her grandmother and me.

We three all have a restlessness that leads us to unknown places and scares us back into security.

And yet, we do not walk the same roads. Hear the same music. Dance the same dance.

Because we each are also unalike.

We are each incomparable.

First thoughts have tremendous energy. It is the way the mind first flashes on something. The internal censor usually squelches them, so we live in the realm of the second and third thoughts, thoughts on thought, twice and three times removed from the direct connection of the first fresh flash.
• • • Natalie Goldberg

I close my eyes. This meditation stuff lowers blood pressures, stress levels, and usually my ability to concentrate. But I will give it a shot. Hmmm. Once I get past thinking how hard it is to keep my eyelids shut, I move to bigger water. What do I see? The skeleton of the door frame, I am facing a window and the light seems to still penetrate my eyes. I think of sleep, but merely entertain and dance with the thought. Sounds encircle, shape, and brush against my fine arm hairs, tickling me. The air moves me about so wildly I stand still. I think: what if someone walked in? I lose concentration but keep my eyes closed. I wonder what animals see when they are blind. My thoughts simmer and rise to a ruthless boil. I wonder: why can't I float when it feels as though I could when I am motionless, elated, or enraged? How long can my heart beat without the supply of breath? What am I breathing? Why do people smoke? Do our body parts experience pain as we do? Would I exchange the ability to feel pleasure for the ability to not feel pain? Would some exchange pleasure for pain? Will violence end, will there truly be a day without war, guns, poverty? What would the world look like if I were to float across it in a bubble? I take that belly-sucking-in cleansing breath as instructed, squint at the light as I refocus on the present time. I am not sure what I learned but it felt good to have a mind recess and to lie on my dirty carpet, which I now need to vacuum.

Just go out there and do what you have to do.

• • • Martina Navratilova

I'm working up courage for my annual physical exam. Each year I tell myself to just go do it without getting into a state of nerves. But every year, I worry that something seriously wrong with me is going to show up. Last year when the clinic called for a second mammogram because something "questionable" appeared on the films, I panicked. Turned out to be a fold of skin or some such thing.

And last year I had to return for an ultrasound to look at a potentially serious lump. It was a harmless cyst. Each time my anxiety level shot up like a thermometer on a hot August day. How many times can I get lucky? I considered not keeping this appointment, but here I am pulling into the medical building parking ramp. Maybe I'll shake this dread if I give myself something to look forward to, like the kids who get lollipops for being brave for doctors.

I park, get out, and lock the car, take a deep breath, and walk toward the elevator, where another woman also waits. "I'll have lunch at that new coffee house," I say. "That's what I'll do." To the woman, I say, "Oops. Sorry. Didn't mean to be talking aloud."

She smiles. "It's all right. To get me here, I promised myself a jaunt across town to the Mall of America and a new pair of shoes."

Love without intimacy, she knew, was an unsung tune. It was all in your head.

• • • Lorrie Moore

The turquoise blended into the blue, which folded into the green waves. I sang him a cute love song as I danced around his beach chair. My carefully chosen purple wrap flew around my tanned thighs. The more I sang, the more loneliness emptied out of my soul.

So I sang louder. Until his eyes said, "You are making a spectacle of yourself."

I plunked down in the sand. Stroked his arm. Ordered him another Corona, with lime. I hummed to myself and thought, "I will dance my dance. Sing my song. I just have to learn to choose my next audience more carefully."

Language uses us as much as we use language.

• • • Robin Lakoff

I'm vacationing in Mexico, and my camera's not working. I find a photo supply and repair shop and stop at the counter nearest the door. A dark-eyed young girl smiles and fans her hand toward the display of film on the wall behind her. "Número?" she asks, assuming I've come to buy film.

I shake my head, say "No," and start to add "número," but the "r" refuses to roll out, clinging like peanut butter to the roof of my mouth. I hold the camera up for her to see and press down on the shutter release, which doesn't move. "Doesn't work," I say in English. She calls out, "Madre," and translates my problem into melodic Spanish.

A woman comes from a back room of the shop, takes the camera, and flips open the back cover, silencing my "No, no. I have film in there," with a smiling "Sí, sí." She adjusts the film intake and closes the camera, which responds with its Instamatic purr.

I fumble out an awkward "Gracias." While I wrestle the camera into its snug-fitting case, mother and daughter speak to one another in the language that unites them. I feel chillingly isolated as they converse. The thought comes to me that I'm experiencing a tiny taste of the fearful loneliness refugee women in my city must feel, especially when faced with the often-heard criticism: "The least they could do is learn the language."

Death and taxes and childbirth! There's never a convenient time for any of them.

• • • Margaret Mitchell

We'd put it off so many times. Until I get a job. Until we buy a house. Then our bodies didn't want it to happen. It took years for me to get pregnant. I am over forty now. We had almost given up. But today, I, we, are going to have a baby! I can't wait to tell my husband.

I make his favorite lasagna. "Smells good. On a Tuesday. What's up?"

I jump a little jump and throw my arms around his neck. "I was going to save the news for dessert. But I can't. I'm pregnant!"

A bit shocked, he pulls back, "When?"

"October 18th."

"But that's the week I go hunting every year." I drop my arms. I cry. "Sorry, honey, just kidding."

He wasn't kidding. I know his voice and face too well to believe it. But I pretend that I do. The first lie to give the baby a good life.

That was thirty years ago. Many more lies, not big ones, followed. Thirty years of absorbing the tension so that there would be peace for my children. I paid a price. Migraine headaches, anti-depressants, let my career pass me by. Was it worth it? Would I do it over again in the same way?

I don't know. There just never seemed to be a convenient time to tell the truth.

Our wedding plans please everybody as if we were fertilizing the earth and creating social luck.

• • • Marge Piercy

I have thought of this day since I was six; he, for sixteen months. We sort through the last of the invitations, returned with the dove stamp we chose, over lunch at a restaurant in town where the chair back was as soft as flannel, the food as bland as air, and the service as mean as the cliques in my sixth-grade class. This wedding, beautifully simple, my dress handmade by a friend, the tux (not really a tux, for that would be stuffy), flowers large enough to climb in and slumber, a cake (not just a cake, a layered sponge bath you could dive into and be immersed in chocolate, raspberry, and amaretto), music from the reggae club down the street. A party of all parties.

It is the morning of the day we thought would never arrive. I see my mother, his mother, our grandmothers. We kiss them and say, "Have a great day—we will think of you the entire time."

Plane tickets in hand, luggage over the back, we sweep ourselves to the romantic adventure of our dreams. "But the wedding!" you say. "The one you had planned since you were a child!"

Our response: "I was six!"

Only yourself can heal you. Only yourself can lead you.

• • • Sara Teasdale

Betty's thirty-six-year marriage ended when Craig left her for a woman fifteen years younger than Betty. She's stopped going to the church we've attended since we were kids. I want her back. She's said, "I don't need a bricks and mortar religion. Leave it alone." But I don't. Instead, I invite her to this conference on aging.

We take our seats; the presenter begins: "As years add up, we need to forgive ourselves for mistakes we've made and lean on our spirituality." Betty quickly scans his bio in the day's program—a minister who works with people healing from death or divorce.

"He's a church guy. I'm out of here," she says, snatching up her coat and striding out into the parking lot, where I have to almost run to keep up. In the car, Betty gives the key a vicious twist, and we move toward the freeway—tension riding along like a rhino, sucking up the air until I can barely breathe.

After a mile or so, I say, "All right, Betty, I did the wrong thing. You've told me to back off on this church stuff, and I promise I will, but you have to promise to let me know how I can help heal the hurt you're feeling. I'll follow your lead."

I wait.

With a misty grin, she gives my hand a squeeze, and flips on a CD. The rhino leaves, and I inhale to the sound of soft jazz.

Where there is a woman there is magic.

. . . Ntozake Shange

She tells me her stories of the power felt by women in her care. She tells me that their strength blooms with each push; with every contraction a new form of inner spirit is formed. She tells me that her role is not to count, not to order, not to worry, but to accommodate. She tells me that this is her life work. I believe her because she loves women as she breathes air. She trusts that beauty is not vain, that anger is not strewed with ill intent, that questioning authority is not purposeless rebellion. She is the mother of five women whom she birthed not in the presence of foreign doctors, multiple nurses, and illusive medical equipment, but in the presence of her own walls, her familiar smells, her husband, her home. She would like people to believe that all women have the power to do as she did. It is no mystery that so many women choose to have her in their presence when they embark upon motherhood.

It has long been my boast that I can read or eat anything.

. . . Katharine Whitehorn

I am eating breakfast. I don't even notice when my partner Susan sits down at the table.

"Good morning," she says. I don't really even hear her.

"Good morning." This time I register a faint noise, far away, not needing a response.

"Again, I say good morning!" she says. This time it penetrates. I look up and smile at her.

"Oh, are you talking to me?" I ask.

"Yeah, who else is here?"

"I'm sorry. I was reading and got lost in my thoughts."

Susan rolls her eyes. "You are reading the Pop Tarts box!"

"I haven't found a word yet I didn't want to read."

"True," Susan says. "That's one of the reasons I love you."

I go back to my reading, thankful that Pop Tarts, words, and Susan are in my life.

A cat is, by and large, sophisticated and complex, and capable of creating three-act plays around any single piece of action.

• • • Gladys Taber

Ten pounds consisting of equal portions flesh and fur. She is not a lover of all, doesn't even show tolerance on some days. Thundercloud gray, marshmallow-striped nose, gargantuan tail, small paws for her size, and eyes green as watered copper. She lives her life day in, day out, drinking from anything that contains a hole large enough for her head, including the toilet in our shared bathroom.

We moved to an efficiency apartment six months ago. Like me, she played in the city, was out late at night, had parties to attend, dates to keep, sex to enjoy.

That life is over for the both of us now. Like most who lead a full, mismatched life, we have time on our hands, not during the waking hours but during those "for private eyes only" hours. We remain in the city, in an apartment so high that the thought of jumping into the tree whose branches tempt by scraping the window seems ridiculous even in the presence of nine lives. Yup, we have each other and for now that is as comforting as a hug from a lover, a card from the past, a picture of my sister.

I'm going to call my dad to tell him I love him—and listen to him say, "This call is costing you a fortune," and hang up.

• • • Erma Bombeck

His lankiness uses every inch of the La-Z-Boy where he reclines, puffing on his forbidden cigar, blowing smoke rings with a satisfied "Ahh." I settle into another living room chair and say, "Well, old friend, I see you're never going to give up those stogies."

"What the hell. My legs don't work too good. My eyes are giving out. A good cigar's the only enjoyment I've got left," he says.

Just then Jenny drops in. "How are ya, Dad?" she asks and gets his usual reply: "Well, pension check's in the bank."

She bends over, pecks his cheek, and returns his morbid humor: "You know what? I'm going to buy you a dictionary. You better read it and come up with something new to say." His eyes brighten. His grin widens, and Jenny winks at me. "I'm on the run today, so I'll put these medications on your chest of drawers and be on my way," she says and disappears down the hall to his bedroom.

"You kids coming on Wednesday?" he calls out.

"Sure," Jenny answers, "whether you want us or not."

He chuckles, and I hear the love in the verbal give and take. "You are one spoiled fellow," I say.

He takes the stogie from his mouth and replies softly, "I know."

Oppressive language does more than represent violence; it is violence; does more than represent the limits of knowledge; it limits knowledge.

• • • Toni Morrison

I hear us on the bus, in the boardrooms, on the news, in the grocery store, walking down the street, on the beach, in a restaurant, waiting in line at the movies, playground, airplane, bowling alleys, in books, the discount store, at a fashion show, the Senate, in the voting line, the county fair, the art gallery, in church, in mosques, synagogues, other holy places
    speaking words
    that kill, maim, marginalize, shred, demolish,
       devastate, diminish, explode, sear, trample, decapitate,
       beat, bruise, bury, annihilate,
    Violently, violently
    Put down
    Kill
    Keep poor
    Starve
    the other.
    Because if we learn new words, we will have new thoughts,
       if we have new thoughts we will
    open up
    bow peacefully to each other
    passing bread
    and water, clean
    from each to each.

Her sarcasm was so quick, so fine at the point—it was like being touched by a metal so cold that one doesn't know whether one is burned or chilled.

・ ・ ・ Willa Cather

He shot liquid daggers of words so far-reaching he had no place to go but to retreat to the hills. Sitting back, controlled, motionless, with one leg crossed over the other, he strategically planned his attack, a ravenous lion needing this kill for survival. He waited with bated breath until the most vulnerable of the pack moved their lips; steam blasted from his nostrils, his eyes turned tomato-juice red, he moistened his straight lips, and, elongating his spine, scratched his chin with a pointy-edged finger.

I was his target, the baby, the one who was sure to say something foolish. This time I felt his heat, I sensed his anticipation. My brother's hand nudged me in a sign of support, barely into the battleground we call Sunday brunch. I packed my shoulder bag with the smile that enraged him, the sincerity that made him howl, and the imagination that was his pouncing ground. I said good-bye to my loved ones, thought of the happy memories, said my confessions, and began to open my mouth. I took two steps in his direction. I plunged into the ring, jumped on his unexpecting lap, and said, "Uncle, I love you." Ahh, the gratification, the intelligence, the insanity. He wiped the Bonne Bell lip gloss from his powerful cheek. Stunned, he wobbled away, wounded, dizzy from the trauma. The ring cleared, my successors chanted my name. It is victorious to beat the wrath of insincerity with love—cheesy though it may be, it works. I zipped my backpack, tossed the lip gloss, and ate a strawberry. It was a good day. Don't underestimate the mind of a thirteen-year-old.

There is no "ever after" for parents whose children decide to end a marriage.

• • • Marjorie A. Slavin

It came without warning: the midlife breakup. Made for each other, her parents had said. Certainly seems so, I said as anniversaries counted upward.

Dismay, guilt (somehow it's my fault), failure, shame barricade all avenues to reasonable thinking. Other people's children divorce. Not mine. How do those other mothers, from a generation when divorce wasn't an option, cope with the grief, loss, and helplessness? I look for answers.

"It broke my heart when Greg divorced. She shouldn't have married him; she didn't know what she wanted," my friend Marilyn says. (It's "her" fault.)

"I've got four kids and nine marriages," Judy says. "Kim accounts for three of them. Life's not been good to her." (It's fate.)

"I've got every mix and match this generation can come up with: Kay's single and has a baby; Joe's married and doesn't want kids; Tom's married and living alone; Sherry's not married and not living alone," says Marge. (It's the times.)

"One solid marriage and three divorces, and my son asks, 'What happened to our family?'" Helen says with a shrug, "As though I know." (Resignation. Dismissal.)

I decide that blame has no place in how I feel. I envy Helen's ability to just say, "I don't know. How could I?" and let it go. Maybe with time. For now I'll cling to the hope that this new turn in the road for two people I love will bring them happiness.

Sorrow has its reward. It never leaves us where it found us.

• • • Mary Baker Eddy

He told me when we got home from a marriage encounter meeting. He told me because his therapist (what therapist?) said he should.

"How long has this affair been going on?"

"For over a year."

The ceiling fell on my head. I felt the dust plug up my nose, heavy pieces crushed my skull, ragged edges severed my heart.

The story is a long one that you have probably heard before. Separation, counseling, kids in chaos, anger, tears, reconciliation.

Nothing was ever the same after that. It looks the same but isn't. Because I am not. I am no longer afraid. I don't duck. I stand. I don't tolerate. I act. I don't ignore. I love.

The word "feminist" is now used most often to divide women from their own interests and, worse, against one another.

• • • Suzy McKee Charnas

"Women and Sexuality" is the topic for the senior women's discussion group. Together, Clara and I tackle the worksheet (three eras of women's attitudes on sex in marriage).

(1) Our great-grandmothers at quilting bees whispered about "marital duties"; forgave men their boys-will-be-boys transgressions; told their daughters the way to a man's heart is through his stomach. "They knew their role in life; it worked for them," Clara says.

I say, "They were pulling their weight as pioneers. Why would they settle for less than fidelity in men?"

(2) Our grandmothers and mothers bobbed their hair; shortened their skirts; got the vote; reared the women who worked during World War II. They caution daughters not to count on a slice of apple pie with cheddar to keep a man's heart. "If you take care of the bedroom," they said, "the kitchen will take care of itself."

"Most women were homemakers. Men were head of the house. Those were secure times for women," says Clara.

"Why, then, did they encourage education for their daughters so they'd have something 'to fall back on'?" I argue.

(3) The feminist era: Women decide they and their daughters have the right to shift focus from bedroom to boardroom—and back again—and to speak up for what they want in both places. Has the feminist movement been good for women? "No," says Clara. "It's gone too far."

"Yes," I say. "Women still have miles to go. Feminist is not a four-letter word."

**There is a privacy about it which no other season gives you . . .
only in the winter, in the country, can you have longer, quiet stretches
when you can savor belonging to yourself.**
• • • Ruth Stout

The snow drifts like sand dunes over the acre garden that my
husband spends the summer tending. Corn stalks stick out of
the snow. Like people trying to rise again.

I don't like it here. I almost hate it. I don't tell my husband
that. The job is here. Why make us both miserable?

I grew up in Los Angeles. This small eastern farm town has
a Mozart rhythm. I like reggae.

But I am learning. Learning how to be alone. How to slow
down. Like the winter, I pull a comforter over myself and wait.
Wait to hear a robin sing. Wait to see green. In the waiting there
is me. I enjoy myself alone. Without the parties, the malls, and
the fast pace.

Which to me is, like the first snowfall, a great quiet surprise.

Privacy—like eating and breathing—is one of life's basic requirements.
• • • Katherine Neville

I travel to places where many live in poverty, and I also travel to places where most do not. One thing I realized is food, health care, and shelter often go hand in hand with the amount of privacy that one receives. Interesting, is it not, that if you have less, in a way you have more to reveal, more that you are made to feel ashamed of, to hide away? I think of some people I know with a lot of money. They converse in low voices, wear tailored clothes that hide lumps and bumps, and makeup that makes everything but their eyeballs vanish. They buy things with cards to prevent people from stealing their wallets or knowing how much they really have. I am not bitter, just interested in why it seems that we know so much about what "our poor population" do with their money—not government money, not taxpayers' money, but their money, the little they may have—but if you have a lot of money, it is considered taboo to disclose any of those truths. I would like to challenge those who live a private life to come with me for a week, verbalize your reality, and I will challenge myself to live in your shoes—who knows what we could learn?

**Sometimes we find the kind of true friend . . . that will winter us
and summer us, grieve, rejoice, and travel with us.**

• • • Barbara Holland

I hurry past the promo poster upright on the front counter
of the card shop. Then I go back, and turn it face down on the
polished glass.

A salesclerk moves quickly to set it up again, perhaps expecting an apology from me, which she doesn't get. The poster photo
of two white-haired women, their slightly rounded shoulders
betraying the burden of age, walking arm-in-arm along a park
path with its caption "Friendship Is Forever" raises angry grief,
long-buried within me. I leave without buying the birthday card
I came in to get. If Laura's spirit could speak, she'd ask, "Now,
what good did that do?"

And I'd sob, "No good. I just get so mad! We're supposed to be
like those two on life's path together, grayed and bowed, friends
forever."

But Laura's spirit doesn't speak. And I don't sob but blend
my way into the pedestrian flow of the busy mall. I let myself
be with Laura awhile, sharing childhood times, marriage, and
parenting days—lucky to have had her—even though our path
ended far short of forever.

I retrace my steps and buy the birthday card.

People who eat white bread have no dreams.

• • • Diana Vreeland

Whole-grain bread. I smell it as I pass the bakery. Little wheat and rye kernels nestled in the air spaces of the flour and milk. I smell memories of my mother's kitchen. Predawn, before the rest of us were up, she pulled gray pans out of the oven. Left cornmeal-dusted loaves on the aqua countertop to cool.

Then she went to work in town as a bank clerk. Maybe she wanted to stay home. To tend the house and her chickens. Maybe she wanted to be a sculptor. I don't know. I never asked. She never said. I wish she had told me. I wish I had asked.

She did dream dreams.

I know that, because the texture of her bread was so complex.

If you cannot tell the truth about yourself, you cannot tell it about other people.

• • • Virginia Woolf

Gossip. Confabulations spread through this working institution expeditiously. The female bees spreading urgent messages not of oncoming beekeepers or a deprived pollen situation but about the tardy one, the called-in-sick one, the guess-who-is-pregnant one, the one-step-behind one, and the all-time-new one. As a self-prescribed witness to the daily buzz conferences, I speculate on the relevance of poisonous chatter. To deliberate, analyze, or inquire seems condescending since my purposeful removal from the colony. This stance comes with consequences. I may not be invited to the working-bee ball or asked to dine in the bumble lounge, or given the latest information about the trendy wing care products. I fly alone most days.

Am I lonely? Not particularly. I clutch my knowledge of the harm done by spewing indecencies about fellow honey makers. I refuse to steal the truths of lives that are not asking to be heard. I decline the opportunity to prostitute one life and reap the temporary reward of fame a.k.a. conformity. I dedicate my time to my profession, my truth, and the pride I gain from knowing that I will fly longer, collect honey longer, bee longer without disease-causing stress resulting from Gossip.

Truth like surgery may hurt, but it cures.

• • •   Han Suyin

For her sixteenth birthday, Carey wants one gift—to find her birth mother. She's fantasized that her mother's a beautiful singing artist, because she has a clear, soprano voice for which she is getting lessons and coaching. I want to save my child from heartbreak, but I contact her birth mother. On a hot July afternoon we go to a midtown park to meet the woman who left Carey, unfed and unwashed, in a smelly crib.

She doesn't rise from her bench, nor drop her cigarette as we approach. Her dress clings to her too-thin frame; dark roots deny the authenticity of her blond hair. She looks at Carey and says, "You seem to have done all right."

Carey sits, turns toward her, tells her about her singing, and asks if she's a singer too. "What a laugh that is!" she says, with a deep draw on her cigarette.

Carey pauses and asks, "Were you ever sorry you gave me away?" I feel my heart doing double time.

Slowly, she says, "Nope. I didn't have time for a kid then. And don't now."

Carey rises, folds her arms, and stares down at her. Turning to me, she says, "We can go home now," links her arm in mine, doesn't look back at the woman exhaling smoke puffs that fade to nothing—like a fantasy dispelled.

I am my own University, I my own professor.

• • • Sylvia Ashton-Warner

She sits across from me in lecture. She marks her notebook with coordinated tabs matching the appropriate chapter in her text: blue, pink, purple, and orange. I don't read the text. I take notes, skim the handouts, and learn from the lecture. Maybe I am not smart enough, diligent or committed enough. She is a real student, the kind who deserves a diploma. I could try harder, look more organized, adapt to that world. I love to learn—don't get me wrong—I just can't do that.

She sits across from me in lecture. She never brings anything but her notebook. She probably doesn't even need to read her text, only skims her handouts that I have turned into mosaics of highlighters. I wish I entertained the thought of enjoying studying, learning. I revel for the day that I would choose to come to class. I do learn best by keeping focused on organization. I am sure she thinks I am anal and rigid—she is the real student, absorbing it all without effort. I am just trying to hold on, to make it, to understand.

There seems to be so much more winter than we need this year.

. . . Kathleen Norris

I can't take a walk. Why? Because I go onto the icy sidewalks and start thinking like an old woman. "Watch your step or you'll break a hip."

I won't go to the mall. Why? Because now I have to wear a tight-fitting hat and a massive, wooly scarf. When I was younger, my hair shone against the snow as I entered the mall with my short coat open to show off my fuzzy sweater. Not anymore. And I refuse to go into a store with old-person flat winter hair.

I don't answer the door when the bell rings unexpectedly. Why? Because I ache and smell like that stuff my grandmother rubbed into her joints all winter. That's because now I rub the stuff into my joints. No one should know I smell like that.

I used to wonder why old people moved to Arizona or Florida. Now I know. It's easier to forget your age when there isn't so much winter.

Every murderer is probably somebody's old friend.

• • • Agatha Christie

I watch movies that prohibit sleep. They encapsulate my deepest fears, death by the hands of a person who hates me for breathing, for being a woman, or for not being a man, for wearing lipstick, for looking like their third-grade teacher who hit them with a ruler, and the worst reason, for being the mistaken identity of the hated person. At times I am frightened by my interest, especially when I start memorizing the lines. I was drawn to Lecter from *Silence of the Lambs,* for example. Not that I want to have dinner with him sometime, don't get me wrong. But I can see what makes him tick. We are all one step away from being vigilantes, if not so close to eating body parts. Why did the creators of the movie make him a pseudo hero, or is it my sick mind that makes me think that way? I do not condone falling in love with men in jail, especially admitted murderers, but I do think that there is a fascinating aspect to our minds, the ability to forget about right and wrong, to do what you feel is most important. When a news report announces the name of a killer, I think, "That was someone's child. A lot of people sat next to him in school, ate lunch with him, had a crush on him in college." Why is this interesting? I guess because all humans have a different mind-set, but they are no less human—this is not a moral issue, I have no score to settle, no message to send, it was just a thought.

She listens to her own tales. Laughs at her own jokes and follows her own advice.

• • • Ama Ata Aidoo

I detest the self-help prophecies that guide rituals, pleasures, love, food, thought. I am a self-taught shoe-tying, book-reading, relationship-engaging, truth-telling, lie-telling, chocolate-eating woman. Life is life. My policy remains: only give what you can or want to and accept what you need. Many books tell you to wake up and make a list of what is important. What exactly has happened to the world that you might forget your purpose— what you like, how to live? Love, eat, think, and by all means read—the rest, including morals, will follow.

You are not as bright as you feel, after the second drink.

• • • Peg Bracken

We've been at the bar for two hours now. I am with my young staff from work. I know that the words are harder to get out. They think I don't know. I pretend that they don't notice. Why do I do this? To relax? To fit in? Does it matter?

It will matter to me tomorrow when I am their boss again. I will wonder if they respect my decision on the Fraser account less because I am slurring now. Or if they will accept it more readily because I am one of the gang tonight.

The waitress interrupts my somewhat foggy musings.

"Do you want another round here?"

"Sure, all around," the marketing assistant replies.

I motion to the waitress. Quietly I say, "Make mine coffee, black."

And who shall separate the dust which later we shall be?

• • • Georgia Douglas Johnson

I look out at the group I've come to tell my story to. I will tell them about our flight from our Vietnam home after the Americans left, about my father and my husband who helped the soldiers out of quagmires and jungles during the war.

They are good, solid citizens. It is in their church that I speak to them. When they say, "My great-grandparents came here, learned the language, and worked hard to become Americans. How are you doing that?" I will show them the pictures on the screen of our people in English-as-a-Second-Language classes, elders struggling with what children learn quickly.

When they ask, "Why don't you work toward blending into our society?" I will show them more pictures of my people, helping at the food shelf and taking the work of their hands—the colorful quilts that tell a story—and the food they grow to markets for all to buy.

They do not mean to hurt me when the questions become sharp-edged. They are proud of their immigrant ancestors who once fled to a new land, bringing with them customs and traditions that enriched the society they now enjoy. So shall my children and grandchildren be proud of their ancestors.

I am nervous about the questions, but I will stand firmly in place and answer them.

february...

Memory is to love what the saucer is to the cup.

• • • Elizabeth Bowen

I'm drinking my lukewarm decaf. The cup sticks to the saucer. I wiggle it free. I am having a fit of melancholy. I don't know what it is. My cranky boss? My husband's comfortable neglect? Last year's dress being too tight? Maybe lost dreams. Maybe nothing.

In the past, I would have been on the phone in a minute with Janelle. For more than twenty-five years we've shared almost everything. But in the last six months, we haven't talked much. I'm not sure we know why. I'm more tired in this decade of my life; no energy for those youthful, intense relationship talks.

I will handle this myself. But I don't want to.

Maybe I'll call my daughter. Not appropriate.

My mom. Won't get what I want.

My husband. Ri-ight!

Other friends. No, they don't know my dark corners.

I put the cup down. It slides comfortably into the saucer. I pick up the phone. "Hi, Janelle. I feel just lousy."

"So, what else is new?" she answers, laughing.

Vinegar he poured on me all his life; I am well marinated; how can I be honey now?

• • • Tillie Olsen

He held my hand in his as we crossed the street, dashing with traffic. He was old compared to the fathers of my classmates, but kids taunting never diminished the feeling of his rough hand against my creamy skin. We enjoyed walking, the same path every twilight, without Mom, without thoughts, just motion, a connection in deed.

We walked the same path every twilight. An apricot pit rose to the top of my throat in anticipation of completing the stroll down Wilson Street, one block left until we reach home. Most nights I bent over to tie my shoes, struggling to make a loop for at least five minutes, trying to extend the inevitable. "Come on, honey, you know we need to go home," he'd say.

As he dropped the tight grasp of my fingers I felt the love loosen. The moment my feet touched the threshold of our minute home, anger spilled from his large unforgiving mouth. Most sentences were prefaced not by honey anymore, but instead *why couldn't you, how could you,* or the worst, *how dare you.* Constant, predictable, futile rage permeated my soul's happiness and ability to soar above reality.

On my nineteenth birthday I let go of his grasp before we rounded the corner. In his hand I placed a note that said, "I can't be loved and hated at the same time, and I can't love and hate at the same time—Good-bye Dad," signed, "Your twilight honey."

What used to be old is middle-aged now.

   • • • Joyce Brothers

On her seventieth birthday a chortling Marianne told her kids, "If I stand still long enough, you'll catch up with me."

Today she calls, and I hear, "Well, she's done it."

"Who's 'she,' and what's she done?" I ask.

"Kathy. She's caught up with me. She turned fifty-one today," she says. "She came over, waving her AARP [American Association of Retired People] membership card in the air, singing out, 'Discounts, Discounts, Discounts.'"

"Kathy's fifty-one?! I can hardly believe it. Seems it was just yesterday she was heading out to protests, saying you brought her up to be her own person. Remember that? Those sixties kids sure shook up the universe."

"Fine," Marianne says. "But they're still doing it. Shakes you up plenty to find out you're mom to a senior citizen."

A career is wonderful. But you can't curl up with a career on a cold night.

• • • Marilyn Monroe

Everyone knows what Marilyn was talking about. A man. One who loves, listens to, and comforts you. *That would be wonderful,* I think to myself after a hard day at the office. My mother's generation worked in small and dramatic ways so that I can have a career where, in the past, women feared to tread.

I am thankful to them.

But tonight I am alone. I look around. My apartment is a little messy but it is still me. With candles, prints, and furniture just where I want them.

I wouldn't mind curling up with a man, if it enriched me.

But another thing my mother and her peers taught me is that the music playing, the warmed-up soup, the book next to my cozy bed, my independence and belief in myself are of great comfort on any night, cold or warm.

We can go into a quiet retirement, which is the traditional stereotype of a 65-year-old, or we can take a risk and put ourselves out where the action is.

• • • Satenig St. Marie

I reach the bowling lanes where it's my first day of substituting for a friend who's wintering in Arizona. I hurry in out of the cold, behind two young moms who shepherd their toddlers into the downstairs nursery promising lunch at McDonald's.

I lace on my bowling shoes, embarrassed by all the youngness around me. At age seventy-five, why have I put myself here? I wish I owned a pair of jeans, or at least had worn slacks, instead of my outdated split skirt.

Jackie, twenty-three, a nanny to two school-age boys, flops down next to me with a tired sigh.

"I'm beat," she says. "Cody, the twelve-year-old, had a hockey game last night. His mom and dad couldn't go, so I went. Turned out it was grandparents' night. There I was, half the age of most of the people around me, feeling really out of place. But not for long.

"They knew more about hockey than I ever will. And they knew how to enjoy the game. No criticizing the officials, no one-sided cheering. They made the night fun for me, and I had a blast!"

I chuckle to think she worried about being young, and I'm worrying about being old. An unexpected way to connect, but her story erases the time gap for me. I take my practice shot, and throw a pin-scattering strike.

After all, tomorrow is another day.

• • • Margaret Mitchell, *Gone with the Wind*

I could never do cartwheels as well as the others. In gym I failed as a partner in softball, floor hockey, tennis, football, and for sure dodgeball. For the most part I was not athletic; I lived in a family where athleticism was admired as much as Communism. We loved trees, books, peace, broccoli, literature, art, music, most of the time each other. I cannot complain about the kids in my class teasing me. I was different. I read instead of swinging, counted rocks instead of talking, wrote letters to the teacher on how to improve class participation instead of jumping rope. I had a friend once, who for whatever reason loved my glasses, my lack of sense of humor, how I chewed with my mouth open at lunch, how boys never liked me. She thought that gave us more time together, and presented less competition in the long run.

Quirky, uncoordinated, bored, and lonely at times, my life went on; I learned, grew, and developed some social skills, all in all not bad.

Later in life I even ran races, went skydiving, went scuba diving, traveled to faraway places by myself, learned the tango and Tai Chi, practiced massage, wrote a book.

However, I still don't know how to do a cartwheel—that's what tomorrows are for.

Angels come in all sizes and shapes and colors, visible and invisible to the physical eye. But always you are changed from having seen one.

· · · Sophy Burnham

We're on the freeway at dusk in heavy city-bound traffic. Suddenly the car jolts violently and veers to the right, threatening to spin out of control.

I see the outer rim of the front tire swirl through the right lane and out of sight. Stunned into silence, I cling to the dashboard even after the car stops, off the highway safe from the high-speed traffic.

Before my husband can get to the car trunk, a low-slung, black sports model with heavily tinted windows pulls up. A tall, muscular young man in a dark uniform steps out. Horror stories of attacks and robbery on the road flash through my mind.

"Need some help, I see," he says. "You just step aside. This won't take long." He has the tire off, the spare on, bolts tightened in minutes. He tells us he sells tires at a service garage.

He waves away our offer to pay and drives off. With a tip of his cap, he is gone.

I'm convinced forever that angels exist among us. They don't have to have halos that glow. They may have only a cap to tip.

You live but once; you might as well be amusing.

• • • Coco Chanel

She blows bubbles out of her car window in traffic jams. Sends me endless jokes via e-mail that make me smile despite myself. She's been known to wear a bright-red clown nose out in public. Go naked in a hot tub in the snow.

"Lighten up and live longer" is her mantra.

And that is what she is doing. Living longer. A survivor of breast cancer, an eating disorder, and an abusive relationship, she will probably live into her nineties. She tells people about her life's struggles sometimes. When it is helpful to her or someone else.

But most days she is on an adventure of fun and will happily take me along for the ride.

She helps me to find my amusing self, a part I sometimes neglect in my seriousness. With her in my life I lighten up and am grateful for the chance to live once.

A handwritten personal letter has become a genuine modern-day luxury, like a child's pony ride.

. . . Shana Alexander

I reach into the rural-style mailbox and grasp the day's collection of the usual and expected. I turn from the street curb up the walk to the front door. I flip through envelopes, ads, and magazines, all with their precise, computer-generated labels.

I see the familiar handwriting, and my step quickens. I thump the mail onto the kitchen table except for the letter I clasp in my hand like a child hoarding a treat mom says she has to wait until after lunch to eat.

I open the envelope and pause to admire the penmanship that curves and flows rhythmically across the unruled smoothness of my sister's stationery. Two sheets of line after well-spaced line, like frame-ready drawings.

"It seems everyone uses e-mail but me," she writes. "So, I've taken the plunge. I now have a computer. Here's my e-mail address."

I reread the letter slowly, unwilling to part with the perfection of this heart-to-heart art. I gently smooth the folds from its pages and reply to her dot-com address:

"Welcome to cyberspace, but oh, how I'll miss your letters!"

Few people who are hurt once by someone they love respond in the way they might to a singular physical assault by a stranger.

. . . bell hooks

I told him, "No, don't push me that high." On the way up I measured the tip of my toes against the trees. If I went above the robin's nest in the sugar maple, I immediately jumped off. He made me go higher than I wanted to, he flipped me over, twisted the rope, twisted my hair, twisted my shoe laces, twisted my words, twisted my insides. He hurt me and all I wanted to say was "Stop." I said it again and again with my eyes, with every drop of my being, I screamed "Never," with my blood as it soaked the sheets, I curled my fingers into a fist grasping the soil, the sheets, the tub water. He stabbed, kneaded, permeated my body sometimes with only a glance or a thought.

All I could do then was say, "Stop pushing me."

To this day I hate heights and for the most part men, but one thing I enjoy is myself, my safety, and my ability to never let that happen to me again.

> "Marilla," she demanded presently, "do you think that I shall ever have a bosom friend in Avonlea?"
>
> "A—a what kind of a friend?"
>
> "A bosom friend—an intimate friend, you know—a really kindred spirit to whom I can confide my inmost soul."
>
> • • • Lucy Maud Montgomery, *Anne of Green Gables*

My first friend, Tricia, died at thirty-three from complications from domestic abuse. I read this at her funeral.

"Remembering Tricia—freckles and braids and sashed plaid dresses and a grin. Little, we huddled on porches in thunderstorms, giggling away our fears; ran through sprinklers; ate my dad's potato chips; played alley softball and streetlight hide-and-seek.

"Remembering Tricia—struggling with reading, getting A's in fun. Dreaming big dreams about being big and eating all of the free samples at Jansen's store. Tricia said, "You're smart, but way too serious," and made me laugh.

"Remembering Tricia—letters from boarding school; boyfriends, love, marriage; hurt. She fought from coma to walking again, a big person now trying to make sense out of the nonsensical.

"Remembering Tricia—forgetting the last five minutes, but always remembering my birthday; sharing old stories over and over again; recalling parts of us that I forgot; lifting up her busy friend with memories of where we began."

What I couldn't say at the funeral was how angry I was at her husband, who beat her over and over, sending the blood clot to her brain where it exploded. But maybe it was better that way. Just to remember her friendship, strength, and laughter.

You'd have done fine at track meets. Especially if they'd had an event called Jumping to Conclusions.

. . . Kristin Hunter

A co-worker asks, "How have you been feeling about the Jack thing?" Translation: She wants to know if I am able to keep a relationship and if I am strong enough to break up with such a jerk.

My mother asks, "Is this job one that fits your lifestyle?" Translation: Are you going to make enough money to support yourself or should I cancel my acupuncture appointment and send a check?

Jack asks, "Do you want to do something relaxing this evening?" Translation: Give it up; it has been a long time.

The waiter asks, "Can I get you anything else here?" Translation: Could I recommend the treadmill or Stairmaster for dessert?"

The hair designer states, "I think if we do the layer thing it will give your hair a little boost." Translation: Did you notice what people look like here, one of these things looks just like the others, *one of these things is just not the same.*

Linguistics. I am a pro. The art of focusing on myself, cutting myself down, doubting the intent of everyone, and having an excuse not to socialize takes years and years to develop. I am offering a one-time course titled "Everyone hates me . . ." It is free; please join me.

The world, after all, is not Noah's ark; you don't have to be in pairs to be allowed.

• • • Ruth Stein

Marge and I are on our way to shop for a sixtieth wedding anniversary gift.

"You know, if you and Tim weren't going to this affair, I'd skip it," says Marge. "We were close friends with Therese and Len, or so I thought. But after my Jim died, they never invited me to anything.

"And they're not the only ones. I quickly discovered that it's a two-by-two world. Once you're not half of a duo, the phone rings less; and when it does, it's the female side of the duos you once buddied with saying, 'Let's do lunch sometime.' Threes, fives, sevens, and nines make for odd-number gatherings that just don't work."

"But, Marge, people sometimes place limits on themselves," I say. "Like when I ask widowed friends to parties, or to go somewhere with Tim and me, they'll say they'd feel out of place: 'It will be all couples.' I'm so glad you don't do that. We'd miss you."

Marge sighs. "I hear what you're saying, but you do feel like a fifth wheel when everyone's paired off. You and Tim have a way of making it easier to be that third man odd. You're like a pair of old shoes you never want to part with—so comfortable to be with."

Her simile makes me grin. "To that I say thanks, I think. Anyway, Marge, let's get the shopping done and get set to have a good time tonight."

Love is a great beautifier.

• • • Louisa May Alcott

I pause in the medical building lobby to pull on my gloves and fish my car keys out of my purse. An older couple sit on a bench next to the open-door pharmacy.

The woman's slender, blue-veined hands tremble slightly as she adjusts her head scarf and buttons her coat, getting ready to go out into the cold. She reaches for her cane and begins to get up.

Her husband, a slim, white-haired gentleman rises and gently says, "Where are you going? Sit there until I get a cab."

"I'm just going to go in here to the drugstore to get you a chocolate bar," she says. Looking up at him, coquettishly, she adds, "That is, unless you don't want one."

He rests his hand lightly on her shoulder, kisses her cheek, lets his lips linger a moment, and in a lover's voice, says, "You go ahead."

I resent like hell that I was maybe eighteen before I heard the L word. It would have made all the difference for me had I grown up knowing that the reason I didn't fit in was because they hadn't told me there were more categories to fit into.

• • • Michelle Shocked

I read labels: extra crunchy, brightens whites, UV protection. They often enhance the product, minimizing its worth through exaggeration. Today I hold her hand, I slide my motion in between hers, I thirst for the touch of her and now I read my label: Lesbian. I am sure that most wonder about our love. I do. I am sure that most think, that is different. I do. How polar an idea. I love my likeness.

I snake my way through life, detaching layers of myself that I cannot fit into anymore. I leave behind the childhood of a girl who felt disgusting, wrong, and confused about boys. I stomp on the layer of my life where I met women who courted me with violence and their insecurities. I pulverized the idea that being like everyone else is the most important part of being a mother. This tall-grass path is dark, filled with venom. I rely on my senses, my instincts, the core that I cannot shed. Eyes closed, senses keen I travel in search of familiar. I find her, my woman, my home, my eternity, my passion, my forever, my permanent skin. Our worth—the indescribable tingling as she places a mere fingerprint on me—cannot be labeled, categorized with a codification, except the generic, overused word: love.

In the country of pain we are each alone.

• • • May Sarton

No one knows by looking at me. Even if they ask, I am tired of telling them how I am.

I am just plain tired. Flu-like malaise that doesn't go away. The pain is . . . like I'm in a vise, pulling, stabbing, burning. Does it matter?

Fibromyalgia won't kill me. There are people much worse off, I tell myself. Get over it. Quit being a baby. Sleep more. Sleep less. Exercise. Don't exercise. Eat this. Take this supplement or don't.

I have a job that is flexible. Family. Friends. How lucky I am . . .

And, yet, when I wake up another day spent, sad, hurting enough to cry, I feel mostly alone. Alone with an insidious leech that sucks out my essence. I can't concentrate so I watch stupid TV shows. Fall asleep. Wake up. Push myself and the leech out the door and down the street to prove I am.

Perhaps I could learn to be its friend. I don't want to. I want it to give me back my life juices. Then I want it to wither and die and I will blow it away. And I will be free.

**Her satisfaction rose to the surface like the thick golden cream
on the milk pans.**

• • • Marjorie Kinnan Rawlings

He whizzes by me, pushing the pedal way past the speed limit,
puts his hand out the window, and with an overuse of his middle
finger, yells, "Get off the road, granny." Raucous laughter trails
behind like vapor from the exhaust, as the car full of high school
kids disappears over a rise in the highway.

"So much for letting my hair go white. It sets me up for jokers
like those," I say to my granddaughter as I keep her hand off the
horn. "But I bet he doesn't know about the speed trap on the
other side of the hill."

Sure enough, we come over the rise to see blue lights flashing,
and the red sports car pulled over on the side of the road, a state
cop approaching the driver's window.

Susie laughs, and the hotshots in the car become just another
bump in the road.

The appetite grows for what it feeds on.

· · · Ida B. Wells

White potato chunks, orange carrot circles, little green peas, strings of fresh chicken, onion, garlic, basil, salt, pepper in a long-simmered broth. I lift each spoonful from the blue ceramic bowl to my lips. Remembering that I am at the local diner, not by myself, I keep my ecstasy quiet. Yummmm. Mmmmm. Ahhh.

It is the first of the month. For the past three days, I ate what was left in my fridge and cupboards. Peanut butter, bread, jelly, can of corn, crackers, an apple, banana, two tins of tuna. It kept me going. But coming home from work tonight, I thought, "I am truly hungry." That doesn't happen to me often. But I had some unexpected bills this month. The car broke down and the heating bill was huge.

"Before I go grocery shopping, I'm going to get something to eat." I imagined ordering roast beef with potatoes and gravy.

I sat down, opened the menu. The roast beef, stuffed chicken, fish and chips all seemed like too much.

My hunger said, "Feed me something simple."

I told the waitress, "I'll have a bowl of soup."

It tastes so good.

By inventing the phone we've damaged the chance of telepathy.

• • • Dorothy M. Richardson

My mother, a woman of so much intelligence, so many skills, so much intuition, so much common sense, is totally and irreversibly hating advancing technology. I watch her purposeful hand as she types with her pointer finger and her confusion as she reaches for her address book to find the number to retrieve her voice mail messages, listen to her perturbation as her cordless phone beeps throughout our conversation. She is not simple, just practical: intellectually capable, intellectually refusing. She now has two phones because one doesn't ring and the other jumbles voices so my grandmother sounds like Darth Vader. She has a computer with a printer that requires you to lean on the left corner, force-feed it paper of a flavor it doesn't particularly enjoy, and chat with it as it is warming up. The untouched, recently purchased cell phone in the box sent me over the edge. I attempted calling. She yelled into the phone, "Call back in thirty seconds; I will plug in the other phone." On my way over to her house I collected an appropriate box, string, the perfect quote, and some sage. One by one we packed up the frail pieces of equipment and tied the box with a lavender ribbon. Holding hands, we sang our peaceful journey song, and sprinkled sage on the remains. The attendant at the dump yard said there was no hope, but my mom said, "Quite the contrary, my life is just looking up."

I shall be glad to see thee back, daughter, for I miss thee dreadfully. I wish I did not.

• • • Hannah Whitall Smith

I pull up in front of the house. She is in there. She left last night in a fury.

I sit, wishing it could be the days when my sparkling little girl ran to greet me, and we melted into love.

I no longer think that this time I will make it different. I have run out of different. I will start a conversation. She will explode and I will explode back. She's only sixteen years old. She knows about drugs, violence, sex. Worlds that I've only read about.

I go through my litany of guilt. If only I had worked less, nagged less, been available more. I try to absolve myself. I've loved her, been honest, tried to understand. It doesn't work. I can neither assume the blame nor forgive myself.

I am angry, sad, exhausted. But I am relieved. Because, when I open her door, I see her eyes peeking out from her comforter cocoon. I cry for her, and am in love with her, again. She is still here. We have more time to try. To be glad.

Sex is perhaps like culture—a luxury that only becomes an art after generations of leisurely acquaintance.

• • • Alice B. Toklas

The scene's a cozy one. I've kicked off my shoes. Feet up on the ottoman, I page through the evening paper. Across the room, he's settled into Monday night football.

"Um," I murmur, "that's interesting. Says here that men in their midlife crises go astray because they one day look at the women they married thirty years ago and say to themselves, 'Her age is really showing. I don't feel that old,' and to prove the point, they go off in search of youthful sex."

No comment from the game watcher, so I say, louder this time, "Hey, honey, do you think I've aged a lot in the past thirty years?"

"Hell, no," he fires back, without taking his eyes from the TV, "but you made an old man out of me."

"Very funny," I say. "Not to worry, hon. This study shows that sex is good for you even into old age and helps control weight. One session burns up as many calories as are in a slice of lemon pie."

"Humph," he says, finger on the remote, and eyes fastened to the screen.

I fold the paper, slip into my shoes, and get up to leave.

"Where you going?" he asks.

"To make a lemon pie," I answer.

One should always act from one's inner sense of rhythm.

• • • Rosamond Lehmann

Carrying my precautionary groceries—cat food, tampons, chocolate, light bulbs, and overnight zit zapper crème, heading toward home, I hear a precarious noise in the distance. Lost in my usual sidewalk thoughts, I hear the noise again and this time, awkwardly strain my neck over my surprisingly tall right shoulder. A tall man with dark hair and a face that doesn't seem crooked from this distance is flapping his giant hands, attempting to capture my glance. Wearing my hospital scrubs that lived up to their name when I formally introduced them to my kitchen and bathroom floors, a fluorescent orange hunting jacket left from the year that Michael Jackson went hip hop, and tennis shoes with laces like hounds' ears, I try to pretend this man is invisible or that I have suddenly lost my hearing. On some days I would think, maybe, yeah, there is a slight chance that he wants to invest his time in me, but today I recognize that the vibes that attract a hungry mosquito to my arm are not with me. I wish I could turn my feminine hygiene wings into a plane and be gone, not out of embarrassment for me but for him, I mean really. Some days I think this world knows nothing, zilch, about timing.

Food for all is a necessity. Food should not be a merchandise, to be bought and sold as jewels are bought and sold by those who have the money to buy. Food is a human necessity, like water and air, and it should be as available.

• • • Pearl S. Buck

We are in a market in Kenya. Not the kind in safari brochures with colorful women smiling sweetly behind neat rows of cabbages and mangoes. The people's market. Goods spread on the earth. More sellers than buyers. Tattered people, eyes cast down.

My friend and I are shopping for used clothes for the children in the street kids' project. In front of us two women walk, their thin babies wrapped onto their backs.

My friend opens a package of crackers. I take one. It breaks off and half of it falls.

I don't notice the sound of it hitting the ground but the two young women do. Their heads twist like nervous birds. We walk ahead of them. Discreetly, we turn around. One woman swoops up the cracker piece. She breaks it in two. Puts some on the lips of each baby. Who swallow it, without chewing. They are so hungry.

What would happen if we each gave 10 percent of each grocery receipt to help someone who is starving to eat? Things would change.

If peaches had arms surely they would hold one another in their peach sleep.

• • • Sandra Cisneros

He is fuzzy by all definition. I hold his hand and purr. I wrap my dangly extremities around his middle and suddenly doubt the invention of blankets, or clothing. I picture a fuzzy fruit, a lass, the peach. I must admit that I am not a true connoisseur of this round, voluptuous, vitamin-C-enriched treat, but I know him, and I say he is the reincarnated southern peach. This plump man with his edible interior is covered by a layer of fuzz that if not counteracted with a sweet center would not be worth the time it takes to open my jaw. The season for this delicious morsel depends on many forces beyond the scope of my control or the planets, it seems. If I had to do all over, I would request the help of a specialist, a gardenologist of sorts. I want the exact recipe for picking a sweet yet tangy, juicy yet firm, attractive yet natural peach that I can put in my crisper drawer, take out in times of need and be able to replace it with an identical pleasantly plump, preferably not related peach. I tend to feel sorry for people and often inanimate objects or fruit. I realize he came from a community where everyone had fuzz and needed a tempered climate. I can only imagine the warmth two round peaches could produce. I cannot be something I am not. In order to counteract this guilt. I will always keep two pieces in my crisper.

The incredible gift of the ordinary! Glory comes streaming from the table of daily life.

• • • Macrina Wiederkehr

I sit at my dining-area table lingering over after-dinner coffee, gazing out at the lighted windows of neighboring houses. Just beyond the fenced yard, I see Jean putting dishes into a kitchen cabinet.

In the house next door to Jean's, Mike puts his briefcase on the table, loosens his tie and greets Carrie with a peck on the cheek. Next to them, the kitchen light comes on at Neil and Rick's. Home from their jobs, they'll hustle up an evening meal.

Tomorrow, the day care kids arrive at Jean's. Mike goes off to okay home loans at the bank. Carrie sees their kids off on the school bus and reappears as a teacher's aide. Neil leaves for his hospital shift, and Rick buses to the government center to pick up the caseload of juveniles in trouble.

At the day's close, the view from my window replays like scenes from Wilder's *Our Town.* And I marvel again at the extra-ordinariness of ordinary people.

All human beings hold the tools of their own destruction.

• • • Barbara Gordon

I tell my clients as I am making the deal that I am a functioning alcoholic. My husband tells me that my web of lashes traps others' attention leading them directly into my butterscotch eyes. I like to believe the irony of my admitted irresponsibility and the demonstration of my organizational intelligence lead people into my trap. I sell vacation property to people for whom I have no respect. I like money; they want to admit they have nothing in order to spend less. I like sophistication; they want it but do not want to pay for it. My life lacks the flamboyance I felt when I was six in my grandmother's room prancing in her boas. I tell my clients I am crazy, wild, in attempt to counteract the previous evening I spent watching *The Great Outdoors* highlighting bass fishing trips, with my husband of seven years, who has apparently built a contraption to break out of my web. Fragmented means having a whole somewhere, that is how I think of myself. I wake, drink, work, drink, and wake again. When I am not consuming a liquid that contains at least 6 percent shame rinsing and 8 percent bad memory erasing, I am planning a different way of being. I want to laugh because something tickles me, I want to make friends because of my genuineness, I want to make a sale because I can be just intelligent, not ironic. The pain of life is warming in my belly like a casserole I am bringing to the family picnic. I want it out, a new recipe, maybe a cold salad. I am shedding the dishonorable badge of "functioning alcoholic" and changing it to "functioning." That is reality and I want to be part of it again.

There is only one real deprivation, I decided this morning, and that is not to be able to give one's gifts to those one loves most.

• • • May Sarton

The morning light melts yellow onto the rose pillow cases. I snuggle into his neck.

"I want to make love to you," I say.

"Why would you want to do that?" he asks, turning his head to the wall.

"Because I love you."

"How could you possibly want to love an old man like me?"

"I've loved you for twenty-eight years. I'm not stopping now."

Not now, I think, in his shunning's empty silence. Not when the doctors say that the cancer will take him from me in a year. Not when the chemo is stripping him of his hair and potency. Not now. Not ever.

"Don't pity me. I won't have it." He pulls the blankets around him like a shroud. End of conversation.

Soft yellow changes to blinding light. I blink tears in its glare as I get up to make breakfast.

Later I will offer him dry toast and weak tea.

I hope he will accept it.

It is a curious thought, but it is only when you see people looking ridiculous that you realize just how much you love them.

• • • Agatha Christie

"Anyone who manufactures slacks larger than size ten should be jailed," a French designer says at an exclusive showing. Everyone knows American women tourists by their "overstuffed posteriors," he declares.

At lunch, I tell my brother about his remarks. I say I have to admit that a lot of us tend to get pear-shaped as we age, putting a little strain on the fit of our slacks. With love in his voice, he says, "Yep, like my pear-shaped darlin'."

"You should have seen us last week when Marge strained a back muscle. She wouldn't go to the doctor without her girdle on, or figure-control garment, whatever you call them now. She couldn't get into the thing because of her sore back. So I offered to help.

"I tugged and pulled. I'd get one side of her stuffed in, and the other side bulged out. I poked that side back in, the other'd roll out and over." He puts down his fork, looks straight at me, and asks, "Have you ever tried putting twenty pounds of sugar into a ten-pound sack?"

I try not to laugh, but as I give up and totally lose it, I note he said "sugar." And I tell him, "That French guy's going to learn that it's the stuff we're made of, not the packaging that counts."

**In the dark / Defiant even now, it tugs and moans /
To be untangled from these mother's bones.**

• • • Genevieve Taggard

I carry an excitable bundle with me wherever I go. I walk with
the weight of a second heart and the knowledge of a second
mind. I breathe for both with the capacity of one and sleep
for one with the capacity of two. I look down at my rumbling
insides. I know you until now, and I know that tomorrow you
will say, "I want to play in the real world. I want to breathe
for me, eat for me, and begin to see."

I will birth you in sixty days, two flips of a large calendar
filled with important days. Eyes, heart, liver, legs, arms, brain.
You are so excited, my darling one, to open up this life and begin
the walk, but I ask for two short flips of the dated pages that
you stay tight inside of the dark place you call home. I promise
to not eat garlic: that makes you rumble. I promise to swim: that
makes you whirl. I promise to sing the song that glides you into
the corner of my ribs and belly and casts you to sleep. This is a
team effort calling for indescribable patience. Once you are here
you will never stop the living; you will never go back to this
place you leave behind. So take a good look, relax a while, and
plan your journey. I will see you in sixty days.

march...

Dreams can be relentless tyrants.

• • • Morgan Llywelyn, *Bard*

I watch him play at night. He sensually strokes his guitar, sings his creative lyrics, and reveals his soul with every note. I blend into the dark-blue walls every Thursday and watch him from afar. I picture him singing to me and then picture myself suddenly acquiring the ability to sing back to him. As the room fills this Thursday night, my red sweater shines in the dark. The lights dim, smoke and background laughter make a haze between me and his deep blue eyes. I step forward, leaving my comfortably distant corner. I approach the stage and he looks at me, right at me. The entire room feels our connection; they are looking at me and back at him and then back at me again. We have finally connected, at last. He reaches for my hand and guides me to the stage. I float to him. In the audience, people are pointing at me. I look down and realize the red sweater is all I am wearing.

BEEP. BEEP. BEEP. It's 7 a.m. My morning alarm vibrates through my head—time to go to work. I think I'll wear red today.

Pistachio nuts, the red ones, cure any problem.

• • • Paula Danziger

I push the green grocery cart down the aisle. The cart is wet from the rain I walked six blocks in to get to the store. The wet plastic handle makes my hands and spirits grow even colder.

I hate this. Stretching money to feed the kids. Off to the mac and cheese aisle, as usual.

I pass a bin filled with red pistachios. I remember, years ago, telling a boyfriend I liked them. One night, when we went to the movies, he brought a big bag of pistachios. I ate all of them. I never felt so delicious.

They're too expensive, I think, passing them by.

Then I inch my cart backwards. I put five pistachios into my jacket pocket. As I toss boxes of macaroni into my cart, I take out one pistachio. I pry open the red shell and chew its delectable seed.

For a minute, I forget where I am. I see a movie screen, feel my boyfriend's arm around me, hear music from *West Side Story.*

And I feel "pretty, oh so pretty," right there in the middle of Super Foods.

When you cease to make a contribution you begin to die.

• • • Eleanor Roosevelt

For twenty years, Mary's been doing the lion's share of organizing an annual high school reunion for more than 500 people. A huge job. She sits in with each new committee and helps choose the place and menu. She makes a floor plan for seating arrangements, and tracks the reservations and the money on her computer system.

This year she had a quadruple bypass, and Chet, the chair, is trying to get her to slow down. *Good luck,* I think, as I watch him take Mary on in front of the whole organizing committee.

"We suggest that we give you some help only because we think you're working too hard," he says.

"I've been doing this since the 1970s. I don't have a death wish. I take care of myself. I'm a widow. I hate housework, so I do what I like to do. Help would be in the way. Trust me."

She grins. "Unless you have a single man available. That I might consider."

She wins. The buzz in the room goes back to selecting a date. Mary makes a note of it.

I think all great innovations are built on rejection.

• • • Louise Nevelson

These crumbling brick streets are walked by folks who lived
in places their bodies could tolerate but their being could not.
In this town west of the key, I hear stories that remind me of
the *MASH* episodes I grew up watching. I talk to people who
previously inhabited lands filled with ideals that bleached their
souls and left them an empty white sheet blowing in the breezes
of distrust. This town pops with one-act shows, drag queens,
painters, intellectuals, hippies, and the not so hippies. There is
no boundary here to creativity. The plan is to live. If you need
to hang upside down in a glass house while drinking grass milk,
then fine. If you need to wake up every morning and swallow
Rolaids with a rinse of J&B, then fine. If you need to push an
imaginary cart and mumble fragments of conversations of the
past to yourself, then fine.

In the midst of it all, I see the usual amongst the progressive:
strip clubs, wet T-shirt contests, even shorter shorts stamped
"crazy" for the left cheek and "chick" for the right. Despite the
throwback to a world without regulations I still walk a street
that tells me I am beautiful and my body is up for grabs. The soul
of the town breaks the glass menagerie of tourist hot spots. I feel
comforted that the folks walking into the spa are being ridiculed
by the local intellectuals who profit on their ignorance. This area
is deep and resourceful—if you do not watch yourself, you will
leave here either a little less conservative or with a lot less money.

You marry into a certain amount of madness when you marry a person with pets.

. . . Nora Ephron

At the dog show, my husband and I meet Carl, who raises spaniels. He tells us he's hoping again for "best in show" and asks if we have a dog.

"Oh, yes," I answer. "I have a boxer. She's beautiful and smart." I tell him about how she knows the sounds of when I'm getting ready for work: the shower, the hair dryer, drawers and closets opening and closing. "When she hears the spurts of hair spray, she knows that's the final touch and heads for her old, soft chair in the rec room. She'll stay there until I get home."

My husband concentrates on the evening's program, and I go on about the dog. "If we're watching television and ignore her signals to go outside, telling her, 'Wait until the commercial,' she squats in front of the TV threatening to take care of things right there. It works; we both jump up to let her out. But if the inside door is open, she can even let herself out; she just pushes down on the latch of the outside door and she's out."

My husband, with a wink at Carl, says, "Tell him about the time she missed the latch and put her paw through the glass, which cost a door repair and a vet bill."

Laughing, Carl says, "Even so, she sounds like an intelligent dog." He turns to my husband and asks, "Do you ever show her?"

Drily he answers, "As little as possible."

Solitude is one thing and loneliness is another.

• • • May Sarton

I take the bus. Sit among the other riders. We speak many languages. A mother counts on her child's toes, "Uno. Dos. Tres. Quatro. Cinco." A woman wrapped in Eastern African cloth writes in a notebook. Young women talk about their brother being shot on the street. "For no good reason," they say. A woman living in her own world hears many people's voices and argues with them. The man behind her reads his Bible.

We are all together. Riding the same bus. I think about our commonalities. And, yet, I am alone. So different from being lonely. I take in the view from my solitude.

Having someone wonder where you are when you don't come home at night is a very old human need.

• • • Margaret Mead

I am not a fuzzy person. I like to walk to the pier at midnight. Despite propaganda telling women that leaving your house past sunset might result in severe bodily harm, I waive the consent form and keep on chugging. I do not particularly enjoy cuddling. Too much warmth for too long makes me itch. Frankly, I like to get the entire sex thing over with. It is fun and all, but it sure doesn't replace a warm bubble bath and a scrumptious novel.

With these ideas I find that I am mistaken for a relationship grouch. To admit the truth may cleanse me, so here it goes. I have never had problems finding an appealing male. If conversation went well I might exchange a phone number. We might have lunch, and possibly date for up to six months. The crap of a relationship ended when *I* stopped returning phone calls. Six months, tops, that was it.

Until this one. Scary as it may sound, I found a person as defiant as I am. He hates holding hands, thinks it causes chafing. He thinks showering together seems unsanitary and takes up time better used by reading the paper and having a cup of coffee. He believes that some short men who look like women are more at risk walking at night than I am. He leaves the light on, and when I return at half past one, I know that inside is a man who would not be able to read his paper or drink his coffee if I were missing. I sleep well knowing that I am loved in the way I need.

**We propose to speak / your language / but not abandon ours; /
we insist that you understand / that you do not / understand us. /
You may begin / by not shouting— / we are tired of the noise.**

• • • Pamela Mordecai

I lead a dozen women into the city council meeting. We have the figures for the cost of adequate lighting in our neighborhood. We also know the costs of the lack of lighting: drug dealing, assaults, robberies. The meeting begins. Item one: A dog park in the affluent part of town. Item two: Funding a professional sports arena. Long discussions. Finally, the president says, "We are tabling the lighting discussion due to time."

I say, "This is the second month we've been pushed aside."

"You are not being excluded. We have time constraints."

"Not for the puppies' park. We listened to two hours of that. Meanwhile our babies cry because they hear gunshots outside their windows."

"You are out of order!" the president shouts.

"I am asking to be put into the order of business. We all vote too."

A council woman whispers to the president. He yells, "It seems we can extend this evening's business."

I say, "We will begin. Unless you need time to calm down. We could wait for that."

Age is something that doesn't matter unless you are a cheese.
· · · Billie Burke

Some people make you feel like a kid again. Like my two aunts. When I stopped by to see my ninety-three-year-old Aunt Frances on my seventieth birthday, she gave me a bear hug and said, "Oh, to be seventy again!" as though it were the prime time of life.

The next week, when I was leaving the house to keep a lunch date with Aunt Gert, who's ninety-one, the phone rang. I answered, and without even saying, "How are you?" to my best friend, I said, "Could I call you back? I'm on my way out the door to meet my elderly aunt for lunch."

When I put the phone down, my husband said, "You know, sweetie, you're elderly."

"Well," I said, "I guess someone forgot to tell me."

There is no way in which to understand the world without first detecting it through the radar-net of our senses.
• • • Diane Ackerman

I am no superwoman. I do not detect the whimper of a child drowning in a swimming pool three states away. Sitting at a coffee shop, I smell the air. Standing in an emergency room, I smell the air. Obvious differences obtained through a rapid sniff, but subtleties that go unnoticed if not analyzed. The woman to my left drinking a cup of chamomile tea slumps over the cup resembling a microwaved celery stick. Her shirt buttoned, but off by one. Her bag overflowing with Web MD resources printed from a not-so-hot home printer. A cookie with one bite small enough that the cookie could be returned to the case and resold. I deduce that she is ill. The tea relaxes the acidic stomach produced by the chemotherapy she is receiving for her metastatic breast cancer.

Later in the day I travel to the hospital to deliver flowers to a friend who just birthed her first child. I see the tea woman. She awaits the calling out of her name in the cancer center. I cannot be sure about my diagnosis, but I feel confirmed in my observational powers. The next week at the coffee shop I bring with me a box of homemade flat bread and a tin of tea decorated by my niece. I place it in front of the tea woman and say, "I hope you enjoy this and your day goes smoothly." She looks up at me, confused and elated, and says, "Thank you."

There is nothing stronger in the world than gentleness.

· · · Han Suyin

It is in the way he moves. He doesn't bolt. He steps so quietly that sometimes he seems to appear out of thin air. It's in the softness in his eyes. In his mellowed voice when he talks about children or cats or hears you are sick or sad. It's in his simplicity of expression. Not too many words that invade you. Soothing words that comfort you. Because he takes time, to give the words the silence they need to settle on.

He is a gentle man, my son. A strong, gentle man.

If we all tried to make other people's paths easy, our own feet would have a smooth, even place to walk on.
• • • Myrtle Reed

She's medium height and carries some extra midlife weight; wears her gray-streaked dark hair in a loose upswept topknot. Like Katharine Hepburn but without the high-cheek-boned elegance.

She takes the chair I offer her and begins to relax as she tells her story.

She's spent thirty of her fifty-eight years as a homemaker, wife of a revered small-town doctor. With her three children grown and living miles away, she at last found the courage to leave the man who bruised her body and stifled her soul.

The town rallied around the man who had spanked breath into their babies. Long-term friends pulled away, testimony to the expertise she'd developed in hiding cruelty under carefully applied makeup and cover-up fashion. How dare she ask for alimony that would cost him the good life he'd given her and that he deserved to keep?

The decree awarded alimony for two years, time in which she is to develop skills that will lead to self-supporting income. In the months it has taken her to move and find an apartment she can afford, rumors of abusive relationships with younger women have become fact. The doctor's façade of heroic goodness has crumbled.

Her wounds deep, and unhealed, Breta feels no vindication, only the need to put her feet on a new path. We look at what she knows and start to build a résumé. Breta leaves with a spring in her step and the names of three more women she can see who will introduce her to others, a woven safety net ready to catch her should her steps falter.

Energy is the power that drives every human being. It is not lost by exertion but maintained by it, for it is a faculty of the psyche.

• • • Germaine Greer

I watch her as she gathers his shirts, socks, favorite pairs of tennis shoes. Tomorrow he will be in surgery for upwards of eighteen hours. According to him, Spiderman is coming to open his brain and teach him how to climb buildings. Despite the endless hours of explanation, the heart of a six-year-old would rather focus on a dream than a nightmare.

The struggle she faces every day: Her son lying in a bed, hooked up to machines, eating hospital food decorated on the tray to turn every meal into a "happy meal" regardless of his appetite. She diligently collects the urine samples, monitors the heart rate machine, prevents him from sleepwalking and disconnecting his IV. He is a six-year-old diagnosed with brain cancer. She is a thirty-six-year-old diagnosed with fate worse than death.

I rush to find his slippers in an attempt to ease her load. I cook a stir-fry, thinking it is a light meal so she will be able to sleep. I arrange a massage for her the day after the surgery so she will get away for at least an hour. I clean her house while she is gone. I will hold her hand tomorrow for twenty-four hours if that is what it takes to get her through the longest day without her son. She stays busy, running a mile in between his naps, knitting in the night-shift hours, running her business from her cellular phone, and in her spare time creating puzzles for her son to solve after his procedures. I want to make her stop, but if I did, I would make her slow down enough to think. For now I watch her spin furiously, and plan to catch her when she falls.

You never find yourself until you face the truth.

. . . Pearl Bailey

It's over. The day I dreaded for a year. I put my hand over my heart. It is still beating. I feel my lungs fill up with air. I'm breathing. I can't say I am surprised or relieved that life still courses through my veins. I didn't have a vision of what after today would be.

Rick offered to live with me and Helen. Such a sweet man. We've separated three times, come back together. At first I thought I needed more space. Then I thought I needed to go back to school. Then, oh then, I made up some other excuse. He loved me through it all. Still does. So much that today when I tell him my truth, he puts away his heterosexuality and offers to just "be with you. To continue to love you and fix the roof. I understand. I won't interfere with your love of Helen."

"It wouldn't work," I say. "But thank you." I don't say *there is no way you can understand* because I am just beginning to. My whole life is just starting to make sense. I can believe that I am a lesbian. It isn't a sentence. It is a joy—when I am with Helen, when I imagine life not dressed up like a heterosexual on the outside or the inside.

I take his hands, the ones that caught our three children as they emerged from the womb. "I will always love you," I say. "I'm sorry it hurts so much. But I need to stop dying a little every day. I have found me and I am gay."

I married him for better or for worse, but not every day for lunch.

. . . Hazel Weiss

Daily lunches don't worry me. My computer does. Before retirement, my husband felt about computers the way he did about the clothes chute. Holding up two mate-missing socks, he'd say, "Don't ever put anything of mine down there; it never comes back up."

But now he's software buying. He put a version of Wheel of Fortune, solitaire, and poker on my hard drive, which holds much of my office work, since I'm still employed. Just games, I tell myself.

When he added a Spanish course; the NFL schedule for the year; "Improve Your Golf on a Championship Course"; and "Ten Steps to a Better Sex Life," I checked the PC's memory.

Today, I flip the on switch, and a winking flasher in a phony falsetto voice asks, "Don't you just love this instrument?" I resolve to have a talk with hubby and click to open my "Office Budget" file.

Blank spreadsheets fill the screen. Weeks of work not there. With all the calm I can muster, I ask, "Dear, did you use my accounting program today?"

"I tried," he says. "Thought I could put household accounts on. I poked around. But I don't know enough yet. So I just pressed delete."

"Look," I tell him. "Before I delete this marriage, I'm rephrasing a vow. It's this: For better or for worse, but not in my hard drive."

The older you get, the harder it is to lose weight, because your body has made friends with your fat.

• • • Lynne Alpern and Esther Blumenfeld

According to my mother and grandmother, I am not amongst the aged. But according to the amount of food I can consume to maintain my body's weight, I am not an unripe pear. If all I ate was pears, of which there are many varieties, would I benefit? How about tomatoes?

On most days I would claim to be a healthy eater. Writing down my food choices only makes me feel bad and realize how much I have eaten. Exercise is the key to my happiness—probably the serotonin; I heard that on *Oprah.* It just seems unfair at times to separate the fat from its home. Fat is a very lucrative business in this shell of mine—it owns a lot of property, especially on the coastal regions and in the middle inland areas. I equate my body to California. If I keep building I will eventually crack and fall into the ocean. I am sorry that I have to separate an element of my body, but fat, you and me: well, it just isn't working out. I have asked you to leave and now I am resorting to extreme measures. I am kick-boxing you out of here. For good.

Many true words are spoken in jest.

• • • Dinah Maria Mulock Craik

I make my way through the large, crowded restaurant looking for the main exit. Failing to find it on my own, I stop a waitress on her way to serving a table.

"Could you point me in the direction of the door to the parking lot?" I ask.

"Sure, but I can't point 'cause I have my hands full," she says and nods her head in the direction of the exit. "Right over there," she says. "Just go toward the light."

"Oh, no thanks," I say, smiling, "Not yet."

Her face flushes. Her eyes open wide, and she says, "Oh, I didn't mean . . ." and then lets the humor of it take over as I move on toward the . . . door.

I have a theory that every time you make an important choice, the part you left behind continues the other life you could have had.

. . . Jeanette Winterson

Black roots with yellow ends, torn daisy dukes, three-inch stiletto heels, legs thinner than her wishbone-sized arms, a purse flapping in air as fast as her discombobulated words. She worked on the same corner I caught my bus. I watched her, and she watched me. We never talked, only stared. We were the same age, only driven apart by misfortune, misguidance, misunderstanding.

I watched her soul wobble as her ankles did down the uneven road. She smiled when she was sad and cried when she was happy. She sang the same song every day—"Amazing Grace." She whispered in the ears of shoddy men with thoughts that enraged mothers, sisters, friends. She kissed the mouths of those who spewed only hatred for people "like her." People had sex on her, not with her, and left a deposit to her soul-for-sale membership.

I watched her. Afraid that one day I would not see her. Hoping that I would see her. *I see you,* I thought. *Every day for the last two years, I have watched you grow thin; have seen your eyes become colorful like a thunderstorm, blue, lavender, and eventually orange, then white again. I see your pain, I notice your innocence; I know you do this because you have to today, tomorrow, and the next day. As you walk away, I see a line of color follow you from the tip of your heel to the door of a foreign car. Your energy, your passion, your intellect are apparent to those who want to know you, and I do.* I placed this story in her hand—she crumpled it and threw it to the ground. It fell to the gutter, swam in the rain water, and followed the light of her heel.

Grief can sometimes only be expressed in platitudes. We are original in our happy moments. Sorrow has only one voice, one cry.

• • • Ruth Rendell

I am calling the florist to send my friend sympathy flowers. I will give addresses and my Visa numbers. I will ask for something colorful but simple. I don't know what words to send. So I wait until the florist asks, "How do you want the card to read?" Then I have to say something. A something that I file along with other things that I failed at this week or this lifetime.

This time it is a friend whose brother died in a car accident. But whatever the loss, mother, daughter, grandfather, it doesn't matter. I can never rise to the challenge of consolation.

When my friend receives the flowers and the platitudes, she calls me.

Her grief pours through the phone, drowning my doubt and self-centeredness. "I don't know if I can stay sane," she sobs. "This is the first time I've cried."

Together we swim the channels of her grief. My stillness holds her as she thrashes through the murky pain.

She reaches the shore and collapses.

"I'm a little better. Thanks," she gasps.

It is not necessary to find the right words, I see. It is my presence that comforts.

Never go to bed mad. Stay up and fight.

• • • Phyllis Diller

Anger, indignation, annoyance, outrage, inrage, inflammation, the bitterest chocolate with a shot of vinegar. 9 p.m. I prepare dinner. Not a simple one, for that would be . . . simple. Cookbooks, measuring utensils, exotic spices, many pots, many pans, many "oops"es. This time, the grand finale will shine. This time the food's aroma will intoxicate inhibitions, love will be made, the future will continue: peace, warmth, and him.

The stage is set. One cardboard box draped with the sarong I wore on our Mexican vacation one year ago; two dishes (unmatched); two forks (unmatched); one used votive candle; lilacs from the neighbor's yard in a blue sparkling-water bottle; a mug (for me) and our one wine glass (for him). We just moved; it's been tense. The romance still packed in a box in the basement is full of mildew, and neither of us wants to repackage it.

He walks in tired from work. Tonight, I don't want to hear about the day—I want him, us, me, to eat, to whisper, to dance, to touch, to revel.

He doesn't notice the box, the glasses, the aroma, me. He changes into basketball shorts, grabs his keys and a handful of pretzels, and walks out the door. I don't try to stop him as I usually would. I sit at my box, pack his place setting away, eat dinner, clean up, and wait. This is what I promised, to find energy when all I want is to hide underneath the layers of my sadness and feathered comforter. To believe that things will be cured by midnight feels unrealistic; I will plan my words, believe in them, and by all means share them, no matter the hour.

I'm forty-nine but I could be twenty-five except for my face and legs.

• • • Nadine Gordimer

I throw on a blue batik dress, slip silver hoops into my ears, wisp my bangs, and bus over to the government center. Today I am applying for a passport. I am leaving in six weeks for Greece, alone—pretty daring for someone turning fifty.

"You're only as old as you feel," I tell myself. I often think in clichés when I need courage.

I fill out the forms, stand in front of the miniature camera, sit down, and wait.

"Number thirty-five," the clerk calls out. He hands me a set of photographs.

"Whose face is this?" I wonder. "This person with the turkey throat, wrinkled forehead, and drooping eyelids looks something like my mother but . . ."

Suddenly my denial mechanism crashes. This is me!

"Oh, well, beauty is only skin deep," I think out loud as I head for the nearest store that sells anti-aging cream.

Courage is fear that has said its prayers.

• • • Anne Lamott

The "C" word moves into my life with terms like "serious but operable," and I begin the presurgery treatments at the cancer center.

"They're just too young to be here," I think about the young women coming and going for their treatment regime, some with small children in tow. As though it's okay for someone in her seventh decade.

I have to push back at the fears of family and friends when medical journals publish a study dispelling faith and prayer as aids to recovery. I choose to reject those findings and assure the worried that "prayer works."

At home I've filled my feeders, centered in a circle of young, growing pines where the birds gather. I know my winged friends will chatter and chirp their thanks. They're the sounds of spring in the midst of winter that await me each time I return.

Being driven by someone else is an ordeal, for there are only three types of drivers: the too fast, the timid, and oneself.

. . . Virginia Graham

The topic is driving. At lunch, Lorraine tells us about her daughter's visit last week. Lorraine wanted to pick her up at the airport. But her daughter said, "No, Mom, I'd rather you wouldn't be fighting that traffic. I'll just rent a car."

Lorraine said, "Fine." The first two days of her visit, daughter drove. Third day, when they were to visit the Mall of America, daughter said, "Mom, would you mind driving today? I'm low on gas."

Lorraine chuckles. "I knew she wanted to see if old Mom could still handle driving. I guess I passed the test, because from then until she left, I drove."

I say, " The retirees' meeting last week had an aging comedian for the program. She cracked us up with her line about driving: 'I know I'm old. I don't see well, and I can't hear, but thank God I can still drive.'"

"My mother's ninety-six and still drives," Christine says.

In unison, three voices ask, "Which days?"

**We do not die of anguish, we live on. We continue to suffer.
We drink the cup drop by drop.**

• • • George Sand

Sunday. Named for the day, not the date, for that goes unknown. We met him on a Monday. He is fifteen. He dines on a chicken head traded for carrying massive water jugs for foreigners at the local hotel. He makes a fire with garbage instead of curling up under blankets at night. His eyes stopped hoping years ago. Whose wouldn't, living in an alley, starving, not attending school, living a forgotten life? His friends smoke glue to keep their sanity. He doesn't touch it. What is the purpose of this? Why is this his life and not mine? There is no fear in his eyes—wonder, perplexity. Why not anger?

I cannot speak his language; he does not want to speak mine, but he follows us, strangers, people willing to help. The doctor draws his blood; the results will be back by 8 p.m. The local diner serves a plate larger than his weight. He doesn't breathe, just inhales, inhales. For god's sake he is starving. He is fifteen, he is growing, he needs food. We say, "Meet us by 8 p.m.," for he is independent, used to living alone. We wonder if he will show.

He peers from a corner, walks with us, gets medicine for malaria, typhoid, and worms. He thanks us and walks into the night. We will follow up, but I cannot be his mother, he cannot be my son; it is not permitted. He will eat, go to school, and someday not live in an alley.

I stop at times. The air is silent, but if I pause long enough I feel his small, tiring heart; he is crying. From afar I write, send school fees, anything so he finds shelter in some place other than hell, where he currently resides.

March 24

Nature doesn't move in a straight line, and as part of nature, neither do we.

• • • Gloria Steinem

White snow, blown into light peaked drifts. Rosy ivory sand curves on the beach as the water laps the shore. A raining downpour here, but not on the other side of the street. Squirrels collecting acorns, storing them in a place they will forget. Leaves, scarlet, yellow, orange raging with beauty today, brown and dead tomorrow. The smallest thin-needled pine tree in the shadowed woods holds up through the storm that levels the huge oak.

So much to learn about the mystery of my own life. About being patient with my own timing, imperfections, softness, strength.

In a great romance, each person basically plays a part that the other really likes.

• • • Elizabeth Ashley

He had the kind of good looks that turn female heads. He liked classic art, music, and antiques; loved my Italian cooking; and knew how to court a woman on one well-planned date after another.

I fell in love.

When he said he didn't want kids, I agreed. Who needed more than each other? When he said we'd live on the second floor of the old house he was remodeling, I agreed. So what if we moved from one wallboard, paint, and varnish mess to another, living in fixer-uppers until they were ready to rent or sell?

And what if he did budget the money—an allowance for me and for household expenses—and then asked for an accounting of how I spent it? I loved the guy.

Ten years into marriage I found myself pregnant. His response was tender concern for me and a surprise house with a yard, which he chose and bought, ending our nomads-in-the-city existence. I fell in love again, a love that's lasted forty years.

When friends ask if I didn't ever resent his captain-of-the-ship-attitude, I say, "Sometimes." When I did, I'd go into a closet, muffle a scream into the clothes rack, and emerge ready to live and love.

Let us linger in the foolishness of things.

● ● ● Anonymous

In the dim light of a classy bar, with magenta stools, pewter fixtures, a hundred kinds of martinis, and a sushi happy hour, inappropriate sounds are coming from one corner.

The sophisticated clientele try not to notice. Lift glasses to their lips, shifting their eyes sideways over the rims, looking at and commenting about the commotion.

Which is, of course, where my friends and I are. We are spitting out martinis, not on purpose at these prices, but because we are laughing so hard. We are doubled over the little, round, shiny tables shaking them with our guffawing. We snort, hoot, talk too loudly.

We just got there. We're not drunk. We all work together for child protection. It was one of those days when things that should be unimaginable happened to kids we know. Someone said something sort of funny, and we let go, let go of the pain, anger, frustration, despair, hopelessness, that we carried in. We spit it out like poison into the jazzed air.

Just before the manager asked us to leave, we got quiet, and we lingered.

There is no human relationship more intimate than that of nurse and patient, one in which the essentials of character are more rawly revealed.

. . . Dorothy Canfield Fisher

Her stomach is swollen yet from the large baby. I walk into the room; she cradles the infant as though she practiced in her room with the door closed, holding a pillow swaddled in a blanket, soothing its temper and rocking it to sleep. It is now a she. A she who needs her. A her who was yesterday a girl. A girl who today is a mother. Her milk fresh. The baby warm. Uncarved territory. She is alone but wise. Wise but alone. I want to walk with her. I want her to walk with me. The infant with no father but with one. The father with an infant but without one. The mother lives without family but created one. She: the mother, infant, daughter. One breath, one blood, relying on each other for love, food, and company. They are not mine to keep, for they have their own path to create, but I wish they were, even for just a day.

One arm full with bags, the other with life, she walks through the door. I think to myself, *I will think of you often.* "I believe in you," I say.

The greatest thing I ever was able to do was give a welfare check back. I brought it back and said, "Here. I don't need this anymore."

• • • Whoopi Goldberg

The only break in the green-gray drabness of the room is white-bordered signs proclaiming, "November is potato month." Apparently the thinking is that people who are dependent on food stamps couldn't possibly know that potatoes are a good buy.

A woman seated at the lone desk gives me a number. "Take a seat," she says. I move to a bench along the wall. A man makes room for me. He's too thin for his height, with more than a day's growth of beard—his clothing unkempt. In a behind-the-hand whisper he asks, "Did you get anything?"

His question throws me back to the waning years of the Great Depression. At age fourteen I stood in a long line that moved slowly toward the front door of these same offices where a brusque county employee ushered me through and nudged me forward.

I sat on the hard bench and waited for a social worker to deem what my family's monthly clothing and food allowance should be. As each person exited from the partitions behind the one desk, I heard the hope-filled "Did you get anything?"

I vowed never to be here again. But I am, on behalf of a nursing home patient who has spent all of her own money and now needs to plead for medical aid. No longer the young girl in the sturdy, styleless welfare shoes, but a woman feeling again the humiliation of poverty, and the symbolic rigidity of the bench along the wall.

I turn back to the man and answer, "Not yet. I just got here. I'm hoping."

March 29

**Never fail yourself / Never commit to limits . . . / Follow /
The particulars of your spirit / As they pull you . . .**
• • • Veronica D. Cunningham

The aroma of cheap, canned, yet freshly brewed coffee fills my apartment. It is a typical Sunday, only this day has no sun. My mind needs a moment of reprieve, a second of nonsense that jumpstarts the imagination I packed away with my letter jacket and other high school trophies.

As I am folding my last pair of line-dried laundry, I pretend that I am the piece of lint I pick off my cotton briefs. Lint. Not a particular color. A floral fresh or raindrop aroma might be nice. A piece that travels from the pants of one to the shirt pocket of another. I like to travel. To go where their feet go; to be with but not heard. I would find my way into the purse of the rich, fancy, lacy type and move to the vinyl coin container of a different variety. Move from the dryer of a large spin-cycle, to the outside wire connected by two chiclet trees warmed by the sun.

You need not return me for I will find my way, somewhere, anywhere. I am not sad but curious and ready, packed with my essential, hope and a plastic bag in case of rain. I have no objections to planes, trains, or automobiles. All I ask is keep me warm and dry, for this adventure is beginning, and we all know what happens to wet lint.

I try to live a "poetic existence." That means I take responsibility for the air I breathe and the space I take up. I try to be immediate, to be totally present in my work.

• • • Maya Angelou

In the garden, in the laundry room, at the office, going for a walk, helping my kids with their homework, making love, writing a letter, watching a movie, staring out the window, reading a book, listening to music, cooking, ironing, arranging a bouquet, visiting my parents, playing Scrabble, petting my cat, swimming, talking to a friend on the phone, listening to the neighbor woman, cleaning the house, washing the dishes, shoveling the snow, mowing the grass, painting the house, making a sand castle, refinishing a table, embroidering, hanging a picture, taking pictures, being in the picture, laughing, laughing, crying, crying, crying, breathing, breathing, living, living, living in the present.

april...

Cover my Earth Mother four times with many flowers.

• • • From a Zuni song

A week ago, Teresa woke and heard birds singing in the damp April air. Their mild melodies filled her with melancholy as she remembered the same date forty years ago when her mother walked into little Teresa's bedroom. Teresa expected her to say, "Happy birthday, eight-year-old girl." Instead she screamed, "Your father just died! You have to help me!" From that day on, Teresa helped many people—her mother and sister, the poor, children, and us, her loving band of women friends. We called her our earth mother.

A week ago, it was Teresa's birthday. "Someday," she whispered to her husband, "I hope spring sounds will make me happy." She stroked his hair, gasped deeply, and died.

For six days, we have cupped each other's tears in our lonely hearts. Today, we sprinkle water and drop red, dewy flower petals on a heap of earth that covers her body. And, in the damp April air, we sing songs that we hope will make Teresa happy.

I am glad it cannot happen twice, the fever of first love.

. . . Daphne du Maurier

I slept next to him in oversized overalls, matched with a long-sleeved fleece shirt, a large sweater, and socks. We knew each other through the restaurant. I loved his wit; he loved my hair, eyes, and legs. Me, the non-drinking, straitlaced college girl who looked pretty but didn't know how to have fun. He, the guzzling, slightly overweight, college-hating boy who was smart enough to not have the kind of fun he had. We hit it off. Lying with our arms interlinked in a room with no heat, we provided the new way. Sharing childhood laughter, realizing our trust, breaking the barriers of the unknown, he swept me off my feet and landed me on my head. This one, the one of ones, will not be, should not be, was never. We were different intrinsically. He was so tall, so smart, so charming, but my oh my, not the one to throw a barrel of water laced with trust, for he would drink the contents and simply excrete the nutrients without a second look.

**The past is written! Close the book / On pages sad and gray. /
Within the future do not look, / But live today today.**

▪ ▪ ▪ Lydia Avery Coonley Ward

I arrive at the monthly bridge game just in time to hear Liz say,
"Did you know that the man down the street died yesterday?
The one who just bought Arnie's house?"

"No! What happened?" seven of us ask, almost in unison.

"I only know it was totally unexpected," says Liz. "He just
turned sixty-five, retired, and bought the house. He loved gardening, so he wanted the big yard."

"What a shame. None of us even got to know him," says Carol.

"You just never know, do you?" says Nina.

While Liz deals the cards, I wonder if the man who died had
fun paging through the seed catalogs and plotting his garden.
Or did he sacrifice living to planning for the tomorrow that never
came? I look around at the faces of my friends and settle in to
enjoy the afternoon.

As Nina said, you just never know, do you?

The brother that gets me is going to get one hell of a fabulous woman.

• • • Aretha Franklin

Watch couples walking down the street. If she is pretty, he is handsome. If he is dumpy, so is she. If one walks with her chin up in the air, so does the other one. If one slouches, the same.

Not me and my guy. He is knock-'em-dead gorgeous. I'm not saying this because I love him. Ask anybody. They'll tell you that women swoon when he enters a room.

I went right from baby fat to middle-age sprawl. I have acne older than I am. I am short and not in that perky way. My nose is too long and my lips too small.

But you know what, I am one of the most fascinating, dynamic, loving people on the planet. And if you aren't looking in the wrong places, I'm so attractive.

My guy knows it. "How did I get so lucky as to get you?" he asks me at least once a week.

So when heads turn and I see them asking, "How did she ever catch him?" I say to myself, "He was running my way. As fast as he could!"

One reason that cats are happier than people is that they have no newspapers.

• • • Gwendolyn Brooks

I am an activist. Always working on the next cause to save the world. I petitioned for the whales, marched for peace, donated to feed starving children, wrote letters to the editor about the schools, ran a 5K race against breast cancer. I teach migrant children.

But I never feel as if I have done enough. Some days I get very tired, in my bones and in my soul.

I used to say that I wanted to come back in the next life as Gandhi or Mother Teresa. So I could be more effective in doing good.

But yesterday, on my fifty-second birthday, I thought, "The older I get, the more often I think I'd like to come back as a pampered cat, with lots of time to curl up, nap, and purr."

Old friends go away, one way or another. New friends come along when we give them a chance.

• • • Sue Schoening-Roess

She phones today and says, "I'm calling about the Georgia O'Keeffe exhibit at the Art Institute. Would you like to go?"

"Love to," I say. "Thanks for thinking of me."

I put down the phone, feeling so good that I hug myself.

Her name's Rosie. We met when I joined the local women's golf league where Rosie's been a member on a team with three longtime friends for several years. One friend moved out of town, so they needed a fill-in. The league manager gave them me.

"I hope I do okay. I've been golfing only seven years. Since I retired," I poured out in rapid, nervous chatter.

"Hey," said Rosie. "Don't worry. I've got the highest handicap around."

I learned that isn't true. But who couldn't forgive a comforting fib from someone willing to be a friend?

If he ain't willing to strap on the rubber bridle, then I ain't willin' to ride.

• • • Calamity Wronsky and Belle Bendall

I have spent upwards of $200 on pregnancy kits. I call them "Please, please don't let me be pregnant" kits. $100 worth of $10 co-pays. I check the dates of my last period, double-check, triple-check, check them one more time.

This free clinic is full of bouncing legs, anxious stomachs churning (often misinterpreted as an active fetus). The signs state statistics about the effectiveness of the "pull-out method." Depending on the reason for my visit, I think, *who would ever just rely on that?* or *I really hope that I am in the 15 percent.*

Multiple phone conversations with sympathetic friends, cutting back on caffeine "just in case," trying to avoid sex, and money that I could use for many other things. All of my friends and I have avoided the inevitable so far. Knowing that invisible bugs live in our secretions, I realize my risk is not just the possibility of being pregnant, but whether I will live or die, spread horrible diseases, or be at a higher rate of cervical cancer.

This game of roulette is nasty. I give up. For Christmas I am asking Santa for a Trojan horse. Maybe I will buy stock in the company and make money on the deal. This time I will not sacrifice my health for pleasure that is not mine. I will cope with the extra thought—he will cope with a healthy partner who is not afraid to make love anymore, who is willing to try new positions, who won't yell out, "Did you, inside of me?" and jump out of bed and begin the flushing process.

Yup, condoms. That is the answer.

I wonder if she knows how much I miss her . . . the girl that I used to be.

• • • Flavia

"I've found a great editor," says my daughter, Mary. "She's talented. Writes poetry, works for a publisher. She's young."

"How young?" I ask.

"Mid-twenties," Mary says, and I groan.

While Mary's out of town, I take our manuscript to the editor. She stands when I enter her office—her tall slimness interrupted by the slight bulge of early pregnancy. She brushes back a strand of dark hair and greets me by name.

Memory strikes. I'm twenty-four again, mother of two. I've pulled my shoulder-length dark hair back into a bun to look older. In love with words and eager to show a prospective employer that I could write, that I could even edit.

Why was he insisting I was too young and that child care could be a problem?

What was wrong with being young?

"I'm excited about working on this," says the editor.

I reply, "And you're just the person for the job."

The essence of volunteerism is not giving part of a surplus one doesn't need, but giving part of one's self. Such giving is more than a duty of the heart, but a way that people help themselves by satisfying the deeper spiritual needs that represent the best that is in us.

• • • Kathleen Kennedy Townsend

They came to my apartment to hear the stories from Africa, heart-wrenching stories of people just like us. Creative, intelligent, hard-working people who love their children and honor their parents. The only difference is that they don't have enough food to eat, clean water to drink, medical care, or a way to make a living. The women in my apartment listened. Some of them cried. They were carefully picked friends of many ages with skills, security, and spirit.

Those friends who returned to the next meeting and the next are young women. Much younger than I. They work and work. Year after year for no monetary compensation. They make a difference in the lives of people far away.

They humble me. Fascinate me. Why do they do it?

At one meeting, Amanda said it for all of them, "I do it for myself as much as for the people in Africa. This work fills something inside of me. My need to be my best self."

Bad judgment and carelessness are not punishable by rape.

• • • Pearl Cleage

At a park in a car at 4 a.m. A simple "no," a contradicting motion, a stabbing pain, a rush of liquid plasma soaking the cushion. The police arrive—past park hours, they say; he's arrested, reason unknown, tabs expired, outstanding warrants, we find out later. The cops say to drive the car home for him. "Sure," I say, as a puddle of my inners forms in front of them. I gasp, trying to steal an unfair percentage of oxygen from the air, faster, faster I try until I black out at a red light, almost every red light. I dash to the front door. I was not allowed to see him, to be out this late, a lie that unmasks many others. This time I cannot continue. I tell Father, "I had sex and I won't stop bleeding." He replies, "Do you want me to get Mom?" As I fall to the floor, I see the blood-stained finger strokes I left on the door.

(Did I say no or yes? I did say yes because I was there, I loved the idea of being with him, exciting, dangerous, not painful, bloody, nonconsensual.)

My older brother carries me to the emergency room, where they ask, "Why didn't you use a condom?" How do I respond? It was his fist. The watch he was wearing did this. No need for a condom. I have never had sex before. As the doctor finishes sewing, he asks, "Was this your first time? Sometimes this can happen." I think it feels like a chili pepper exploded inside of my vagina. "This can happen—" why? to whom? how often? I faint twice.

I tell no one until my brother holds my hand (the hand that drove the car to the impound lot, his pants covered in my blood). I tell him. He says, "I love you and you are safe now."

We do not want them to have less. But it is only natural that we should think we have not enough. We drive on, we drive on.

• • • Gwendolyn Brooks

Workers spew out of downtown buildings, bracing against a surprise April snow. I notice a thin Hispanic woman standing in water-soaked sandals at a busy intersection. Her long, black hair rests on the front of the thin sweater she wears. An ankle-length, wet skirt clings to her legs. She holds a baby wrapped in a coat.

I stop. "Could I give you a ride somewhere?" I ask. Her fear-filled eyes tell me she doesn't understand. I plead, "Let me take you home."

She understands "home," and hands me a slip of paper on which is her name, Teresa, and her address. I nod. She gets into the car. We arrive at an old frame building, once a small grocery before the freeway raped the neighborhood, leaving a few run-down houses and buildings such as this.

A young man comes and takes the baby, says, "Muchas gracias," and then in English, "We came to plant apple trees, but the weather is not good. We found a doctor to see the baby. We did not think it would snow like winter."

Smiling, they both wave from the storefront door. I drive on, vowing to offer my friendship to Teresa, feeling rescued from the smugness of plenty.

When they want to overpay you, there's usually a reason.

• • • Diana Vreeland

My daughter, a senior in high school, sighs one of those "Ask me what is wrong with *you*" sighs as I hang up the phone.

"So," I ask her. "What's the groaning about?"

"It's eleven o'clock at night. You've been on the phone about your job for three hours. Don't even tell me that you have a lot of responsibilities and people counting on you and it's a good thing you do because that's what puts clothes on my back and food on our table."

"Okay. I won't," I answer. But I am so exhausted, I don't want to get into it with her.

She continues, "You were happy on your other job. You remember, the one that still let you see your family occasionally?"

"Yes, but—" As she interrupts me, I think, *But you don't understand that I didn't make enough money to give you what you want and I think you need.*

On she goes, "Yes, but—this one is for the money. To quote you, 'For once in my life I'm going for the gold.' That's not you, Mom. And it's going to drive us all crazy."

"I'm sorry, I do what I think is best. Shouldn't you go to bed?"
"Sure."

I sit down at my desk to finish more work. I hear her brushing her teeth, climbing into her bed. I go to her room. "Thanks, honey. You're right. I'm going to figure something out."

"Mom, you know what I love best about you?"
"What?"
"That you know when to apologize."

I love the abandonment to impulse, I act from impulse only, and I love to madness that others do the same by me.

• • • Julie de Lespinasse

My discombobulation is referred to by others as disorganization, ADD, caffeine-induced chaos, immaturity, anxiety. The difference between how I make decisions and how someone else might is that often there is no reason for mine. The motion that drives my thoughts feels like something outside of me rather than inside. I am the type to plan my next trip—by *plan,* I mean book the tickets today. I am the type to plan a haircut—by *plan,* I mean walk into a salon the same day. I am the type to plan my future— by *plan,* I mean work hard in school, take adventures that inspire me, strive to help as many people in one sitting as I can, and when that is done, move on to putting an end to world poverty. Random, well-intentioned, traveled, I follow a path of random-ness. The road to impulsiveness can be a lonely one. The lovely people that accompany me breathe the energy of my motion, and I do the same. The scattered approach I take is not that of my select group of companions. It creates swirls of frustration in their heads, but they come with me, step by leap, leap by bounds. I risk the inevitable, myself, my time, my humility. I do not know where to go at times, but I sway with the movement left by others' excursions, well planned and all. There is one thing I consistently plan: to live my life one bounce, one energy thrust at a time.

If you rest, you rust.

• • • Helen Hayes

We've come, Leona and I, to meet three friends we've known for more than a half century for Sunday brunch—and to bask in the elegance of an early 1900s mansion with its shining silver and fragile china and crystal chandeliers.

With the formality of a well-trained house servant, the waiter seats us at the window table we've reserved. Looking up from the silk-corded menu he hands us, we see a pair of cute young beagles in the park across the way.

"There's a walker that's set quite a pace for herself," I say.

"Dogs are better than treadmills to keep you exercising," Leona says. "No treadmill's going to come with a leash in its mouth begging for a walk."

"Don't need a dog," says our friend Julia. "I've got one of those exercise pads that folds into the size of big briefcase." With a tender smile that spells appreciation, she adds, "And my beloved Marie, here, to see that I use it."

"Listening to this conversation, you'd think we were thirty-something, instead of pushing eighty, " says Gloria. Raising her wine glass in salute, she adds, "Isn't that grand?"

Laugh and the world laughs with you. Cry and you cry with your girlfriends.

• • • Laurie Kuslansky

Girlfriends. Friends from my girlhood. Remembering how we laughed until we spit the cherry Coke across the ice cream parlor counter. How we hated the pretty new girl on the block. How we camped in the back yard and got scared to be so far away from home. Had lemonade stands. Played baseball in the alley. Went to the Saturday matinees, sneaking in our own popcorn.

We are at my father's wake. No one, but no one, would be allowed to laugh with me here. Except my girlfriends. The ones he would tease because they had freckles. Buy ice cream cones for. Build a sandbox for. The ones who envied me because I had a dad who loved my mother. Who came home from work on time and sober. Who shoveled the sidewalk and mowed the grass. A father who did what fathers should do and didn't think about it much.

They who loved him with me can laugh and cry, and cry, and cry with me.

Dolly used to get almost tipsy upon sunshine. The weather is as much part of some people's lives as the minor events which happen to them.

• • • Miss Thackeray

I spent my childhood watching her. Her house, painted purple. Her shutters, an ocean blue. Her lawn, spray-painted the color of the setting sun. The sea-colored wood faced us all winter. She never left her home once the snow fell. We'd know the day of her descent was coming when she chopped off her long graying braids. It was my job to gather her mail, place it in the white wicker basket, and present it the first day of spring.

I wondered why she wouldn't prepare, save money, cancel her paper and catalogs, ask us to shovel her walk. I wrote letters to her asking her to try sledding, hot chocolate, reading one of her *Reader's Digests* in front of our fireplace. The desire to reach her consumed me.

One morning I heard the familiar shattering of icicles on the concrete sidewalk. I gathered her basket plump with typed information of a season gone by. I put my snow boots on, took the plate of cookies saved from the holidays out of the freezer, wrapped them in yellow cellophane, and in a daring move packaged the letters I saved for her all of those years. I placed them on her stoop and dragged through knee-deep banks back to my warm home. Later that evening it snowed again. I realized with every frozen flake that it would be days before I saw the sunshine woman.

On my way out for school I found my wicker basket on the porch stairs, in it a fuzzy yellow quilt. Footprints in the snow led to her home. She wrote, "I had to do something with all of that hair, and the leftover spray paint for my yard. Thanks, kid. See you in the sun."

One day I have chicken to eat and the next day the feathers.

• • •   Calamity Jane

I do not mean to insult anyone or their ways, but may I just ask a few questions? If adult stomachs are similar in size, why does it take some six courses to fill the pouch and some a piece of bread and a cup of tea? I watch them come to play tennis at the club across the street from my work. The teams: wealthy and wealthier. The uniform, diamond rings with a sparkle noticeable from across the street, cars with seats like armchairs covered in animal skin, workout attire purposefully dressed down but never worn, water bottles filled with drops of mist from international waterfalls, and the infamous card—small enough to be a credit card but rounded by the gluttony of affluence—that grants them access to the pearly gates called a health club. Is tennis then the game that monitors the stocks and bonds of each player, not the serve?

I am a person who grew up with what people with this much would see as nothing. I want to be at a place where I can eat and read at the same time, play in the muddy park with the same sweatshirt I painted in last night, take the city bus not because I have to but out of respect for the environment.

I was poor by all practical terms but, my goodness, the soul that grows from hunger, thirst, fear, and inadequacy is like the richest cream soup, indescribably delicious. I do not judge; that is never fair. I just admire the differences of all of us, our backgrounds, our futures, and all the stuff in between. I may introduce myself to them, the fancy ones across the street, just to sample the tastes of their soup, and let them savor my flavor.

Each child has one extra line to your heart, which no other child can replace.

• • • Marguerite Kelly and Ella Parsons, *The Mother's Almanac*

At a bridal shower for my son's fiancée, his future mother-in-law smiled at me and said, "I guess this wedding can't be all joy for you. You know the old saying, "A son's your son 'til he gets him a wife. A daughter's your daughter all her life."

I wondered if remarks like that are what make in-laws barely tolerate one another. I returned her smile without comment. Of my three children, the son she warned me I was losing was the middle child. When his baby brother cried, he was the one who asked if it was time to feed him. The one who said, "You've gotta be kidding" when I told him I already had and explained breast-feeding.

When the newly installed furnace had not yet warmed the house on the day my husband left for the Korean War, he was the one who said, "Mommy, don't cry. I'll keep you warm," and tried to with all the strength of a five-year-old's hug—thinking the tears I shed were because I was cold.

He was the one who, at age ten, lugged home discarded evergreens, in bundles as tall as he was, from the tree lot near his school, and worked at shaping them into wire clothes hangers to make holiday wreaths for gifts, when there was no money to buy them.

He is the one in the middle who elbowed a space in my heart between a sister and a brother that only he can fill. He'll always be there.

The first time I see a jogger smiling, I'll consider it.

• • • Joan Rivers

I know that women my age jog. I see them running around the nearby lake. Wearing black shorts and tank tops.

I encouraged my children to always do one thing for their bodies. Probably because I didn't form the habit as a child and wanted them to be healthier.

One of them jogs seriously. The other two sort of jog and work out regularly. I am very happy about that.

However, there is also some guilt connected with having active offspring. I feel not only slothful but also—well, not with it, old.

So I tried jogging for a while. I had almost convinced myself that I liked pounding around the lake when I got shin splints. Really, really bad ones!

I went to my doctor. She said, "Some people shouldn't jog. Your body just isn't made for it. Stick to walking."

Who says doctors are overpaid?

We are not amused!

• • • Queen Victoria

My twelve-year-old spent the week at his friend's family's lake cabin. He's perched on a stool in the kitchen telling me about all the sunnies they caught—those small, colorful fish that make good eating when pan-fried and served up crisp on the outside, tender on the inside. "Sounds like you had a really good time," I say.

"Yeah, it was fun," he says, snatching a strawberry from the salad I'm making, "except one day when Gordie's mom fried the fish wrong."

"What do you mean she fried the fish wrong? That's not easy to do for a good cook, and she's a good cook."

"I thought they were good, but Gordie's dad said, 'What did you do to these fish? Did you cook them covered? They're not very crisp.' His mom said, 'Here, let me fix that,' and took 'em back. She did it twice before his dad said, 'That's much better.'

"Boy, was I getting nervous," he says.

"Why?" I ask.

"I kept waiting for her to say, 'You know what? Why don't you fry your own damn fish?'"

I put my spoon down and ask, "What made you think she'd ever say that?"

Ducking out of my reach, with a grin, he says, "You would," and scampers out the door, out of reach, letting it slam behind him.

I decided as usual that justice lay in the middle—that is to say nowhere.
· · · Antonia Fraser

We kissed good-bye on the lips. I love that about her. She came for the weekend; oh, my heart pulsed through my chest in anticipation. This semester, a long maze of work, every corner I turn, more reading, more research, more sleepless nights. When she comes to town, I can sleep as though I am five again waiting to be tucked in.

She never saw it coming, they think. A vehicle with eighteen wheels; why they call it a semi, I do not know because it fully destroyed my life. The driver, charged with driving under the influence, obviously not of wisdom at that moment, or consideration for others' lives. The grief so intense I melt as though butter on hot pancakes, our favorite meal together. I am five again, and dammit I want my mom, here, not in spirit, by my side.

The court date. Cleansing: not the word I would use. Closure of a wound so deep I have to tape myself together in the mornings: not possible. I stare at his back wondering what he looked like as a child, if his mother is here somewhere, what he had to drink, how it tasted, if he has a daughter.

I do not wish him a shortened life, or even a harder one, at this moment when I tell him that she is my heart, and when she left I stopped breathing: what could be harder? What else could you do to a person? He will do his time, and so will I, and so will my mom. No justice, only memories, permanent scars. "Good luck to you. You now realize your power, a life taken. Please recapture yours, for me, and for my mom."

It has begun to occur to me that life is a stage I'm going through.

• • • Erma Bombeck

My thirty-year-old son answered the phone.

How can it be that this is my son, the one with the responsible deep voice? Why, just yesterday he squeaked his first words, or so it seems.

"I was really calling to talk to Tyler. To wish him a happy second birthday," I say.

"Sure, Mom. But before you are grandma, I could use a little mothering."

"What's the matter?"

"I'm feeling kind of sad and can't shake it."

"About what?"

"I'm not sure you will understand."

"Try me."

"Well, Tyler is two years old already. You just have no idea how quickly time goes by."

Luckily, I remember to be respectful, as I chuckle to myself.

"I'm sorry you are feeling sad. But it's just one of those parental stages," I say.

That never ends, I think.

When we were children we used to think that when we were grown up we would no longer be vulnerable. But to grow up is to accept vulnerability.

• • • Madeleine L'Engle

I don't remember a time when my mother said that I had done something well, that I was pretty, or that she loved me. I guess some kids would have rebelled; I spent my childhood trying to please her, trying to be the perfect child that Mom could love. I'd clear the table without being told and wash the dishes with extra care, hoping that Mom would say "good job." Like the other kids, I'd make Mother's Day cards at school and take them home eagerly. "Hmph," she'd say, and set them aside to go into the recycling.

My mother is old now. I visit her, bring her perfectly prepared food and perfectly arranged flowers and listen to her say, "What did you bring those for?" I know that a gentle word of thanks will never come, and I shrug off the spike of hurt I feel.

My brother asks me why I bother, and I say, "I do it for me. I can't just not care."

Show me a woman who doesn't feel guilty and I'll show you a man.

• • • Erica Jong

Utterly phenomenal. The take he has on situations never ceases to amaze me and all of my senses. In classic guilt-provoking situations, he feels nothing. The stage is set. We enter the restaurant. Two hungry people, in jolly moods. Restaurant popping at the seams, servers running like rats escaped from a fourth-grader's science experiment. We are seated, the menus are in hand, the server drips by, finally slides across the floor on another puddle of sweat (produced by the manager, I believe), and arrives without rattling anything. *Impressive,* I think; my companion thinks nothing of it. Our drink order taken and the server is off. I watch the ballet of servers set at the pace of ska music. They have many close collision calls, and then our friendly sweaty server crashes into his other table, spilling a dark-red substance on top of them. At this point, the gratuity I plan to leave instantly doubles, but my lovable male friend feels nothing. He may say, "Wow, that sucks for him," but he won't feel induced to change his behavior (or his tip) on the basis of someone else's bad luck. Guilt: what a strange phenomenon. I think that at times I confuse it with being responsible, compassionate, or nice. What an uncomplicated life I could have, what freedom, how much money I would save without it. But he spilt the drinks all over them; I have to do something—right?

If high heels were so wonderful, men would be wearing them."

• • • Sue Grafton, *I Is for Innocence*

"You really shouldn't wear those high heels. They throw your whole body out of sync," I say to the young receptionist who's busy straightening the magazines in the wall rack at the dental office.

"I wear them all the time," she says. "My boyfriend hates flat shoes on women. High heels are just sexier."

I pick up a copy of *Time* to read, but I keep thinking about what she said. Sexy was never a word I applied to shoes, though I surrendered the comfort of penny loafers for high heels when I entered the world of employment. They were the fashion with skirts and dresses. Even when pants suits for women gained approval for the workplace, we women wore heels for the feminine touch.

About the time a generation decided "Gentlemen prefer Hanes" was sexist, not factual, women put their feet closer to the ground in shoes that spared spine and ankles. The rest is history playing itself out in the clunky, comfort-stressing shoes that gained popularity in the 1990s and into the twenty-first century.

That was a break for women who bore the pain and strain of the high-heel era. I stretch my feet out and look down at my Mother Superior-style shoes, soft and wide for wiggle room on thick, gummy soles that cushion the pebbles of life. Not so out of fashion, after all.

Blows are sarcasms turned stupid.

• • • George Eliot

I tell myself that if he ever hit me I would leave.

I would. I know I would.

He is coming downstairs now. I can hear his measured steps. My stomach tightens. He said after he finished working we would talk about some things he has on his mind.

I don't know what things he means. I do know I will have to defend or duck. Either counter his sarcasm with my own or accept what is being said. I can lose a ten-round fight by a wide decision, because he is the champion. Or I can take a knockout in the first round. I can't imagine a way out of the ring.

"I don't suppose you've ever given any logical thought to this . . . ," he starts.

I counter with, "I did have a logical thought once, about ten years ago." It looks like ten rounds coming up.

But if he ever hits me. That's it.

"I don't know if there's anything in the world I can't do . . .
In my creative source, whatever that is, I don't see why I can't sculpt.
Why shouldn't I? Human beings sculpt. I'm a human being."
• • • Maya Angelou

I tune into the Oprah Winfrey show. Maya Angelou is on, celebrating her seventy-fifth birthday. I look her up in a reference
book, which lists her as a U.S. poet, writer, entertainer, dancer,
producer. I'm in awe of her. She's done so much and plans to do
more, ignoring her age and living her life.

She and Oprah connect as only black women can. So genuinely
affectionate is the touch of Oprah's hand on Maya's arm that a
shiver goes through me. I feel like an eavesdropper.

Oprah surprises Maya with a videotape of her son, in which
he thanks his mother for his life, and in loving tribute celebrates
hers. This woman of almost superhuman accomplishments weeps
with joy and love.

My tears join hers as though my son were on the screen. I feel
her humanity, and I'm no longer a stranger looking in from the
outside. We are connected, after all, Maya and I, in the common-
ality of motherhood.

You may say that I'm a dreamer. But I'm not the only one.

• • • John Lennon

My brother loves John Lennon. He sings him, has photos of him, reads about him.

Thinks like him. He is a dreamer who often wonders if he is the only one.

I am eight years older than he is. I have worried about him since the day he was born. Today, I watched him look at a sunset over the ocean. Listened to him as he shared his struggles. I won't worry any more. It is not my place. I can't control his happiness through my worry. I have to respect him enough to know he will lead the life that makes him happy.

Instead I hope for him. I hope someday he will know that although there aren't as many who dream his dreams as don't, we are here. And we wish him peace and love.

We perceive silence where, in fact, there is a muffler.

• • • Louise Bernikow

We are like a fruit rollup—she is the plastic and I am the pressed fruit—strawberry, I think. We separate but cannot retain our form without each other. We have love, great sex, commonalities, the sharing of our lives. We struggle for money because it seems like the romantic thing to add to a controversial relationship, and it gives us character. She tells me it is due to the fact we don't have any, but I like to believe otherwise. We use our intuition to connect and our tempers to disengage.

I can feel the situation coming to a boil. I fear heat, for I know I will melt and surrender portions of my texture, durability, and elasticity. She stalks the apartment, pillaging, ranting. I am not the victim but a pedestrian adjacent to a freeway with no sidewalk. She warns me with a beep of her horn, and I leap for the ditch. She follows me and hovers, beating her large black wings. I am prey at these moments. My insides dart from side to side. I hear her stomach rumble. My heart skips four beats. She raises her neck and erects her back, but just as she plans her swoop, a piece of yesterday's paper blows into my bunker. Snatching it from the ground, I overextend my rattling arm, a white flag. A squawk from her beak guarantees safe passage.

I am not afraid, just resourceful: to engage means building armor. I have not the time nor the energy to war against the woman with whom I want to share a bubble bath and a glass of cheap scotch.

The heresy of one age becomes the orthodoxy of the next.

• • • Helen Keller

The year is 1943, I'm a northern girl newly arrived in a southern city. I've taken the bus into downtown to shop. In a store, I stop to look at buttons on display. A black woman steps aside to pass me and bumps my elbow. She backs away, bowing, "Pardon me, ma'am. I'm sorry. I'm sorry," she says.

I reach out to her, saying, "Oh, it was my fault. I stopped abruptly." She quickly moves away to avoid my touch.

The experience stuns me. I take the next bus home to a house an aging southern gentleman generously shares with army couples, where black servants cook and serve his meals and care for his personal needs. Empty seats surround me; "coloreds" stand in the back.

Years later, at a civil rights meeting, a black teenager sums up racism differences in the South and North. She says, "In the South you whites don't care how close we get, just so we don't get too big. In the North you don't care how big we get, just so we don't get too close."

I remember a woman, her dark hair beginning to tinge with white, bowing to a nineteen-year-old witnessing the humiliation of a people, and I wonder: Do we see the wrong in that yet?

may...

You were courted and got married in the magic world, but you had your baby in the real one.

• • • Bess Streeter Aldrich

I am two weeks away from my twenty-seventh birthday. A meaningless age except that it's inching closer to that very meaningful thirtieth. This year I will share my celebration with my new little bundle of joy (as my mother refers to her). She was born just three weeks ago. Prior to having her I was the CEO of a large human resources firm, had a romantic love life with my husband, took Pilates classes at the YMCA twice a week, got my hair cut once a month, and wore a size eight. Now I stay at home, fall asleep and dream about romance with my husband, bounce the baby for exercise, haven't had a haircut in two months, and wear a size twelve.

I never thought any of those external things were important and wrote them off as superficial. However, in their absence I am finding new ways to re-create who I am and how I make myself feel good. I look at this little miracle in my hands and remember worrying if I could even get pregnant. She is the answer to that question. Now I stare into her eyes and wonder, *Can I be a parent? Will I know how to answer those questions I always wondered about as a child?* "Why is the sky blue? Why is there war? What is God?" I sit here thinking, *I never answered any of those questions for myself! Why did I put myself in the situation of being the grown-up if I wasn't prepared?*

I remember what the nurses, my grandmother, and my sister told me: at this moment, treat parenting as your own birthing process, sleep a lot, eat well, accept love and guidance, and eventually put one foot in front of the other. That is where I will begin. For this moment, I will sleep.

I have been asked to pose for *Penthouse* on my hundredth birthday. Everybody is going to be sorry.

· · · Dolly Parton

I want to live long enough for old to be beautiful. Not the "I think the wrinkles on that old woman's face are so interesting" kind of beautiful. But rather, "heads turn when she walks down the street" beautiful.

When men, and women, will look at an aging body and truly believe that it is as awesome as a twenty-year-old's.

When the folds of the skin at the belly and the sloping down of the breasts, the fullness of the arms, the rich blue leg veins, and the dark hand spots will be seen as lovely.

I have no idea what will make that happen. But I want to be there.

Guilt is the teacher, love is the lesson.

• • • Joan Borysenko

He had just returned from a year-long trip. He looked gray, fatigued, but happy to be home. While he was in Central and South America he spoke the language, ate the food, felt their pain. He was a smart man, a mere nineteen, and I, his younger sister, only sixteen. We were tight. We performed dance videos on the ragged living room couch, played "queen of the hill" to be fair to me, laughed at the breakfast table until milk came out of our noses and loved, oh loved, each other until it hurt. He is my only brother and my friend—at times my only friend.

It had been a couple of days since his return. I invited a friend over to make monster cookies for the family party that weekend. My brother complained of a stomach pain, plopped himself in the middle of the living room floor, groaned as he did when he played dead, and wiggled around like a worm looking for soil.

He often became dramatic when he carried a bug inside of him, similar to my father, who wore a wool sock around his neck when he had a sniffle. I wasn't paying attention to him, not because I was mad, simply because I thought it would pass.

We waited until the wee hours of the night, our family stiff with worry. The sweat-soaked surgeon removed his mask, wiped his brow, knelt down on one leg, and said, "I have some bad news."

He recovered after a year of chemo. He is about to be a father for the first time.

I will stand by his side, cry holding his hand, love him with every drop of my being, again and again and again.

She would not measure living by the many who had less but always by the few who had more than she had.

• • • Faith Baldwin

My father rarely brought a gift to my mother. But something about Easter the year I was thirteen moved him to buy a hydrangea plant for her and a corsage of carnations for my sister and me.

We pinned the flowers to our new spring coats. Then we waited for Mama to come out of the bedroom so we could leave for church. We gasped when we saw three beribboned hydrangea blooms, resting on her shoulder. She had made a corsage from the plant.

Papa shrugged his shoulders, but said nothing. Not a church-goer, he sat down to read the Sunday paper. Mama said, "Let's go, girls."

The shattered plant sent a message, one I couldn't decode. Did she want to show people her husband had given her flowers? Did she want to scorn his gift, let him know he'd made the wrong choice, given her a lesser gift than he gave my sister and me?

I wanted my mother to be happy. He was the reason she wasn't. But for the first time, I felt within me the stirrings of understanding that there was another side to this conflict they called a marriage.

When love comes it comes without effort, like perfect weather.

• • • Helen Yglesias

My first marriage was like the weather in the Midwest. Wait a minute and it changed.

Sunny warm days, thunderstorms, sleet, blistering hot spells, cold below zero time, pleasant breezes.

Like the Midwest it was mostly friendly. My husband died suddenly, young, forty-eight years old.

My friends and family gave me what they considered to be the appropriate grieving time. Then they started to ask, "Do you think you will get married again?"

"I don't know," I answered. But I thought, *No, it was too much work. Being alert to those incoming fronts is exhausting. Not to mention how much energy it would take to navigate a new relationship.*

One night I went to a friend's for dinner. There, once again, was a single man among the guests. I carefully avoided the ploy.

The next day he called. We went out for dinner. Candles, wine, flaming desserts. He took me by the hand to a place where the temperature is always in the seventies, the clouds are fluffy, and it rains only when we are in bed.

I don't watch the weather station any more. I just wake up and enjoy each day.

That is the best — to laugh with someone because you both think the same things are funny.

• • • Gloria Vanderbilt

I stop at a popular wine, cheese, and bread shop in a retirement village and make my way to the red wines section. The aisles are narrow, so I'm close to a couple who pause often to adjust bifocals and read labels.

She makes the selections. He makes comments.

"This looks like a good Bordeaux," she says and puts a bottle into her shopping cart.

"Did you hold it up to the light?" he asks. "Did you look at the date?"

"Here's a blackberry Merlot Sharon told me to try," she says.

"Just because she likes it doesn't mean it's good," he says. "Probably too sweet."

"Probably," she agrees pleasantly as she puts the bottle in her cart, and comments to me: "Love him. But what a pain he can be. Thinks he's a real wine expert. Drives me nuts."

"If that's the only thing that drives her nuts, I guess we've got it made," he says.

I meet them again at the cheese counter. He's saying, "Who cares if we have brie or edam, sharp cheddar or mild cheddar? Cheese is cheese."

"I care," she says. "And cheese is not just cheese. It has to go with the wine."

They look at me and smile. "Thinks she's a real cheese expert," he says. "Drives me nuts."

 May 6

Learning too soon our limitations, we never learn our powers.

• • • Mignon McLaughlin

I practice courage before attempting something new, in small imaginary ways. For example: I walk around the edge teetering on the brink of disaster. I am fearful because the feeling of falling is limitless, the ground so far away I may never reach it. As I continue on the quest, I discover ridges, valleys, large puddles with no fish and no vegetation, just salt—pure, grainy, coarse. The ground I climb over trembles and sways. I find the movement from below an added obstacle. One sharp movement to the left, I grasp with bones in my toes that have never moved, muscles in my thigh that twist like an orange slice. I find a twine woven into a rope with a knot as large as the one in my stomach. I grasp with my ankles, swing, and climb. This journey with the unknown frightens me, but I move on. As I make the last thrust I freefall into a massive straw hammock; it gently rocks my muscles, swings my mood to elation. Here I am: I sit atop my hat. I have imagined climbing. For me, imagining is believing and believing is doing— what is my hat today is a mountain tomorrow.

"Daughter" is not a lifetime assignment.

• • • Shirley Abbott

My daughter votes Republican, stays home with her children, lives in the suburbs, wears makeup and heels, watches the soaps.

Where did I go wrong? I ask myself. I raised her to be a feminist. To go out into the world and make her mark. To challenge stereotypes. We didn't have a TV. I sent her to karate lessons instead of ballet. Barbie couldn't live in our house.

I raised her to be her own woman.

Just a minute. I guess she is.

Yes, Mother . . . I can see you are flawed. You have not hidden it. That is your greatest gift to me.

• • • Alice Walker

The local paper wants people to help build a feature story for Mother's Day. "Tell us your 'Mom' moments" headlines the request. What the feature writer wants are answers to "Have you ever found yourself thinking, in midsentence: 'Oh, my, I've become my mother!'?"

The writer will probably have lots to choose from. Some women will write about their mothers as role models who did everything right—happy to know they've copycatted some of Mom's sayings and habits.

Some will manage to make their answers into glowing tributes that come from guilt feelings for even thinking that mom wasn't always right. Some will drip sentimentality for mothers who have died and thus earned sainthood—proud to hear themselves saying what their mothers once said or did.

But what to do with those who find themselves thinking in midsentence, not "Oh, my," but "Oh, NO, I've become my mother!"

Maybe they won't write. After all, the story runs on Mother's Day.

You've been brought up to be nice—and that is a dangerous profession.

• • • Phyllis Bottome

Nice a.k.a.: accurate, agreeable, appealing, charming, choosy, cordial, dainty, decent, delightful, discerning, elegant, exquisite, fastidious, finicky, fussy, gratifying, likable, lovely, particular, peachy, picky, pleasing, precious, precise, refined, respectable, skillful, subtle, swell, warmhearted.

Independent a.k.a.: autonomous, free, liberated, nonaligned, self-governing, self-reliant, self-sufficient, sovereign, uncontrolled, unrestricted.

I try hard to be both. There are no commonalities, no mutual ground. I think of myself as nice but I sure ain't dainty, peachy, subtle, or genteel. Most days I'm not correct or accurate either. I place my hand on my forehead, lean gently, thinking, pondering. Nope, I would still much rather be independent than live as a "nice girl."

How do I convey to the cashier at the grocery store that I appreciate her smile, to the postal worker that I appreciate the consistent service, to the bank teller that I appreciate her not closing my account when I had five cents in it for a year, without adhering to the definition of nice? As a previous nice person I am reforming my disposition to include independent compassion.

Compassion a.k.a.: consideration, empathy, humanity, tenderness, benevolence, HEART.

If you don't understand how a woman could both love her sister dearly and want to wring her neck at the same time, then you were probably an only child.

• • • Linda Sunshine

Small talk rides the heat waves of a handheld hair dryer as Greta dries and fluffs Bea's sparse curls with her brush.

"I don't think my youngest sister will ever grow up. I went to her apartment yesterday, helped her straighten it up, and then we talked budget," Greta says. "She's a job hopper—always has her own good reason for quitting and 'moving on,' as she calls it."

"Just a minute now," Bea says, admiring her new "do" in the mirror as Greta spins her around. "You're an older sister; I'm the younger of two, so I'm on your sister's side. Older sisters never think younger ones grow up.

"To this day, my sister says things like, 'You know what I'd change if I had your house?' Or she points out a spot on the carpet or a streak on a mirror that I may have missed. Or she looks at my new car and says, 'Don't you think this is a bad time for you to buy a car?' She'd never say any of that to anyone else."

"Well, was it a bad time?" Greta asks.

"No," Bea laughs. "You're hopeless. I guess some things will never change."

If you can't live without me, why aren't you dead yet?

. . . Cynthia Heimel

Seventy-nine hours exactly. Not long in the course of a breakup. (Why break up, why not break down, or break into particles?) I can handle this. I maintained myself through much, much worse.

They call and console as always, but after four and a half years of breaking, what is left to say? I tell them I picture myself not only stepping off a plane to see him (tall, warm, with his sweaty palms for the first time in two weeks), but also sitting in his efficiency apartment four days after my arrival looking at his stuff that I once lived with, listening to the silence that hangs in the air around us, both of us afraid to move our mouths in case a comment attaches itself to our lips.

Where do we have to go, we, they, everyone asks, marriage was the next step, and apparently breakup the other.

What's behind curtain number one, Jack? Tonight, ugly sweat pants, my cat, a yoga tape, two liters of caffeinated soda and the hot-air popcorn popper I bought for myself today. It's not the love machine I was hoping for, but unlike this relationship it won't add inches to my waist, make a lot of noise, or require cleaning— and best of all, I can unplug it.

Nothing is old / About us yet; / We are still waiting.

• • • Wendy Rose

It's sunset and I am driving home from an appointment with my gynecologist. Lavender and pink color the green hills and reflect my musing mood.

"You're getting to that age," the doctor says, in a paternalistic tone that I was taught to love but am growing to hate. "You need to face it and get on hormones before everything shrivels up."

"I'll think about it," I said.

I often think about this time of life when the annoying but formerly reliable period doesn't come; the silk blouse I wear to a meeting becomes a sponge for hot-flash sweat; heart palpitations are not related to looking at a gorgeous man; the kids still need me, but my husband doesn't. And my parents are getting grouchy.

I don't know for sure what will happen next.

But, for tonight, I decide to look at the muted sunset and just be.

Memories are our doors of escape, our compensation.

• • • Dorothy Dix

One of the best deals we get with age is a large memory bank. On days when I don't feel like being in the present, I go back and pull out a memory to live again. A favorite is about Mother's Day.

My son sent me roses each year for the occasion. One year I planned to be in San Francisco that weekend. A few days before I left, he called to ask about the trip and to wish me happy traveling and a happy Mother's Day.

Days later I stood waiting my turn in the registration line at a California hotel. I looked around at the lobby admiring the décor and the plantings. Into my vision came a large bouquet of roses just behind a potted palm—then the hand that held them—and then the figure of my son.

I hurried across the lobby. As I neared the palm he stepped out, put the roses into my hands, and said, "They wouldn't deliver." Roses never had a sweeter scent, and it lingers among the memories that carry me through the not so happy times.

"The sooner you 'settle' the sooner you'll be allowed home" was the **ruling logic; and "if you can't adapt yourself to living in a mental hospital, how do you expect to be able to live 'out in the world'?" How indeed?**

• • • Janet Frame

Sun up. Back down. Sun up. Back down. Sun up. Back down. Moon. No moon. Moon. No moon. Ridiculous redundancies, my saving grace while hospitalized. An adequate place to do almost anything except get well. The carpet screams at us here of feet heavy with the pressure of runaway life. The walls torment your dreams with shadows of souls needing attention, ousted by drugs meant to calm, making me cold and clammy, not considerate. The beds have stacks of past beings—we all sleep one on top of each other; as they turn, one falls off, usually me. To describe mayhem feels like putting my mind through a doggie obstacle course, which my doctors tell me not to do. I am here for the third time this year. It is holiday season and the accommodations are hard to come by. I am hoping that some of my friends will be here, but that is not nice, I suppose. I have a job. I have children. I have family. They all want explanations. They all want me to get better. They think this will help.

I have bipolar syndrome. When I am down, like the sun everything goes dark. When it is up I can breathe, I could run a hundred miles, I could bake twenty varieties of cookies and have them ready for the kids when they get home from school. I have no in-between and because of that I find refuge in the mental hospital instead of the local spa. I am here because I have a family, kids, and a job that I want to return to because they love me and know I am strong enough to get through this. This is my job now, I have work to do, for now this is home and I am safe.

You grow up the day you have your first real laugh—at yourself.

. . . Ethel Barrymore

Six tables, set up in the day room at the senior assisted-living center, await weekly card players, due to arrive in a half hour. I'm a first-time volunteer and I've come early to put small dishes of snacks next to pencils and scoring pads on each table where someone else has already placed a carefully folded, lace-trimmed handkerchief.

I hold one up in the direction of Terese, the social committee chair, and ask, "What are these? Prizes?"

"No," she laughs. "When you're the dealer, you unfold the handkerchief and put it on your head so at the end of each hand we remember who dealt last and, then, whose turn is next."

"How ridiculous," I say.

"Oh?" Terese says. "Think about it next time you're playing bridge, and someone says, 'Who dealt that?'"

The following week, I reappear and ask, "Where do I buy one of those hankies?"

The real drawback to "the simple life" is that it is not simple.
If you are living it, you positively can do nothing else. There is not time.

• • • Katharine Fullerton Gerould

It is my forty-fifth birthday. My friends and I eat at my favorite restaurant.

I get a scarf. A cookbook for busy people. Two books on living simply. When I get home, I put the books away. I laugh.

I have a whole shelf of books telling me how to live simply.

There is an industry telling us how to live simply—videos, books, furniture, consultants, paints, organizing systems, magazines, architects. Throw away your old stuff. Replace it with new simple stuff. Get rid of your house. Build a new "small" house that costs twice as much.

Whom are we kidding? Living simply is another choice that we who have so much can make. It may help us feel that we aren't materialistic. However, rather than de-stressing us, it sets up competition about who lives the most simply.

Simple living, which so many people in the world still do, is digging and hoeing, washing clothes in a stream, cooking, cleaning, gathering wood, and flopping into bed exhausted. No time to read that book on simplicity.

I will use my time to help those who have very little to simply live, rather than working on an image of simple living.

For years I wanted to be older, and now I am.

• • • Margaret Atwood

Agnes was the supervisor on my first job. She was twenty years older than I. I respected her knowledge. At the same time, with the audacity of youth, I resented her suggestions. Couldn't she see those details she was so fussy about just didn't matter?

As I moved along in the working world, I met more Agneses. I stopped resenting—listened and learned and promised myself to someday be where they were—when I was old enough. But how old was old enough? I wondered.

With an expanded résumé, I went beyond the Agnes jobs to management and fulfillment of ambitions. Then, in retirement, I left it all behind and found the answer:

Old enough may never be.

The only good teachers for you are those who . . . love you, who think you are interesting, or very important, or wonderfully funny.

• • • Brenda Ueland

"Floppy disk. That's the kind I should have had when mine slipped. Double click? Now I have to tap dance, too? Save as . . . soon as possible."

As I make jokes, I am thinking, *Maybe fifty-two is too old to be trying to jump into the computer age.*

My child, who has known me for thirty-two years, recognizes the tense tittering. It is my low-self-esteem coping mechanism.

"Mom," he says. "There is only one thing that you really need to know about computers."

"What's that?"

"They aren't as smart as you are."

Maybe not, but he is.

I should think that you could be gladder on Monday mornin' than any other day in the week, because 'twould be a whole week before you'd have another one!

• • • Eleanor H. Porter, *Pollyanna*

I hear others wish days away, weeks at a time, months, years, decades. This saddens me. Today, as the late Sunday sun falls to the floor of the sky, my stomach follows. Tomorrow means a lot at this moment. Surely not a regret, just an anticipation. It isn't personal. I have no prejudice against this day overall; I just hate to think of what I could feel like at the end of the "big" day. If I were a person who had the ability, I would capture the feeling by balancing on stilts, each worry I have about tomorrow in an odd-shaped box. A race is set: whoever still has all of the boxes on his or her head still aligned wins. Impossible feat. I think of myself as a random person, but when these feelings intensify to the point of feeling like bugs are crawling through my veins, what some call nerves, I get organized, lay clothes out, pack my bag in advance, follow through with deadlines: another impossible feat. Yes, tomorrow, Monday, we will meet. I mean no offense; if you were a Tuesday I would dread leaving Monday. I will challenge myself tomorrow to enjoy the experiences. I will try to not wish the hours away or complain of the time that my healthy life has. Tomorrow night I will know that at some point I have cherished that day.

**Hearts are there to be broken, and I say that because that seems
to be just part of what happens to hearts. I mean, mine has been broken
so many times that I have lost count. But it seems to be broken open
more and more and more, and it just gets bigger.**

• • • Alice Walker

The young woman leans into the microphone. Her voice is quiet but clear.

"My mother came home from celebrating her birthday with her sisters. As she entered the house, she thought of my little daughter waiting for her.

"My father met her. In an emotional rage, he took his gun and blew her head open. As my child watched.

"I can weep no more. I will be angry no longer.

"But I will tell you that from my mother, who lived her life for the children in our land, and from my father, who got so sick from all of the hate in this land that he couldn't do good anymore, I got the strength to speak to you tonight.

"To tell you that pain should make us love more, not hate, and compel us to fix this world to be a better place."

I clap, along with the 200 other people in the room. I am a friend of the young woman's mother. I know she is here tonight, too, feeling oh so proud.

You know, a heart can be broken, but it keeps on beating, just the same.

• • • Fannie Flagg

I try to comfort her. I tell her that adult children say things they don't mean. Adult children may not understand that you were under stress and that you may have said something hurtful that was far from what you meant to say.

Her pain comes from estrangement from a son she adored who has taken offense from what his mother said at a time of crisis in the family. Her son has refused to visit her new home, the one that replaces the large yard and aging house that she and his father could no longer maintain.

"But doesn't a son know that a mother's love is forever, that words are only words? I have said I am sorry in every way I know how. What more can he demand?" she sobs.

"Maybe," I tell her, "he's just too angry right now. That doesn't mean he will be angry forever. One day you may find him at the door. Home again."

I make money using my brains and lose money listening to my heart. But in the long run my books balance pretty well.

• • • Kate Seredy

I take pride in my accomplishments. I am the mother of one, or two including my husband, as I like to joke. I live in a modest home compared to those on the lakefront. I moved to this small town in honor of my husband's job, and then we had the baby. I would like this world to be a place where I could openly enjoy the money we have worked very hard to attain. I want it to be okay to enjoy the finer things we can afford now in our mid-thirties. The other half of my brain realizes as I drive my SUV to the local market for fresh salmon for dinner, stop at Crate and Barrel to find napkins the color of the fish, and pick up a twenty-five-dollar bottle of wine, that I might not be as charitable as I claim. I try to find a compromise. The path of living among the poor does not seem fair to my daughter, or me.

But the hypocrisy of worrying about homelessness as I lay my head on my down pillow at night spins me so fast I get a migraine—at which point I make an organic herbal tea imported from China, take a steaming bubble bath and fall asleep. After watching a program about the refugee camps in Afghanistan, I decide that I will help in any way possible. I get myself a part-time job. All of the money I make I give away. I feel empowered again. I am contributing. I go home to wealth as compared to many, but at least I am doing something.

There is an unlucky tendency to allow every new invention to add to life's complications, and every new power to increase life's hustling; unless we can dominate the mischief, we are really worse off instead of the better.

· · · Vernon Lee

Last week, after a meeting, I gave a young guy a ride to his downtown office and had headed home, when a shrill, alarm-like sound filled my car.

No warning flashed on the dashboard. So I pulled off the road, checked the doors, fastened and unfastened my seat belt. The sound stopped. A mile or two later, it began again. I tried the seat belt again, and the noise stopped.

Finally home, I found a message from my recent passenger. He had left his cell phone in my car.

I had to laugh at myself, adjusting my seat belt to solve a problem that had nothing to do with seat belts. I retrieved the phone from under the front seat and marveled at the piece of progress I held in my hand. But I also felt glad, wonderful as progress is, that I don't have to succumb to the lure of every bit of it.

Hope is a very unruly emotion.

. . . Gloria Steinem

I tie a tiny pink ribbon in her jet-black hair. I stroke her smooth new skin. I rock her and sing about love. My first grandchild— an ode to hope.

I hope her life goes well. That her pain strengthens her. That her laughter lightens her. That her loves comfort her.

I hope she cares about others, learns from them. Loves herself enough to say who she is. Loves others enough to respect them, to stand in solidarity with them.

I hope she likes pink ribbons and that she raises a little hell.

It is always hard to believe that the will to change something does not produce an immediate change.

Janet Frame

I am the instant gratification queen. I always want to strike a match and have it ignite the first time. I want praise when a good deed is still warm in my hands. If I don't get it right at once, I become a rabbit caught in a squirrel trap. I find an obstacle in every direction I turn. Every roadblock sends a message to the thousands of bees in my stomach that there is a two-for-one pollen sale going on for the next fifteen minutes. Utter excruciating chaos. Caffeine and sugar only enhance the sting.

During times of need, though, I find the patience of a sea manatee. I draw on the power of my childhood waiting the arrival of my brother at the airport, home from studying abroad. When I have to slow my heart to a turtle pace, I do it to respect the ones around me. I do it so my body can recycle the energy it needs to accomplish a million things per day. I believe in personal accountability to create a changeable path for life but I also know that I must slow down long enough to place the beginning and the ending.

So many women don't know how really great they are.

• • • Mary Kay Ash

She arrived for her interview hoping she would come across as confident. She didn't think she'd get this job, because she'd been out of the workplace a few years, and she was in her mid-forties.

What she didn't know is that she was exactly what the job needed—maturity with talent and training. Interview over, she left, passing an incoming younger applicant.

I saw her eyes brighten and her speech quicken when she talked about her experience and education, which fit the job description. Her confidence was there. It needed a bit of success to burnish away the coating of self-depreciation someone, somewhere had layered on like corrosion on metal.

I called. Offered her the job. She hesitated, unbelieving, then accepted with enthusiasm. A multitalented woman was on her way to being all she could be, and enjoying it.

Energy had fastened onto her like a disease.

• • • Ellen Glasgow

God blessed me with high energy. I've always been able to do more than other people. I must admit I like the question "How do you do it?"

People asked it when I carried maximum credits, a part-time job, and the student government presidency, and then graduated from college with honors.

When I raised three kids, worked full-time, volunteered, and gave dinner parties with honors.

When I chair task forces, care for the grandchildren, take water aerobics, and complete graduate classes with honors.

Last week, I said good-bye to a friend. My age, she died in a hospice. As I left her for the last time, she said, "I've always admired you. I just wish I had known you better."

How could she? I don't even know myself.

The things people discard tell more about them than the things they keep.

• • • Hilda Lawrence

The rain blurs my vision, my cat's tail aggravates my nose hairs, the window fogs from the imprint of both of our breaths against the window. If I squint any harder I will lose the ability to open my eyes again. I believe my Montessori teacher told me that to keep me from casting snarling looks during French song time. I am snooping today. From my third-floor window I can make out the figure of a younger woman, dressed in tight sweat pants (black, of course) and a hat stamped "USA." She is carefully destroying household objects by slamming them into the cement, across the street from her duplex. She seems to dance with each large object she carries until she makes it plunge to its death in my parking lot. These objects have no future, innocent pawns caught in the war of love. I remember that same teacher again who said if you stare, your eyes might stay that way or some such thing. I detach my face from the window's suction and plan to visit the site tomorrow. Little pieces of glass, mangled metal, defeathered or feathered—I never get that right—pillows, grated clothing. And a poster of Pamela Anderson. Conclusion, it is obvious but yet poignant: Don't move in with a woman who lives across the street from a parking lot.

Religion is the most widely debated and the least agreed upon phenomenon of human history.

• • • Georgia Harkness

A large meeting room at the community center serves as home for the nondenominational congregation gathering to celebrate Mother's Day. Guitars, tambourines, rhythm instruments, and three good vocalists liven the scene with sounds that have invaded the solemnity of church music since the '60s.

Most of the people in the room are in their thirties, forties, or fifties. When the music stops, they hush the children and settle into rows of folding chairs, eyes riveted on the raised platform at the front of the room where sit five women, ages seventy to eighty-three. Like me, they've witnessed the cultural upheaval of the '60s, which left parents reeling in shock as their children questioned and rejected the religions in which they raised them. They are to speak about mothering as they experienced it (their greatest joys and greatest challenges) and to offer advice they may have for parents today. They tell of bringing their children up in traditional sects with prayer the center of their home lives as they faced the challenges of parenting.

I feel a great pride in these women—believers walking with seekers on a new pathway, lending the strength of their convictions.

That's the definition of poverty. The less choice you have, the poorer you are.

• • • Anzia Yezierska

Her bones protrude like branches hung with thin brown moss. Shoulder blades, knees, arms, cheeks. The human skeleton revealed. It is two years since I saw this young Kenyan woman. She had more flesh then, as did her small child. But the rains didn't come, and neither did the tourists. Everything dried up.

I wonder if she has a disease or is starving.

"Do you eat?" I ask.

"Yes."

"What do you eat?"

"Anything I can get."

Ahh, her disease is starvation. I might, before I went to Africa, have thought that I would never allow my child or myself to starve to death. I would do something about it. I could not have imagined that there are people who have no choices. But now I know that it is true.

It is also true that starvation is 100 percent curable. No research necessary. No pharmaceutical companies needed. I have choices. I can help.

june...

I never painted dreams. I painted my own reality.
• • • Frida Kahlo

Three-year-old Mitchie wears a button as big as her chest that says, "You go, Grandma!"

After attending college for eight years, Grandma Sherry is graduating tonight with a degree in art. She raised seven kids alone after her husband died, by cleaning motel rooms while the kids were at school and stuffing envelopes at the kitchen table while they slept.

On Sundays, after church, Sherry painted. She painted still lifes, portraits, and scenes from movies she'd seen. For her fifty-fifth birthday, her kids surprised her with a scholarship fund for the world's best mom. She still had to work to pay the bills, so it took her a while to finish her degree.

But tonight, with her children clapping and shouting, she and Mitchie are walking across the stage to grab hold of one more job well done.

What people really need is a good listening to.

• • • Mary Lou Casey

When I arrive at the weekly meeting of a forum of active, civic-minded retirees, the week's speaker is already at the microphone. Her forest-green business suit shows off her short auburn hair. Young and efficient, I mentally classify her—no more than thirty. Pictures of children with shortened eyelids or flat and broadened foreheads flash on the screen behind her. These children have fetal alcohol syndrome. Many of them also suffer from heart defects or growth retardation.

If she's at all uneasy about her audience, it doesn't show. But I'm uneasy for her. She faces a room full of forty seniors, thirty-five of them men, old enough to be her grandfather, from a generation that saw babies and children as women's worries. They now have hot-button issues of their own they want heard, such as health care and prescription and housing costs. How receptive will they be?

The speaker tells the children's stories, choking back emotion as she brings her presentation to a close. A standing ovation ends my uneasiness. And I join the applause with pride in the young woman of my granddaughter's generation and from mine—those five women in the audience who know how hard it is to get a good listening to, and thirty-five men who are learning.

With the gift of listening comes the gift of healing.

. . . Catherine de Hueck Doherty

On my way to meet my friend Sherry for coffee, I wonder why I am going. She consistently does all of the talking and I mainly stare at the yuppie clothing store across the street, feeling lonelier than I had been before.

We sit, she chats at me. I have a strange feeling in my stomach. I wonder: is it anxiety? Is it the mocha I had instead of my usual green tea? Is it because this is the third time this week I have heard her tell this story? Regardless of the reason, an uncomfortable vine is growing inside of me. It twists from my stomach, twines around my throat, and finally bursts through my mouth. As Sherry continues her story, I blurt out, "Sherry, Miles beats me. He has for years. I just thought you should know."

With the leftovers of a few words yet spilling from her mouth, she gathers both of our purses and grabs my hand with a mother's force. She puts me in the car, pulls away from the curb, drops me in front of the Women's Center, and waits in the line with me to see a counselor. We have known each other for years, but I never knew she was familiar with such a place. Then again, she never knew my body was covered in bruises. She waits for two hours with me, holding my hand and for the first time saying nothing. After the session she brings me to my house; we pack my things and move them to her house. Life begins again. The road will not be even, I am sure, but nothing could be as bumpy as it had been. This is a true friend, my chatty Sherry, she is a life saver—orange, my favorite flavor.

The opposite of talking isn't listening. The opposite of talking is waiting.

• • • Fran Lebowitz

"I've told her that I wish I hadn't worked so many hours, pushed her to be like me, screamed at her through the closed door when she wouldn't talk."

"And?" my friend asks.

"And she won't answer my phone calls. Won't let me visit her in Chicago. It feels like we're divided by a thick wall with tiny holes that only allow hurt to ooze through."

"What are you going to do?"

"I leave messages telling her I love her. Maybe this time I'll just leave one that says I'm not going to take it anymore."

"Doesn't she write to you and didn't she ask you to write back?"

"Yes, but I'm way too busy and I want her to talk to me. I want meaningful conversation." I gasp. "Did you hear what I just said?"

"Yes."

"I'm still doing the same things to her I've done for twenty-four years."

"Yes."

"Excuse me, but I need to write a letter."

A happy marriage is the union of two forgivers.

· · · Ruth Bell Graham

"A mouth full of cynicism helps the marriage go down, helps the marriage go down." This new version of the Mary Poppins song explains the reason I never allowed my Cabbage Patch doll to marry. My parents never liked each other, the main ingredient in an unhappy family recipe. The next step takes time: set to one side the dissatisfaction and lack of interest in each other, cover it with cheese cloth, and wait. During this time fill the empty moments with things like sex, children and all of their crises, houses, pets, family illnesses, broken-down cars, and really any other available stress you can muster. After about twenty years of turmoil, remove the cheese cloth, contact a lawyer, and file for divorce.

The aggression brewed in twenty years of tension surfaced when I met a man who did not crave the stew my family cooked up. His family's recipe called for silence and lack of communication. Now what? Do I add a step to my home cooking? Do I throw in these new ingredients? The taste for this meal goes deep. We both fall into the comfortable patterns, but when we smell the old-world cooking, we know to call for take-out. Our recipe: love, eat, fight, forgive, and the sweetest of all, make up.

Anyone can be passionate, but it takes real lovers to be silly.

• • • Rose Franken

It's early evening. The maître d' seats a well-put-together man in a dark business suit at a table for two next to where I sit. He orders a martini, three olives please, and a brandy Manhattan. A waiter places the shimmering glasses on the table and leaves.

One person waiting at a table for two feeds the imagination of a people watcher like me. I play with the question of who may be joining him. Is this a business dinner? Is it a lovers' tryst?

A woman arrives, the picture of modern feminine success.

"Whew," she says. "What a day I've had!" The man rises to hold her chair out for her. As she seats herself, she says, "You ordered for me. How nice! What a good husband you are."

He returns to his chair, and with mischief in his voice, leans across the table a little and says, "Do you ever stop to think about how lucky you are to have me?" I lower my gaze, finger the flatware, and listen for her reply.

"Well," she says, leaning back to sip her drink, "I'd have to think long and hard."

"Exactly," he says. She laughs and lifts her glass to meet his. I quickly gaze out the window at the sidewalk traffic, smiling but embarrassed by my eavesdropping, grateful for the lift their intimate humor gave my evening.

My mother and I could always look out the same window without ever seeing the same thing.

• • • Gloria Swanson

A minty, white-chocolate-coated pickle flavor envelops my tongue as I leave my mother's fiftieth birthday party. Our heads and their contents collided throughout my childhood, producing a risky environment for anyone who came within fifteen feet of our battle zone. At eighteen, I created a survey in hopes of unraveling the mystery of who my father really slept with. There is no way that I share any of her genetic makeup, unless feeling alienation and disapproval from your mother is a trait.

Every birthday I attempt to find a card in the local grocery that sums up the collage of events and hurdles we face and manage not to physically hurt each other. I have resorted to blank cards, but there is so much white space available for me to miss the mark on what she is expecting to hear that particular year; I find that gluing complimentary pictures of her looking footloose and fancy-free rings her salivation bell and I can eat my third piece of lacey torte in peace.

I am reminded every Thursday at 4 p.m. sitting across from a therapist in a room filled with dried flowers and the smell of stale coffee, and bookshelves lined with books about the art of teaching self-help, that the personal damage extending from this mismatch runs deep. I ran out of forgiveness doors to open years ago. I know that in order to be sane and a moderately adjusted person, I must face the pain of not melding with the woman who we all know was in labor with me for thirty-six hours. I am trying; that is all I promise myself and my daughters to be.

I am a woman / Who understands / The necessity of an impulse whose goal or origin / Still lies beyond me.

• • • Olga Broumas

Perched high, pillow behind her back, leaning against the old Mexican carved headboard, she reads me her writing. It stuns me with just the right nonconforming sensual images and spiritual similes.

How did it come to be that this daughter of mine learned to speak so? It did not come to be. It always was.

She fought to keep it. She raged, starved, cried, acted out against the world or her parents or teachers or friends, anyone who would steal from her what is her—a magical essence, rooted to the core of the earth and tied gently to the corners of heaven.

She acts, sees, feels, senses, loves, slays injustice, thinks, emotes, articulates, and melds with the untouchable nameless beings that most of us cannot know. She teaches that we need not, often cannot, know the reason for being. But we must fiercely and tenderly be.

Life is worth being lived, but not being discussed all the time.

• • • Isabelle Adjani

Nora and I visit over a cup of tea. She leans forward and says, "Let me tell you what Deb did today." I smile; Nora's stories about her daughter are always full of spice.

"She asked if I wanted to go see a new assisted-living complex that's almost completed. She said the builders are having an open house on Sunday. They expect they'll fill units fast, but they'll have a waiting list," Nora says.

"I reminded her I've been in my condo only five years. And I love it. I told her, 'I know I'm turning eighty, but I'm hardly ready for the *home*.' She said, 'It's not a *home*, Mother. I just thought you might be interested in seeing what's out there.'

"I said I'd think about it. My friend Josie loves Deb—she's always told me how she envied me my daughter—so I'm going to call and ask if—"

I interrupt. "You're going to ask her if she wants to keep Deb?"

Nora laughs. "No. Of course not. Deb's right. I am interested in what's out there. Right now, though, I just want to celebrate being eighty."

Yours is the year that counts no season; / I can never be sure what age you are.

· · · Vita Sackville-West

Always sixty-two. She crosses her legs and sits erect, makes pots of golden broth that tempt the soul, teaches college students how to compose poetic stories, freelances as a résumé writer for ultraprofessionals, dresses up for her husband when he returns from a baseball game, wears just the right shade of red lipstick that also tempts the soul. She is a hot commodity—grace and sophistication compiled with the dexterity of change. She drives across town to return to the city where her daughter insists on residing. She eats at restaurants where she is the only one speaking English. She travels to faraway lands that require an ulcer-provoking plane trip. She writes stories of memories that were never intended for the public eye. She is my grandmother. The one who is so subtly clever that you are apt to miss her quiet analysis as she sits across the room from you. This world is not the one she or her husband thought it would be. I know that decisions I have made have disappointed her. I also know that as I continue to share a world with her I absorb the style that keeps me believing she is always sixty-two.

Ah! If you only knew the peace there is in an accepted sorrow.

• • • Jeanne de la Motte-Guyton

The hospice nurse had done all she could. The slow morphine drip was doing its job. My daughter and I spoke quietly to him, husband and father, telling him what a good person he was, how proud we were of him, how much we loved him.

I leaned close and heard him say, "Ginny, go pack, we have to leave now."

"Seth, I won't be going with you this time," I said.

"Then I'm not going," he replied.

"It's all right, I'll follow." I said. "You go on ahead."

And he did.

A good time for laughing is when you can.

• • • Jessamyn West

Our group laughed uproariously in the halls of the oncology floor.

"You can move into the family waiting room and close the door." The nurse's tone was surprisingly understanding.

Two days earlier, doctors told us that my son Nick had cancer. Twenty-one years old. Out of the blue. Could-kill-him cancer. His best friend Rick, his sisters, and I waited as Nick slept.

Although we usually didn't do dark humor, we laughed about starting "I Can't Cope" groups and visiting the hospice rooms disguised as the angel of death. The more irreverent the talk got the harder we laughed.

Soon after we moved behind closed doors, the nurse told us that Nick was awake.

"We can't tell him what we've been talking about, okay?" We all agreed that it would be much too insensitive.

The minute we walked into Nick's room, we burst into laughter.

"You been having fun without me?" Nick asked. Immediately, we began telling Nick about all of our gruesome plotting. One of us remembered our pact and shhh'ed the rest.

"Don't stop now," Nick said, as laughing tears streamed down his face. "You're giving me a reason to live."

It was enough to just sit without words.

• • • Louise Erdrich

Frank calls, "Come in," in answer to my knock. And I enter the front room of the big, old house on a tree-lined street where bookshelves line the walls and large windows bring a flood of light into where he sits at a drafting table.

Reddish hair, green eyes, and a sprinkle of freckles bridging his nose give him a young-boy look. But he's thirty-four, an architect who recently lost his partner of ten years to AIDS, which now invades his body in its early stages.

He rises, motions me to a small sofa, says, "Have a seat," and turns his chair to face me. Frank has agreed to an interview for the health agency where I volunteer to help in promoting AIDS education.

His sister, who looks enough like him to be his twin, enters the room, and he introduces her. She stands behind him and puts her hands on his shoulders, giving him a quick squeeze.

He reaches up and pats her hand. "I'd rather not be sitting here talking about dying," he says. "But I'm pleased that you came to listen, because I'm grateful to your agency's program, where I learned to care for Craig at home among friends and family. But more than that, I want to put a human face on this horror by telling our story, Craig's and mine."

His sister leans forward to rest her cheek on his ruffled hair. And though his eyes grow misty, he manages a half smile and says, "So let's talk."

I put away my list of questions, unasked but answered, in an outpouring of grief that compels understanding.

Birth control is the means by which woman attains basic freedom.

• • • Margaret Sanger

I have been on birth control pills since I was fifteen. I have tried at least six types. Each creating their own Jekyll and Hyde version of me. Each causing rivers or droughts of periods. Each making me think that there should be a pill that men can take. I know there is a shot not yet on the market that will make the men's sperm temporarily sterile, but "they" do not feel comfortable releasing it to the general public because it has what? Too many side effects.

Now I take the pill not because I do not want children but because my husband of two years and I decided that we wanted to wait to have a family. I know that wearing condoms feels different for him, but honestly, I don't like them either—the latex gives me a rash. I choose to attend graduate school, travel, be an aunt before being a mother, assist with my dying grandmother, balance life. I choose to self-administer a drug that leaves me feeling hollowed. I choose to take the risk of breast cancer instead of cervical. I choose to worry whether or not the pill will hurt my chances of getting pregnant or increase the risk of complications. I am glad for the right to choose, but I am angry about the lack of options.

these hips are big hips / they don't like to be held back / these hips have never been enslaved / they go where they want to go / they do what they want to do / these hips are mighty hips / these hips are magic hips

• • • Lucille Clifton

Good are big lips
Bad are big hips
In is little nose
Out is little boobs
Who cares
Who dares
To be herself?
Graying, belly piercing, socks with sandals, bikini after fifty,
    polyester, natural cotton, little black dress, outrageous red
    dress, stilettos, callused feet, manicured nails, unwaxed brows,
    Bermuda shorts, spandex tights, tofu burger, potato chips,
    makeup brushes, lipstick three for a dollar
Who cares
Who dares
To be free to be?

In the darkness they go, the wise and the lovely.

. . . Edna St. Vincent Millay

This is my first job in a hospital. I see them walk, roll, gasp in. Bald, bruised, exhausted. They want rest from the disease but mostly from the treatments. People die here. I come on shift at ten minutes to 11 p.m. The air feels like I'm in a bag full of sterile bandages and stale bread. There is no movement, no windows to open, all doors shut tight.

I receive my assignment. A patient died one hour before I made it to work, and I have to prepare her body for the undertaker. I have never seen a dead body. My trainer gathers the supplies, a bag stamped Body Bag Equipment. We walk down the hall shutting the doors as we go so as not to alarm the other patients and families. "Not good for business," my co-worker says.

I enter the room, flowers mildewing in the window that she must have faced. Sixty minutes ago she struggled to emit her last exhale; sixty years ago she took her first breath. Her hands send a chill to my feet as I unlink her slender fingers.

A black plastic envelope for her body. I do not feel sick. I do not feel sad. I wonder who she was. What she would want me to do for her now. What her favorite color was. If she wanted to be alone when she died. If she would want me to see her naked. I think, *Please, please come back for one moment and tell me you were not scared and you know we cared for you. Tell me you are safe now.*

We take the elevator, and roll her to the frigid room. When we get back to the floor, her son is there. I sit with him, hug him, and say, "She looked peaceful." There are no words for this job, just actions.

June 16

I have a brain and a uterus, and I use both.

. . . Patricia Schroeder

I'm at the clinic to have stitches removed from a well-healed cut above my right eye, an injury from a sidewalk fall.

A young woman enters the small room where I wait. She wears her straight auburn hair in a short, easy-to-manage style and a smile so friendly it twinkles her eyes. She tells me her first and last name, omitting the prefix, "Doctor." But the "M.D." on the name tag on her white coat tells me she is. "You're here to have some stitches removed?" she asks.

She's about three inches shorter than I am, and several months pregnant. She maneuvers herself around to my right side and stretches to clip the stitches. I'm thinking it would be easier for her if I sat. But she's the doctor.

She clips the stitches and says, "You could have done this yourself, you know." I'd never been to a woman doctor, nor to a physician who would admit I was equal to even the simplest task in his realm.

I feel a surge of pride in this new-generation woman taking on the dual role of mother and physician, to whom I could have said, "Wouldn't this be easier if I sat?"

Before we love with our heart, we already love with our imagination.

• • • Louise Colet

I bring you or someone like you to bed with me every night.
The passionate set I arrange for the two of us serves as our stage.
I rest my lock-filled head next to your shiny straight lines, I move
toward you in the hopes of smelling your mood, I touch your
outside layers softly, in the way I would want to be caressed. The
anticipation of knowing you, reading you, understanding you
overwhelms me. Some nights I leave you be, happy to be in your
presence, elated that I have found you, knowing that tomorrow
I can savor you over and over again. You ask for little—my time,
my ability, language.

Tonight, however, I need you. I open your cover, turn to page
one, and begin reading.

O world, I cannot hold thee close enough!

• • • Edna St. Vincent Millay

Coral pink sky smeared with indigo. Aquamarine organza floating on turquoise. Yards and miles of it edged in chantilly lace, flowing onto powdered pearls. Sky melds with water melds with sand.

Breezes drifting warm. Tiny gray wings gliding at the horizon's edge.

My feet not making prints in the powder. My body not disturbing the wind. My eyes not capturing the colors.

I am allowed to visit this moment. Not to interrupt it or own it.

And I am grateful.

Fortunately the family is a human institution; humans have made it and humans can change it.

• • • Shere Hite

I open the door for Linda and her basket of cleaning supplies. "How've you been this week?" I ask. "Is the new medication helping?"

"Seems to," she says, "but it's a little early to tell. Speaking of 'telling,' though, I have to tell you that I'm dropping my Thursday clients. It's hard to stop working for people I care about, but Granny needs me to take her to clinic appointments."

Unexpectedly, my eyes tear up at her news, but I say, "Granny's lucky to have you, and I'll miss you terribly." I met Linda when I answered her ad for her fledgling cleaning service. For five years she's come to clean, and we've become Thursday friends. She told me she married at twenty, because "that was the expected thing for me to do." When she could no longer deny her sexuality, she left the marriage. In time, she met Ava, and together they formed their family, which includes Linda's two children and Granny, Ava's grandmother, who recently came to live with them.

At age forty-seven, this strong, caring woman, despite the rheumatoid arthritis that plagues her, has built a successful business and a full life. As we part with a hug, she says, "I'll be in touch." I can only reply, "I hope so."

The journey is my home.

. . . Muriel Rukeyser

Unpacking the suitcase and two boxes, I put my underwear on the lower shelf of a carved cherry sheet-music cabinet, deodorant, tooth and eye paraphernalia on the upper shelf.

Photos, a candle, books, and a notepad go on the top.

Jeans and shirts go in the old cedar chest next to the bed. The dresses can stay in the suitcase until I need them. There. All set to learn what this place has to teach me.

I lived in the same suburban house for twenty-seven years. Raised children, had our initial on the front door, made cookies for the neighbors.

And then, the kids left and so did I. It had never been home to me, that sturdy brick place. It was somewhere to do what I needed to do during those years.

Now I travel lighter so that I can go farther.

Whether I'm in a room like this in an old house or a cabin or hotel or hut, I am at home. With myself and the road ahead.

Dreams pass into the reality of action. From the action stems the dream again; and this interdependence produces the highest form of living.

• • • Anais Nin

I am too young to feel like I have not lived and old enough to know that how I live is up to me. I watch many shows where the meaning of life is hard for people to find. I guess I am not looking for anything that specific, just a guide, something to strive toward. So instead of making my grocery list tonight, I order Chinese delivery and write my life dream shopping list. It goes something like this:

- World peace
- Two days off in a row
- A metabolism that is in overdrive and needs cheesecake to build its stamina
- To be able to fly for a day
- To not get seasick
- End world hunger, of course
- To experience the "love" that everyone makes up
- A bookshelf full of unread books that I would classify as "the best book I ever read"
- An honorary doctorate from Maya Angelou
- Paul Simon playing at my birthday party
- The ability to understand my cat's language
- To find out what really happens to people after they die
- To ban my loved ones from dying
- To have the ability to play the violin
- Most importantly, to acquire a singing voice

This list is not filled with reality, but I think it is better than the mundane broccoli, toilet paper, and peanut butter.

We must talk about poverty, because people insulated by their own comfort lose sight of it.

. . . Dorothy Day

Her shoes are tightly tied, but still they flip-flop when she walks. They're just too big. Her dress, too large for her tiny frame, has the faded look of numerous washings. Shoes and dress, the hand-me-downs of poverty.

She clings to her mother's hand as they leave the discount store, passing the Easter display of chocolate bunnies.

"Can we buy a bunny?" she asks.

"No," her mother replies. "They'll be half that price after Easter."

No tears, no temper tantrum, just acceptance. Her bunny will come from the discount store, and not until after Easter.

Where is the magic in that?

There are days when I think I may drown in this constant sea of sorrow.

. . . Ann Reed

My name is Christine. I want you to know that I have a name. Because when you hear about my life, you may think that I don't have a name like you do.

I live in hell's slums. Stench from human waste and wasted humans fills my nostrils. I went to school until I was eight. Then my father died of typhoid, we think. We never know for sure in hell.

I have AIDS. My six-year-old son has AIDS. I married at thirteen. Was widowed at eighteen. My husband died of AIDS. Neither of us knew what it was. He didn't know that sex with other women could hurt us. It always hurt me, of course.

I pick in the garbage. Grow scraggly plants in the filth. Caress my child's rattling body when he coughs. I can't drown in this sorrow. Not until my son does.

I keep swimming in the backwaters. I do not feel sorry for myself. Just so sad, so out of breath.

My name is Christine. What is yours?

Our disabilities may impose limitations, but physical, economic, and political barriers impede us far more.

• • • Laura Hershey

I love diving and found out later I have terrible depth perception. So I have hung up my feet, but the rest of me is kicking. I beat the odds, defied the inevitable, got lucky. The M.D. in the emergency room that night said he had never seen a person fall so hard and retain the partial use of their hands. Not the exciting news I was looking for.

I sound cynical. I am. I just mastered the chair after taking my first step twenty-one years ago. The biggest drawback is not feeling like a celebrity anymore. I am five-foot-ten, but sitting my presence is not as remarkable. People stare as I attempt an icy curb in January. People bow their heads as the automatic door strikes me.

Please do not mistake me for a better person because my spinal cord was severed, but do praise me for putting up with the injustices I face. I miss wowing the crowd. I miss being able to do just about anything with my body. I miss it all. But mostly I miss being listened to. My rights have changed. I long to eat at the restaurant my husband proposed to me in. I desire to shop at the vintage clothing store my sister and I frequented.

I graduated from med school and will finish my residency in one year. My sister petitioned the vintage store to build a ramp, and they obliged. My husband proposed to me again in our new favorite restaurant, this one on the ocean in Mexico. I have the power to live with my new physical being instead of resenting it. There are days I want to hide away, and I do. Don't we all. But I wake up and start again—that is healing, that is power, that is confidence.

Women are not forgiven for aging. Robert Redford's lines of distinction are my old-age wrinkles.

• • • Jane Fonda

I go to the copy room to get copies of a meeting agenda I'd ordered. The young woman there says, "I like your haircut. It makes you look younger."

I reply, "Younger is better?"

Why didn't I just say, "Thank you," and let it go? Because I wanted an answer. And because I was still rankling over a column in the morning paper on how to dress for success. The author strayed from his topic with this bit of wisdom: "Sorry to say this, gals, but in the workplace, white hair on men says 'distinguished.' On women, it says 'old.'"

The stay-forever-young pressure on working women has intensified from hair coloring to face-lifts, body tucks, and Botox treatments that turn faces into emotionless masks. I escaped that. But now I contend with salesmen who ask older men, "Can I help you, sir?" but coyly ask me, "And what can I do for you, young lady?"

When they do, I look all around me as though the question is for someone else, and then sweetly say, "I'm not young," and coyly add, "and in a minute I won't be a lady."

I gave up smoking four years, two weeks, and five days ago. But who misses it?

• • • Sandra Scoppettone

I remember the exact day I said, "No going back this time." I was fifty. My doctor was worried about my cholesterol. "Smoking raises your cholesterol," he said.

For some reason, this got to me. Not the pictures of dirty lungs, or the emphysema warnings on the familiar cellophane pack. Cholesterol.

I had quit 3,791 times before. But I got so crabby. I would tell my husband exactly what I thought about his lack of communication, insensitivity to our kids' needs, putting work before everything else.

I warned him, "This time it's for real."

"I'll be there for you," he said.

That was one year, two weeks, and three days before he left me. For a younger woman. "Who doesn't expect so much," he said.

The smoke smothered my loneliness. Without it my feelings flamed.

Was it worth it?

Who misses him?

Being a woman has only bothered me in climbing trees.

• • • Frances Perkins

"You listen to the sisters," was my mother's standard reply when I whined about unjust discipline or unfair grades when I was a child in parochial school. The word of the nuns, from the principal on down, was law. We kids rose to our feet when a priest visited our classroom and dutifully addressed him as "Father." In my young mind, he was there only because Sister let him be. No one I ever saw entered or left without her permission.

When my grandma got sick, she went to the Catholic hospital, where nuns were boss from bedside care to top administration. "You wait here," my mother would say when we went to see Grandma. "Kids can't go into the hospital rooms." So I'd sit on the hallway bench where she left me and watch with wide-eyed awe as nuns moved briskly in and out of patients' rooms, their flowing white habits putting air in motion around them. Male doctors and priests came and went, but the sisters were the mainstay. Women in charge.

Thus, I grew up with pride in being female, never envying a male's position. When I meet the question of how I can remain in a church that refuses to ordain females, I go back to my early perception: Men were priests because the poor guys couldn't be nuns.

The life of a religious might be compared to the building of a cathedral. Day by day the stones are laid, in the beginning one hardly distinguishable from another . . .

• • • Margaret Wyvill Ecclesine

Royal blue, ruby red, and amber light wash them. Some in the old garb of long scapulars and veils. Others in street clothes and good haircuts. My sisters, with whom I lived and loved and learned for twelve years.

I know each of their idiosyncrasies. This one won't eat butter, that one clicks her teeth. I know their gifts too. The kindest person, the teacher, the cook, the college president.

We are reuniting today in prayer in this chapel to bury one of us.

This chapel full of grace where I wrestled with the decision to stay or to go. With their blessings, I took my leave. To do good in the world without them to lean on. How I've missed them for the past two years.

My new life is good. More in tune with the way I am made.

But in my dreams I am still here, in this cathedral, wondering why my stones wouldn't fit into place.

Damn words; they're just the pots and pans of life, the pails and scrubbing-brushes. I wish I didn't have to think in words.

• • • Edith Wharton

As I walk down the street, people cover their ears, cast their eyes down toward the filth of the sidewalk. I often cover my ears not because they are cold but because I figure they must be trying to tell me something. There are bugs, you know, that get into your ears and lay eggs; I wear earmuffs at night to protect myself. I also know there are large bugs that crawl up your pant leg, and when they bite you they lay their eggs under your skin. I secure plastic bags with the rubber bands that come on my newspaper around my ankles when I am sleeping or even out for the day.

I understand why people look like that when I walk by, but I haven't figured out why they look afraid of me when I am walking or sitting at the bus stop. I know that I have thoughts that they don't. I know that my clothes aren't nice. I have been told by some doctors that I have an illness in my brain that makes me scream, and think I am other people, and sometimes even see things. But the bugs, the eggs, they are real. Maybe people look that way when I walk by because they are warning me; maybe they look scared because they are afraid of something I don't know about. I try to ask them. I have to yell because my hands are over my ears: "Are you afraid?" No one answers.

july...

Your being is full of remembered song!

• • • Bernice Lesbia Kenyon

My husband and I treat ourselves to lunch at a favorite restaurant—a little pricey for our budget. We sit near the large windows that frame outdoor foliage and mid-summer garden blooms and relax into enjoying the Shrimp Louis, good wine, and soft background music.

We don't expect "our" music, but a World War II hit, "Don't Get Around Much Anymore," softly presents itself. The song takes us back to Texas, where he served for a while at Fort Bliss, near the Mexican border. I stayed in nearby El Paso. Our eyes tear up as memories flood in.

The next rendition is "Too Young," another wartime hit, about a couple everyone saw as too young for real love. The story fit us well over fifty years ago, when I was eighteen and he just twenty-two. To the closing lyrics, "they were not too young at all," we raise our glasses. Tears dissolve into grins.

What a kick it's been to have fooled the world.

This is no lake, / it's a flat blue egg. We peel / its shell and climb inside / like four spoons looking for the yolk.

• • • Ethna McKiernan

I clumsily reach for his grasp as we tumble among the forest of grass. The night is coming. The park is emptying. I want to show him that I can be adventurous, but more than that I want to feel the warmed liquid of the lake against my body. This is not legal and I can see he might worry; I reassure there are no rules at this particular lake. The bra flies, the boxers soar, the shoes take off on their own. We are ducks in our private pond feasting off the stars and nibbling on the moon. As I dive beneath the surface I notice the flailing of my companions' feet. He is a great swimmer; there must be a fish or leeches. I extend my neck and body and rise again. A piercing light blinds my eyes; someone is holding a light on us. *How rude,* I think. And then I realize the obvious: a park ranger. Apparently there has been some vandalism in the area and when he spotted our clothes . . .

From the moonlit water I explain that this is something I love to do and what harm is there really and assure him deceitfully that I am a lifeguard, not to worry. He tells us we could be fined, and as I think about replying by asking whether or not we would have to appear naked in court, I feel my partner giving me a swift kick in the shin. The ranger lets us swim that night and as we frolic I think, *That was rude; I should have invited him in.*

Beneath incrusted silences, a seething Etna lies, the fire of whose furnaces may sleep but never dies.

• • • Georgia Douglas Johnson

The office crew put together the end-of-summer picnic—spouses and families invited. Everybody came. Those who had spouses brought them. June, the newest employee, brought Sheila.

June was fun. She cracked us up with stories about Master, her German shepherd, that made him seem more human than canine. We really got into that. Marmaduke cartoons appeared on the bulletin board with Marmaduke crossed out and Master printed in. She worked hard, did more than her share.

She had never mentioned Sheila.

The picnic started the whispered conversations that stopped when she walked into the coffee room, the groups that broke up at the water cooler when she approached, the happy hours after work that didn't include her.

When she announced that she'd be leaving, she said she and Sheila wanted to continue to see the USA. They'd be moving their mobile home out of the trailer park at the edge of town and hitting the byways, stopping to work when they needed to replenish their cash.

No one wanted to be the one to take the last Marmaduke clippings off the board. They yellowed there. We had failed Humanity 101. And we knew it.

She always says she dislikes the abnormal, it is so obvious. She says the normal is so much more simply complicated and interesting.
• • • Gertrude Stein

I like to make apple pie. To make green peeling spirals. To notice how the seeds are perfectly placed. To coat the slim wedges with cinnamon and sugar.

I love my husband. To kiss him before he shaves. To take his muscular arm when we walk down the street. To hear him sigh after a good dinner.

I like the Fourth of July. To smell hot dogs on the grill. To splash in a blue lake. To ooh and aah at the red, white, and blue fireworks.

And I am okay.

You can't prove you're an American by waving Old Glory.

• • • Helen Gahagan Douglas

Helen Gahagan Douglas was a U.S. congresswoman in the 1940s, as well as a singer and an actor. I turn to two reference books, one the "newest" collegiate encyclopedia for more about Helen. Under "Douglas" I find Kirk, actor-producer, and Kirk's son, Michael, actor-producer; from the 1800s a Canadian statesman, a male U.S. jurist, and a male abolitionist. Nothing about Helen.

In 1946, a congresswoman had to have been as lonely as the proverbial petunia in an onion patch. But Helen served three terms—in the FDR, Truman, and Johnson administrations—before she lost to Richard Nixon, who successfully labeled her a communist. She went on to work as an environmentalist until her death at age seventy-nine, and for the following three decades, no Democratic women served in Congress.

Do you feel the outrage I feel that we continue to have to scrape away layers of suppression, like archaeologists digging in ancient ruins, to uncover the footprints on history that so many women put there? They did more than wave Old Glory, and we need their stories.

**We have descended into the garden and caught three hundred slugs.
How I love the mixture of the beautiful and the squalid in gardening.
It makes it so lifelike.**

• • • Evelyn Underhill

"Why do you stay in your neighborhood?" my well-intended friends ask. It used to be one of the "better" parts of town. Everyone had the white wooden fence, rose bushes, and pansy patches I carefully tend each day.

Now the houses flake off paint. Many languages and rhythmic music dance in the air. Sometimes the police come, responding to domestic quarrels and drug exchanges.

"I don't want to move," I tell my friends, who worry about their safety if I invite them to visit.

"There was always domestic violence and drugs," I say. "Plenty of neighbors hurt each other and drank too much or swallowed calming pills. But we never talked about it."

I like this altered place where big families share the same spaces. Where outside gatherings emit spicy, rich cooking smells. Where children call me Mrs. Hanson. Where I can sit on my porch and talk with other women. I love the life-giving mixture of the beautiful and the squalid.

A cheerful woman is one who has cares but doesn't let them get her down.

. . . Beverly Sills

It is the end of our monthly women's group dinner. We chat over coffee about the week's events: work, kids, spouses, books, movies, and, of course, the inevitable physical.

"I had my mammogram this week."

"How I hate those things."

"Well, I can't say that I hate them," one member reflects. "It's just that I feel so, so . . . checked."

Another woman says, "Remember when our bodies were simply alluring, mysterious, and beautiful? Now we have to treat them like our cars, one tune-up after another."

"Oh, well," I say, "we might as well be cheerful when we get those ten-thousand-mile checkups."

**Have you ever felt like nobody, / Just a tiny speck of air? /
When everyone's around you, / And you are just not there.**

· · · Karen Crawford, age nine

One lick, that hardly counts. Two licks, depending on the size,
not a problem. Four or five licks of real ice cream and the math
begins. The calorie counting and guilt set in like thunder and
lightning, although intellectually I realize which comes first
sometimes is impossible to know for sure.

Name a diet; I enhanced it. Name an exercise; I strengthened
it. Counseling consisted of learning the nutritional makeup of
food, realizing "how your metabolism really works," being forced
to eat everything in front of me before acquiring activity privi-
leges. Group sessions for the eating-impaired turned into "recipe
for death" swapping sessions: *What do you do to not feel hungry?*
What do you take to help you throw it up or poop it out? How did you
exercise it away? And my favorite, *How much did you lose this week*
during treatment?

The worst part is, I stopped living, and for what: a lick of ice
cream and, God forbid, four or five. My spirit cannot survive, my
creativity stifled, my sense of humor will diminish, all for the sake
of vanity. As I eat the last bits of ice cream I think, I have come a
long way; maybe in two years I won't even count the licks.

You don't have to be afraid of change. You don't have to worry about what's been taken away. Just look to see what's been added.

• • • Jackie Greer

When I met Paul, he lived with a widowed grandmother who believed in waiting on the man of the house. To his dismay, Grandma got up early and served breakfast, as she always had. She put the carefully folded morning paper next to his coffee cup, where she had placed it for Grandpa.

Paul tried saying, "I'll get breakfast later," but she reacted with such a look of hurt that he accepted the routine. He even tried to manage dinner at home each day, following his granddad's habit of calling to say what time he'd be there.

When we decided to get married, his grandmother delighted in cooking for the two of us. She served up Paul's favorites, and I warned Paul that he might not be ready for the real world after years of such pampering. But Paul convinced his grandmother to sell the aging house and helped her move to a senior complex, near her church and the park she loved. We bought an old two-story with work space for me. Breakfast is coffee by whoever gets to the kitchen first, and dinner's on a "your turn," "my turn" weekly basis.

Day one of my turn, Paul stopped for flowers, picked up wine, and quietly slipped his key in the door, planning to surprise me in the kitchen. But there, instead of me, he found a can of Dinty Moore's beef stew and an opener on the table—with my note: "Here's dinner. Meeting a client. Will be late."

He loves to tell this story of what he calls his initiation into the real world and brags that every so often he still cooks a mean can of stew.

I break up through the skin of awareness a thousand times a day, as dolphins burst through seas, and dive again, and rise, and dive.

• • • Annie Dillard

Since I have slowed down a little in my middle years I am more aware. Aware of myself and where I am. I take time to sense and to feel. For me awareness is seeing the simple beauty of yellow daffodils in a white porcelain vase. Singing "The Sound of Music" in the shower. Sensing the loneliness of the woman across from me on the bus. It is the feeling deeper than melancholy but more elusive than sadness. It is noticing the lightest rose sunset on green leaves. Laughing with a baby. The breeze between me and my skirt. The brush of my lover's skin under the sheets. Grief that doesn't let me exhale. Night dreams of breasts dripping milk. Smelling ingeniousness. Floating on silken possibilities.

We criticize mothers for closeness. We criticize fathers for distance. How many of us have expected less from our fathers and appreciated what they gave us more? How many of us always let them off the hook?

• • • Ellen Goodman

"Have you ever heard a father-in-law joke?" I ask. "One that really slams at a father-in-law?"

"No, I don't think I have," says Millie. "Why?"

"Because those stories about mothers and mothers-in-law as witches causing trouble are a pet peeve of mine, and an ad running on TV lately really gets to me. It's the one where a couple is settling in to watch a movie on television. She says she'll get the snacks. The woman returns from the kitchen with a can of deluxe nuts, the 'no peanuts' on the label kind, when a car pulls up outside. He cautiously peers out the window and says, 'It's your mother.'

"They scurry around to dim lights, hoping Mother will think they're not home. But the doorbell rings. He answers while the woman backs into the kitchen, nuts behind her back, and maneuvers her way around to put the 'good' nuts down and pick up the cheaper brand.

"Now, I ask you, is that funny? And why is it always the mother?"

I believe she keeps on being queenly in her own room, with the door shut.

• • • Edith Wharton

This is typical. She is twelve, I am fourteen. The evidence is clear. I had my shirt yesterday. My little sneaky sibling had an important field trip and needed something "cool" to wear. I tell her, "No matter what you wear you will not look cool! You are scrawny and shy—no one likes that. So, NO, don't even think about touching my clothes, hear me?"

It doesn't matter how mean I am to her; the tears that pour from her lake of hurt are only a plea for attention. This is her pattern; she is the youngest and always gets her way even if she steals MY stuff. She will bang on my door, slip me apology letters mentioning her hurt feelings, and express her love for me, and when none of that works she scurries to her room to pout. Meanwhile I scream through the door at her, "How is the bottom lip workout going? Did you get it even farther this time? I am sure Dad will be real impressed. Give me my shirt! You are sooo immature!"

Reflecting on this situation as an adult, I remember one thing: she was immature. I had a job to do other than grind her childhood into pulverized piles of lost moments. I was the older one. If I had to do it all over I would still not let her borrow my shirt—that is crazy. Yet I might not enjoy my cruelty as much.

All of us need to recognize that we owe our children more than we are giving them.

• • • Hillary Rodham Clinton

If I could live my life over again, if I tell you the truth I would have to say:

I would not have married my husband, made cakes from scratch, had a vegetable garden, quit school, laughed at sexist jokes, given up vacations when I couldn't afford them, kept friends after I outgrew them, worn high heels, or worked for the same company for twenty-five years.

But I would have had my children. I don't know why. But I am sure that I would.

If you have children, be glad. If you don't, let young people into your life. Someday you will say that you would do it all over again.

Fang, my husband, says the only thing domestic about me is that I was born in this country.

• • • Phyllis Diller

I learned something new today. I find it quite alarming. I learned that when I get married in about a year, I will be called a wife. A wife. Yes indeed, this is shocking. I call myself "engaged" but never a "fiancée." I call myself a "girlfriend," but a *wife?*

I think the resistance I have is the connotation. A wife is someone who knows when her husband is hungry and then serves him a sandwich. A wife is someone who knows when her husband needs time alone and then leaves. A wife is someone who puts on lipstick and stays off the phone until her husband has been greeted sufficiently. I see myself knowing when he is hungry, knowing when he needs time alone, and knowing it is nice to spend time together. See, I would say, a great greeting for my husband when he comes home from work would be for me to apply lipstick, figure out what I want to eat, and knowing that I need time alone, to pick up Thai take-out and be home an hour after he gets there. I am not sure how to approach this conversation with my prospective husband, except to say, "Look here, I am no wifey, just me, who I will always be. If you are hungry, eat. If you need to be alone, leave. If you are mad, tell me. And please don't expect me to be your mother." See, I am ready for marriage, no sweat, no fears; it'll be easy, I'm sure.

Anger is a signal, one worth listening to.

• • • Harriet Lerner

I find the matchbook my grandfather lights his pipe with. Over and over again he ignites the flame, inhales the blue cloud, and I smell the sweet leaves burning. My dad has custody of me. My mom left or was told to leave. She inhales other things, my grandfather tells me, things that are against the law.

His matchbook has two red initials stenciled on top of the white shiny surface, "R.J." I have made up many stories about where he gets these: a restaurant or bar is too obvious. My latest theory involves my mom. She works at a dance club and he goes and watches her. I know he likes to watch naked women even if they are family because he watches me all the time. He watches me in the tub, when I am swimming, when I am sleeping, when I am awake. He watches me and puts his hand in his pocket and plays with the coins; I hear them clinking. He frowns almost like he is in pain, but not. I tell my dad that it is weird sometimes and he says, "You girls are all the same, making stuff up. You be nice to your grandfather. He is the only part of your mother you are going to have."

My grandfather always leaves his red hunting hat behind. One night he comes back for it, he sneaks into my bed, and the nightmare begins.

Today, I took his matches and his red hat. I put them in the middle of my bed, thinking to myself, *Not tonight, Grandpa, not ever again.*

I never knew the whole house could burn so quickly. I never knew the power of fire until today.

July 15 ⊚

Anger is protest.

・ ・ ・ Lillian Hellman

The cancer comes, as it always does, unannounced and uninvited. Her doctor says, "We can fix this." But he can't with his first try. So her family waits through a second major surgery, in disbelief.

"She's never sick," they tell each other. "Even when we were kids—aching, coughing, upchucking—whatever the bugs were, they flew right by her."

"Then why didn't she stay well?" a daughter asks, her voice sharp, her eyes fiery. No one tries to answer, and her words die in the heat of her defiance.

She comes with her sister and brother to wait and watch. She's there when the coma that envelops her mother dissipates, like a cloud on a breezy day, leaving behind only remnants of lost time.

At home, her mother misses the calls and visits her daughter no longer makes. She confides her sorrow to a friend who says, "She's lost the healthy mother who was her anchor. She's adrift in her anger at this disease, and she's fighting back in all the wrong ways. When you've won your battle, she'll win hers."

Since we are in the world of the unfinished, the imperfect, let us make the best of its opportunities and enrich ourselves with its faith and hope and love.

• • • Annis Ford Eastman

The three of us push the cart up the cobblestone hill. My young daughter's dress is torn, but her chocolate eyes flash as she talks. My eighteen-year-old son has never been quite right, and now his distorted face is tight with the task of moving forward the cart full of watermelons, pineapple, table, cups, and buckets.

My children are taking me home after fourteen hours of selling fruit.

I am wearing the red and blue embroidered dress that the tourists like to photograph.

I can barely lift my feet, so my daughter lets me lean on her.

Home is a rickety wooden structure. No water or electricity. Cots with blankets. Three chairs and the table from the cart. I will cook corn tortillas tonight.

I pass the tourists who buy my fruit.

I look at their faces. So many of them bored. Some drunk. All with too many things and not enough to worry about.

I try not to judge. I am just happy my daughter can go to school and that my son loves me.

To be content with the world as it is is to be dead.

• • •   Dorothee Solle

I know that I can be too serious, not fun enough, gloomy at times, and rarely cheerful. I get mad when I turn on the television and the news begins with a "human interest" story that revolves around the missing puppy. Her owners have set up triage centers around the city, neighborhood organizations pass out cookies to the volunteers, water companies keep the workers hydrated, and no one, not a soul, has stopped to think that this is out of control. We breathe air filled with particles that massacre our lung tissues; eat vegetables painted with pretty colors that rot our intestines and give us cancer; drink water laced with battery acid and raw sewage; live in a country with high rates of infant mortality but put down Third World countries for their massive reproduction; support a government that keeps itself so quiet that we never truly know whom we are bombing today and why; eat ourselves or starve ourselves to hide the pain we cannot express in this busy world—not to mention heart disease, abuse, sexual assault, animal rights, prejudice, and a malnourished educational system. Yes, I do think that getting married, making cookies, and vacationing at the lake sounds great, but if I never make a sign to protest all of the above, then I feel dead.

Oh my gloomy father, why were you always so silent then?

• • • Ingeborg Bachmann

I peer out at the hospital grounds through the steel mesh that covers my window. I've come here to find an answer to why fear and panic grab at me unexpectedly until I cower, with no place to hide from the pain of it, and cease to function.

I'm thirty-four years old, and I question the relevance of digging into my childhood. But I'm cooperating. I've told the psychiatrists about growing up the child of a marriage full of clashing quarrels that stormed in the night, of a father who drank too much, and a mother who demanded my allegiance.

I've told them my father never showed any love for me, and I felt nothing but fear for him and the drunk he became every payday. When a child, I would pray that a car would hit him as he staggered his way home. "What would you have done if that happened?" the doctors ask. I tell them I would have felt my prayers were answered.

I move away from the window to call out, "Come in," to a tap on the door. A hospital aide enters, carrying a floral arrangement of snowy white and sunny yellow chrysanthemums with red roses tucked in here and there. The card reads, "From Dad."

The doctor comes next. "Who sent those beautiful flowers I followed down the hall?" he asks.

"My father," I reply. And a small seed of recovery sends out a tentative root.

**I doubt if nuns are really as self-sacrificing as we must seem
to be to you . . . . We don't give everything for nothing, you know.
The mystery plays fair.**

• • • Elizabeth Goudge, *Green Dolphin Street*

We just got back from doing the mall. I am plopped in a
chair with my shoes off. My aunt is hustling in the kitchen
starting dinner.

I think about her life. Sixty years a nun, she moved from
school to school to teach biology to kids who live in the country,
in the inner city, on the reservation, or in migrant camps.
Everything she has fits in the trunk of our car.

"I don't get it," I call to her. "I'm forty-two years old and
you're eighty. How do you keep on going and going?"

"No kids, no husband, no bills, no retirement planning.
It's easy."

Spiritual warrior's pledge: Not for myself alone but that all the people may live.

• • • Brooke Medicine Eagle

I am an urban woman living in NYC, a licensed nurse, licensed masseuse, an aunt, a sister, and also a nun. I do not claim to be a virgin of life, however. I like to eat chocolate as often as I drink water. I drink beer and enjoy it to the last drop. I've been known to swear when I am cut off on the 6th Street bridge. I have used my saintly attire to reduce traffic tickets in court. I am not a reincarnate. I firmly believe in the religion I exist in, dine with, and sleep with at night.

My hand kneads a knot of concrete from a six-year-old who is suffering with AIDS. As she collapses into my arms, she sobs. "I do not want to hurt anymore. Please, please make it stop. I have been praying—what else can I do, Sister?" To listen, not to preach; to touch, not to push; to love, not to lecture is the gift I have, the reason I live this life. This is my work. Please do not think that I am less capable, experientially deprived. We walk the same sidewalks; I see the reality of life. I may not digest the same flavors, but I smell them, I react to them, and I savor my role.

You've got to find a way to make people know you're there.

• • • Nikki Giovanni

"Hi," she says. "Gert here. I've been worrying about how your son's doing out in San Francisco with all those floods in California."

"He's fine. Thanks for asking," I say. My Aunt Gert is a ninety-two-year-old witty charmer who jokingly insists she's twenty-nine. She lives alone in her childhood home. She has no children, but she's one lady who will never be one of the forgotten elderly.

"I don't wait for people to call me," she says. "So, if I don't hear from you for a while, you can expect to hear from me."

Today she has a story for me. "Tracy, my nine-year-old neighbor girl, brought over a belated birthday present yesterday. And so-o-o seriously shook her finger at me and said, 'Listen, you can't say you're twenty-nine anymore, because now you're thirty!'"

The actual American childhood is less Norman Rockwell and Walt Disney than Nathaniel Hawthorne and Edgar Allan Poe.
• • • Susan Cheever

She's my friend. We're kids, eleven years old. She's come to my house in the dark and she's carrying Rags, her fox terrier dog. She's crying. "Oh," she says, "I'm so scared. He staggered in the kitchen door. Then he went into the dining room. I don't think he knows where he is. He stood there and peed on the dining room table."

"Who?" I ask.

She sobs. "My dad."

I didn't know her dad was a drinker. She sure hid that from me, and we were together after school every day. I'd have to tell my mom, so she could stay. I was afraid Rags would not be a good idea. But I found out that adults know a lot that kids don't. My mom and dad just said, "Sure, she can sleep with you, and you can take Rags in there."

We're still friends. She's a widow now. She used to say if she married, she was picking a good father for her kids. She wanted them to have what she never had. And they did. But I think of her childhood at Christmas when I hear "Toyland, Toyland, beautiful girl and boy land." It ain't always so.

Anybody who drinks seriously is poor; so poor, poor, extra poor, me.

. . . Caitlin Thomas

We used to drink together. After the kids were in bed. From the jug of Gallo. That was all that we could afford. It started out as a glass or two and moved into too much.

My husband stopped. One night when I offered him "a glass" of wine, he said, "No, thanks. I went to an AA meeting this afternoon."

I didn't ask him why. I stopped too. For one night.

He didn't get any sweeter when he quit. He stayed the same. His same annoys me.

So I drink. Especially on the night he is at AA.

Waking up with a headache annoys me. So I drink.

The kids' college tuition depresses me. So I drink.

My husband never mentions it.

He doesn't even care enough to say anything. So I drink.

If life just wasn't so trying, I wouldn't drink. I don't think.

If you ever do a survey, you'll find that people prefer illusion to reality, ten to one. Twenty, even.

• • • Judith Guest

I am a bartender. I have a water view of the drowning of lives capsized by living lies. Saturday night. The glitter of tight silver dresses budding with breasts of magnolias cut through the chocolate forest sky. Looming in the shadow of this thirst orgy are souls desperate to find citizenship in a land of acceptance. The women wear costumes to enhance femininity; the men to become feminine. The satisfaction with oneself flushed after the emptying of a full bladder temporarily replaced with re-application of lipstick colored with the hue of self-respect. I rage with fury to see mindful people engage in mindless activities that strip them to their raw animalistic characters. They binge (it's called "socializing"), euphoria for three to six hours, wake up, purge, and escape again into animated slumber. Twenty-four hours of mindlessness. The genuine insincerity of interactions brings me back every day, and I return to flush the toxin every night. I tell myself I am only a witness; I collect their generosity and punch out feeling righteous. I revolve instead of evolving. I imagine sobering this reality and ending my life at the same time.

Are anybody's parents typical?

• • • Madeleine L'Engle

She sits at a table for two on the hotel lanai, sips at her coffee, and gazes out at the sparkle of the sunlit ocean. Tables are close together, and I can't help hearing the conversation when another woman joins her.

"Where are your folks?" she asks.

"Oh, Alice," she says. "We'll have to go see the crater without them. Damn TV! My mother says she doesn't want to miss her afternoon soaps, and my dad says, 'If you've seen one mountain, you've seen them all.' I suppose they're pretty typical of parents at this stage of life.

"But, gosh, I stashed away my coffee money for two years and stripped my entertainment budget down to zero, except for the one time when Julie Andrews came to town, just to give them these two weeks in Hawaii."

I pay my check and leave, taking with me, like a photo in my camera, that image of disappointment in paradise as one of the sights to remember if I find myself on the slippery slope to becoming "typical."

Night comes to the desert all at once, as if someone turned off the light.

• • • Joyce Carol Oates

I knew she wanted this trip with the intensity with which I need carbonation and chocolate two days before my period. I am a beach person. There is no water in the desert. She told me that there were mirages, and lots and lots of sand that I could sculpt into my architectural gems. I told her that I felt out of my domain in places where we were the only black people, not to mention the only lesbians. Her response to this was that if everyone felt and behaved that way we would for sure be the only ones of our kind. Okay. It is a vacation. I will not complain. Plus, she sweetened the pot by paying for the hotel accommodations— how can I argue?

I knew not to pack my flip-flops, which were replaced by boots I referred to as feet helmets. What I did not realize is that my lady was in a new phase and wanted to sleep with the earth and rise with the universe. Accommodations that fit into the cloth packs we carried on the plane were not my idea of relaxation. Love, I remember love at these times, and it kept me putting one Gore-tex-lined foot in front of the other.

And then we arrived. Sedona. An exotic breed, like the two of us. Filled with rock praising, mystic poets, nature cherishers, and even a few gay people. My love had once again forced me out of my domain into a land of beauty and intrigue. We hiked and pitched our tent, cooked on a fire, and washed with lake water, and at the same time fell in love all over again. We will be back to this mountainous land that kept me curious and wanting more, just like her.

There is no disorder but the heart's.

. . . Mona Van Duyn

I was an abused little girl. In the tidy house with organdy curtains and cookies baking in the oven, he raped me. From the time I was a baby until I was ten. I didn't remember any of it until a year ago.

But I did remember my childhood as disordered. As nothing being right even though it all looked so right. I remember arranging and rearranging the dolls on my shelves. Thinking they were always in the wrong place.

I vowed, even before I remembered the abuse, that I would put sense and safety into my life when I grew up.

I have. I get to work every day, twenty minutes before I am scheduled to start. I put my purse in my bottom-left desk drawer. Adjust my framed family photos so they look at me at just the right angle.

I go to the coffee room. Three quarters of a cup. Two spoons of sugar. One plain bagel.

I turn on my computer. Take a breath hoping there are no surprises today. Because if there are, I will snip at someone or close my door and weep. No more surprises; my chaotic heart cannot cope with them.

He who laughs, lasts!

• • • Mary Pettibone Poole

We're invited to a "1950s" party. We're to dress in the style of the times. I borrow a poodle skirt a friend has saved. The skirt's a heavy felt and flares from the waist. On one side, an appliqued poodle swirls when I move.

Combined with a pair of penny loafers, I'm highly in style as a teenager in the '40s, which I intend to promote to the '50s. Who's going to notice? Close enough.

My husband, however, approaches the whole theme with more imagination. In the '50s we had our third child, a complicated pregnancy that put me in the hospital for three months. Medical bills mounted. At home we needed help with three children, which we couldn't afford but had to find money for somehow.

We borrowed on everything we owned and lasted it through. So his idea of dressing for the '50s is trousers, a tie at his neck, a blazer, and no shirt.

"Where's your shirt?" I ask. He says, "I lost it in the '50s."

If you know much about your work—why you work, how you work, your aims—you are probably not a poet.

• • • Mary Webb

I paint blue butterflies on a clay pot.

I remember the world I left three years ago at age thirty-eight. I was a legal secretary. Every semicolon in place. I left for the uncharted course of motherhood. And it seems, now, for my art.

I place the finished pot on a shelf. I take the baby for a walk. She sees ferns, ladybugs, a goldfinch. I introduce her to a squirrel.

After she eats lunch, I sing "Somewhere Over the Rainbow" until she is asleep.

Soon, I am back to my art. I pull out a stool covered with faded orange paint.

I see ladybugs among green ferns, goldfinches, a squirrel climbing one of the stool's legs.

In no time, the baby wakes and my husband is home.

Art is so much more real than life. Some art is much more real than some life, I mean.

• • •   Rebecca West

I cut into the piece of clay, gouging the grain and making a path for my tool to follow. I think not about my life but instead focus on the feeling of sweat dripping from the last lock of hair, reaching my back and trickling down to my tail bone. I think not of love that is past but feel the beating of my heart that pulses, charging my fingers forward.

The clay is my ocean, if I were a surfer. Art is my food, if I were a chef.

I have created a land in the garage of my tattered house, a reservoir of motion that remains off limits to reality. I am often asked to describe the work that I do, tell the meaning of the pieces I display. People ask me questions. "There are words here that don't seem to match the meaning entailed in this piece; can you explain that?" "Why did you use such a predictable color? It says nothing about the strength of women—it is so neutral."

I think about the comments, trying to find this pattern others seem to identify. I am lost, wondering why I have no explanation. I try to answer their questions by saying, "If you were to ask me why the sky is blue, I would have no idea. If you were to ask me the meaning of life, I would struggle to make sense of my thoughts. If you ask me either question pertaining to my art, I can only tell you that art is the way I breathe and move. I don't know what is expressed, but that is all it is, expression."

august...

I suspect that in every good marriage there are times when love seems to be over.

• • • Madeleine L'Engle, *Two-Part Invention*

I fell in love eight years ago with a man who drove a fast motorcycle, listened to The Doors, read books I had never heard of, ate exotic foods, and loved me completely. We married and grew two wonderful children. We fought over minute details—who was going to buy the milk, who made dinner last, which TV show the kids were allowed to watch. We never could find words to communicate about the big problems—the lights are off for the third time this month, we don't have any groceries in the fridge, the kids' tuition is overdue, I lost my job.

Like I said, I fell in love eight years ago and almost to the day I am falling out. We've seen counselors despite his opposition. We've read books, made nightly lists of things we like about each other. A few months ago we even agreed to sleep in the garage for a night with the motorcycle, listening to the reminiscent music, and eating exotic foods. Unfortunately, the motorcycle was wheelless and had expired tabs, we ate a mango because they were only a dollar at the Cheap Save down the street, and we couldn't find The Doors so we listened to Ricky Martin on 101 POP. I am about out of things to try to rekindle our passion.

Tonight I decide to go to bed early. I rest my head on my pillow and feel a piece of paper against my cheek. I turn on the old lamp next to the bed and see a picture of us on his motorcycle eight years ago. I flip the picture over and it says, "To the woman I fell in love with eight years ago. I fixed up the bike, sold it, and paid the kids' tuition. We have our memories, darling—let's live for today, let's reinvent our love. Happy anniversary!"

August 1 ⑥

The truth I do not dare to know, I muffle with a jest.

• • •   Emily Dickinson

Today we updated our wills and wrote instructions for our final care. When we were young, we'd joke that whoever left had to take the kids, so no one left. After the kids were gone, whoever left had to take the dog. After six decades together, this was a day when if you didn't laugh you'd cry. So we laughed at a story about a couple married more than sixty years.

They shared everything—kept no secrets except the shoebox in the top of the woman's closet that she cautioned her husband never to open. For years, he forgot about the box, until the woman got very sick. She told him to open the shoebox; it was time he knew its contents.

In it he found two crocheted doilies and $25,000. She explained, "My grandmother told me the secret of a happy marriage was to never argue. If I got angry with you I should keep quiet and crochet a doily."

The man fought back tears. Two doilies meant she'd been angry with him only twice in all those years! "Honey," he said, "that explains the doilies, but what about all this money?"

"Oh," she said, "that's what I made selling doilies."

When I had my daughter, I learned what the sound of one hand clapping is—it's a woman holding an infant in one arm and a pen in the other.

• • • Kate Braverman

The grand announcement. I am going to be a grandmother. Kisses all around. At last I will know this better-than-anything-you-can-imagine experience that all of my friends shout about.

As the months go by, I am getting worried. A widow for a long time, I have built a life different from my friends. It revolves around work—not the home hearth. It takes me on long trips—not to the zoo. I jog—without pushing a stroller.

I'm not sure how thrilled I am about being limited by a totally dependent being. I don't think I am ready for this. But maybe I can be.

I'm a flower, *poa*, a flower opening and reaching for the sun. You are the sun, grandma, you are the sun in my life.

• • • Kitty Tsui

We sit on our friend's sun-warmed deck. It is the annual reunion of our women's group. As we do each year, we say that we should get together more often.

"Let's really set a date so we don't let another year slip by. What about two weeks from today?" I suggest.

One of our members, Bonnie, not known for joking, says, "Sure. You can all come over to watch me give my granddaughter a bath."

"You're not kidding, are you?" says a member who is thirty-something.

"No, why would you think that?" Bonnie asks.

"I guess I just don't get this grandmother thing."

Bonnie laughed. "I guess I am assuming that you would all adore her as much as I do. Which is impossible. I can't explain it. When she looks at me with her brown eyes focused on my face, it is as if we are the only two people in the world. She is asking me to love her more than I have ever loved. And I do."

The difference between weakness and wickedness is much less than people suppose; and the consequences are nearly the same.

• • • Lady Marguerite Blessington

I write everything down: the celery with the teaspoon of peanut butter, the slice of white low-calorie bread, the eight ounces of yogurt, and even the piece of gum. As a thirteen-year-old attending Saturday Weight Watchers meetings I see my destiny in women three, four, or five times my age struggling not to force-feed themselves with chocolate-covered potato chips. I am embarrassed and exhilarated, knowing that I have the weight to lose, and realizing that I will indeed lose it.

I found her waiting in the kitchen when I returned from school. You would expect a grandmother to gravitate toward the youngest child, but I put her over the edge and she wanted to take me down with her. I wore the new baggy black pants my mom bought me after my last weigh-in session. I laid out my snack of rice cakes and jelly with eight ounces of skim milk. Diligently I scratched the food groups out and then stopped. There was a new check mark in my booklet. Apparently that morning I had left the knife I used to butter my toast with out on the counter. My grandmother had put a check next to the fats section in my hidden booklet and stowed it away without saying a thing to me.

I felt myself spinning out of control. I wanted to eat anything in sight. This was even worse than the time she took my siblings to the zoo while I was napping, and said she didn't realize I was home.

My mom stood up for me. We asked my grandmother to stay at a hotel. All hell broke loose, but my diet plan and my self-esteem remained intact.

A name is a solemn thing.

• • • I. T. Meade

"Glen and Carol are naming the baby Candace," says Joyce. "She's our first great-grandchild. I was hoping they'd pick a family name. She'll probably spell it Kandi, or something like that, the way kids do when they start hating their names," she grumbles.

"You mean you'd like Joyce, after a certain great-grandmother?" I ask. "Family names don't always pass the muster, you know. I was at a baptism once when the mother said the baby's name was to be Hazel Marie. The white-haired priest clasped his hands, rolled his eyes heavenward, and said, 'Glory be to God. With all the saints in Heaven, they're naming them after nuts.'

"'Marie' was acceptable as a derivation of Mary so the mother got the name she wanted, which, it turned out, was in honor of two grandmothers, one being Hazel, the other Marie."

"I get it," says Joyce. "She's darling. Her name will be Candace, and I'll love her."

I believe in hard work. It keeps the wrinkles out of the mind and the spirit.
• • • Helena Rubinstein

To crown a person with the title overachiever seems proper, complimentary, a respectable title. Coming from a family fitting this diagnosis, I think otherwise. I equate overachieving with a malnourished self-esteem and diminished self-control. This may seem harsh, but to overdo achieving seems almost impossible to people who claim and dish out the title of "overachiever." How can you achieve beyond what you are capable of *without* overdoing it? Confusing? Truly. The theory is out of whack.

Reach for the stars, be all you can, try your hardest, and you will find success. Slogans tell me that I can exert all of my energy and be accomplished. If I am truly attempting to accomplish things and extending my arms to the point of dislocation, it would be crazy to push the limit if I realize that actually pulling them out of socket would land me in the hospital and seriously deflate my success. I love to be productive—who doesn't? If being productive means that I have more power, a wealth of resources someone else lacks, a motivation that someone will find a year later than I have, then does it automatically mean that I am over-achieving?

I do not want to injure my creativity or stifle the oxygen supplying my dreams in the honor of the word "over." I am an achiever and dream catcher of sorts, and my shoulder is intact.

I feel so agitated all the time, like a hamster in search of a wheel.

• • • Carrie Fisher

Cell phones beepers palm pilots laptops faxes Microsoft Macintosh microwave call waiting voice mail same day delivery .com cd rom dvd floppy disks hard drive data base software security checks cameras digital video walkmans gameboys fast food viruses double click delete you've got mail new saved sent answering exercise espresso machines bread makers electric woks rice cookers four wheel drive suv rv cd vcr word process excel . . . excel, excel, excel.

Life's pace today makes a hamster on a wheel look like a holiday. Relax, relax, relax.

Stress is an ignorant state. It believes that everything is an emergency.

• • • Natalie Goldberg

I wake up at 4:30 every morning. Let me clarify that: seven days a week. I run for forty-five minutes, squeeze fresh orange juice, scrub my body in the shower for exactly twenty minutes, style my hair for fifteen, get dressed in six minutes, and walk to my car in four minutes. I have no children. I wish I had no boyfriend. My family lives 2,000 miles away. My routine in life is to push as hard as I can all of the time until I can't and then I sleep, wake up, and start all over again.

I work on Wall Street. I deal people's money. I make or break their lives by one rub of the nose, one lift of the eyebrow, one stock projection. I have the power to make my clients feel secure or devastated each day.

Stress? I thrive on it. My doctor tells me that no thirty-year-old should have the heart condition I have. No thirty-year-old should have the blood pressure I have. NO thirty-year-old should have the anxiety I have. I am thirty, I have stress, I have high blood pressure, I have a faulty heart, but I have a lot on my mind.

Then the other day I was walking to work. I saw a small group of women in the street. They were holding hands, talking, eating donuts. I woke up with my boyfriend and a cardiologist standing over me in the hospital room. The doctor said, "You are lucky, but you have to take a break if you like it or not." I believed I was invincible, that my body was born to run. I even told people that. I am lonely. I am tired. I am starving for a decent book and a night at the movies. I am happy to be alive. I am thirty years old and I have to learn how to live all over again.

It matters less to venerate things than to live with them on terms of good friendship.

• • • Adrienne Monnier

When we were young, we discussed late into the night what our life would be like. We sat on the green and brown hide-away sofa from his parents' basement. Or drank coffee on the peeling-paint table from the alley.

He wanted teak and rosewood. I would grab a book from the shelves made of bricks and boards, open it, say, "We don't need those things," and sulk.

I wanted to sell the family china to send the kids to school. He didn't. There was no further discussion.

Tonight, we celebrated with the family, ten of us. My mother's eightieth birthday party. I clear the last pink translucent china cup from the teak table.

He washes and carefully dries it. Places it in the rosewood cabinet.

I take a book from the shelves made of bricks and boards. His hand brushes my hair. Gently. I reach up and hold it.

I open the book but I don't sulk. We have held onto each other and some things. And it is fine. Just fine.

Life is about knowing, having to change, taking the moment and making the best of it.

• • • Gilda Radner

She moves slowly, her quick steps gone with her yesterdays. But she's doing what she's always done, graciously serving her guest with the best she has. "This china belonged to Dan's mother," she says. "I love using it."

We dip our forks into the white cloud meringue of her lemon pie. "I miss having you just up the street," she says. "The neighborhood's changed so much. The children hint that I ought to consider something easier to care for. But I'm comfortable. This is my home. Why would I leave it?"

The question's not for me but for her doubting heart to answer. On this visit, I know she'll stay through the confining snow and ice of still another winter and the loud silence of empty rooms.

But spring brings magic. She visits a friend's condo. In the building, a vacant place beckons her—room enough for treasured furnishings—the safety of neighbors nearby.

Her spirit wakens. She readies her house for sale; decides what goes with her and what doesn't, and relishes the admiration in her children's eyes.

There's an ease to her slowness now. She laughs. "I wake in the morning hoping my reservation isn't up and I won't have to leave." Refilling two china cups, she says, "They're from Dan's mother's set. I love using them."

Romantic love has always seemed to me unaccountable, unassailable, unforgettable, and nearly always unattainable.

• • • Margaret Anderson

A night flight. Time's irrelevance magnifying nothingness, producing significant somethings. I am thirty-three, a professional risk taker who wanted to add the Peace Corps to my list. I just stepped foot on a plane that I paid to take me away from my comfortable cocoon of love and I am wondering for what. Our verbals now, since I said I was going to fly, miss each other, we are officially miscommunicating, diverging, and possibly avoiding.

I float above the land we once danced on together and wonder why for this moment our skies cannot touch. Can we create a mutual falling star?

I want us to make the little things disappear, create our own planet, re-create our childhood forts and post a sign: "Two person, maximum occupancy."

Common sense fled the moment we met. Maybe the first time you called. It was gone the day we kissed for sure. I want to be tickled like I am six. I want to giggle like I am twelve. I want to make love like I am twenty-one. Every ounce of me wants to strap a parachute to my back and flee this current scene of independence. The flight attendant pulls up with the mini ice cream containers, strawberry, and a mini wooden spoon. For now I will let the frozen milk melt on my tongue, for now I will find comfort in knowing I would not have done this if it was going to kill me or not make me stronger, for now I stop wondering why our skies can't touch and realize that at 20,000 feet, they do.

The dark is all about us. Our consciousness changes. We step carefully. We know where we are going.

• • • Mary Caroline Richards

A night flight. Seven hundred thirty days ago I sat on the same flight in the opposite direction, holding the same mini ice cream. Today I am remembering the pit I felt in my lower abdomen. I look at the deep, light-speckled sky and remember wanting my sky to touch that of the loved one I was fleeing. Living alone, in a country where food is scarce, water is poisoned, and people are not willing to take tomorrow for granted, I was so nervous to see my surroundings that I clouded my eyes with that dying love. I look at my tattered notebook and read the lines I wrote during the first two months:

Smells, music, tastes that once characterized our time, after all is said and done, now only encompass and guide my wallowing. Agonizing, tearful, bitter tastes once sweet or salty. Music churns stomach muscles once catalyzing happiness, exhilaration. Now a ringing phone stops the heart, deafens the sound of any strengthening separating wisdoms. Why can't our skies touch?

I remember watching movies with you, exaggerated reality: Guns kill more people, skies are more beautiful, animals talk. I do not desire the life of the movie characters, but I want the love they receive. They are cherished. We always want the unattainable; maybe that is why I want you so much tonight. Our skies touch, but I know our souls do not. I am writing to say good-bye to this hold that sucks the oxygen and life out of me. I need to be present in this life I have, far away from you. I kiss my hand, touch the star we picked in the sky and am off to my new me. I will carry our memory in my pocket for a lifetime.

Trust in my affection for you. Tho' I may not display it the way you like and expect it, it is not therefore less deep and sincere.

• • • Anna Jameson

I am in love and admiration with my daughter.

She is an elusive love. Sweet in her considerations. Fierce in her loyalties. Clear in her brilliant intellect. Funny in the most unexpected, sharp-witted ways. I am in love with her.

I am in admiration with her. That is also the elusive part, for me. She knows herself. Intuits and analyzes what works for her. Sets boundaries. She doesn't let you swallow her whole. And I am so good at doing that.

Sometimes we miss each other. Pass each other without recognition. I wish I could have known her as well when she was a child as I am beginning to know her now. I could have given her more comfort, more everything.

But she is more complex than I, and it has taken me this long to learn about her.

I think she understands.

The test for whether or not you can hold a job should not be the arrangement of your chromosomes.

• • • Bella Abzug

In the heat of a 1946 July afternoon, I walk on the long bridge spanning the river that runs through the city on my way to my second job interview of the day.

My feet and legs protest high heels and nylon hose as I push, head down against the hot breeze that whips across the bridge. In one hand I carry my white gloves and purse; with the other I struggle to hold my small hat in place.

My earlier interview, for a job with a large insurance firm, included an unexpected two-hour comprehensive test on everything from basic math to the question "What firm uses the slogan 'We cover the world?'" The question was out of sync with the rest of the test, but I answered it. Then I hurried to be on time for the second interview.

I finally reach the office building I'm looking for. I pause a minute to straighten my hat and dress before I open the door to the personnel office. Inside, one of two men there openly scans me, head to foot, and says to the other, "Nice job you've got interviewing beautiful girls."

Oh, how I hope I passed that test.

A week later I get a postcard from the insurance company congratulating me on the highest test score ever achieved, adding that, with regret, the review board rejected my application. Company policy prohibits hiring mothers of small children.

So much for knowing that Sherwin Williams Paints cover the world.

On one thing professionals agree: mothers can't win.

• • • Margaret Drabble

Katie, my neighbor, stops by to see me, feeling bad. She'd told her small son he couldn't wear his favorite old jeans to school, so he wouldn't let her hug him when he left for the bus.

"I'm sorry you feel bad," I say. "But hugs are a mom thing. We want them to know they're loved. We think they get the message, but sometimes you have to wonder if they ever will. Like when my son was a second-grader at the Catholic school, I sent him off each morning with a gentle hug and a good-bye kiss.

"One day he came running into the house after school, all winded and worried.

"'Boy,' he said, 'is Steve in trouble. He pushed Jim into the radiator at school when we were in line to go home, and Jim cut his head. Sister took Steve to the principal's office and she took him to see Monsignor. Gosh, I just hope they don't tell his mother.'

"Being in trouble with the teacher, the principal, and the priest wouldn't bother Mark, but facing me would.

"Sometimes you just can't win—unless you count giving your child a hug winning. Which I do. It's all in the mothering game."

I firmly believe kids don't want your understanding. They want your trust, your compassion, your blinding love and your car keys, but you try to understand them and you're in big trouble.
• • • Erma Bombeck

Clock tick, tick, ticking. Refrigerator whirring. The cat snoring. An ambulance screaming.

I knew it. I knew I shouldn't let him drive tonight. My mother is going to say, "I told you he was too immature." If there's more than $100 damage, I'll kill him. Oh, my, what am I saying? My baby, how will I live without him?

Ambulance sound fades.

House creaking. Dog stretching. Leaves swishing. Rain dripping, dripping. Police car screeching.

It seems like yesterday that he took his first steps to me. Who would have thought that I would be bailing him out of jail? Poor kid, so scared. He doesn't drink. Or does he? It's that friend with the pierced tongue. That relationship is over.

Siren goes away.

Garage door going up. Key turning in lock. Refrigerator opening. Milk pouring.

"You awake, Mom?"

"Not really, but if you want to talk . . ."

"Nah, everything's cool."

"I knew it would be. Good night."

"Sure. 'Night."

Sometimes when I look at my children I say to myself, "Lillian, you should have stayed a virgin."

• • • Lillian Carter

The radio's tuned to CNN news. Ella and I are moving along the interstate on our way home from an Older Women's League meeting.

The report's about the ongoing turmoil in the British royal family. A spokesman for the royals, in crisp tones, says, "The Queen Mother prefers to be something of an ostrich about it all."

"Way to go, Mum," I murmur.

"What did you say?" asks Ella.

"Oh, I was just sending a message to the Queen Mother," I say.

"Well," Ella says, "maybe that's the secret of her survival for 101 years. Be an ostrich. Put your head in the sand when life's storms hit. You can't do anything about them anyhow, especially if they involve your kids going down a path you wouldn't choose for them."

I'm not frightened of the darkness outside. It's the darkness inside houses I don't like.

. . . Shelagh Delaney

I am twenty-six years old. I have been afraid of the dark ever since I can remember. The truth: I hate being alone. I am the youngest of three independent siblings. They never seemed afraid. Of course, I was always upstairs sleeping, keeping the floor safe: they had nothing to worry about. I knew smart kid stealers knew that the youngest went to bed first, wouldn't that make sense? The familiar heaviness of family feet on the tattered carpeting eventually soothed my palpitating heart; I knew they would protect me. Good night, sheep; I do not need you tonight.

At the age of twenty-six this phobia cannot be diminished by the familiar. I live alone. My ritual prior to sleep entails a short mental conversation about why this is so stupid and unnecessary, at which point I remember a Montel show about women who didn't follow any of the following steps: opening the closet, lifting my loose blankets, punching the shower curtain, looking under the futon and bed, leaving the bathroom light on, and finally crawling into bed. Sometimes it is harder than others to be an independent woman; it is work to feel safe. I will conquer these irrational fears, but for now I enjoy my sleep and really we are only talking about thirty seconds. What's the big deal?

She has no oil on her feathers.

• • • Josephine Tey

I tuck my head under my wing. Totter a little on the rough branch.
I shudder from the cold. No one sees me doing that. Because I
won't let them. No. I spit mean words at them. I find their faults
and pick at them. When they call I don't answer. I dredge up the
past and regurgitate their errors.

I am so afraid. I am afraid that they will pull my feathers out.

The way he did. When I was little. If I don't let anyone near
again, I won't hurt. Never again.

I won't hurt.

Then one day, for no reason, I poke my head out a little. Someone tenderly says hello. She strokes my feathers ever so gently.
And I begin, slowly, to trust again.

We know one another's faults, virtues, catastrophes, mortifications, triumphs, rivalries, desires, and how lone we can each hang by our hands to a bar. We have been banged together under pack codes and tribal laws.
• • • Rose Macaulay

We look young. Our time together has rank on our combined weight. We live on the streets of Tororo, Uganda. We talk to our mothers every day at the river where we wash our clothes. We pretend they are alive and their life is in the rock we use to beat our clothes, or in the ropes that hold the plastic barrels of drinking water we carry on our backs, or in the kernel of rice we eat to fill our stomachs to prevent the pain of emptiness.

We have plans. I want to be a teacher, the other two doctors. There are no schools that will let us in without the school fees for which we have nothing to offer. We dream at times of going to the river to bathe and the water suddenly turns into ripe fruit and vegetables, clean water, and rocks of gold. We do not want to have too much, but it would take a lot before that could even be possible.

I know that my sisters are sick. I can see it in their yellowing eyes. I am strong, but I cannot get a doctor. I have the power to be creative but no tools with which to create. I have the power to learn but no books. By anyone's definition we are not fortunate; I think we are called poor. We laugh at the river while bathing; we hold hands while carrying the full buckets on our backs and skip when returning them empty. We promise not to let ourselves have extra bites of food. We are not better than anyone, but we love each other and know that we will leave this world together with our minds intact and the belief we helped each other through hell.

It was not so long ago that people thought semiconductors were part-time orchestra leaders and microchips were very, very small snack foods.

• • • Geraldine Ferraro

On a ten-minute writing seminar break, a few of us talk about the subject coming up—our ever-changing language.

"Kids are major change makers," someone says. "When they use a word a lot, it filters upward into adult use. Like 'cool,' which seems to describe most anything—from great art to the latest pop music. Who needs descriptive adjectives? Just use 'cool' like a one-size-fits-all kind of word."

"If adults adopt their words, kids think of new ones to claim as their own," I say. "A few years back, my friend Jack asked his fourteen-year-old to do him a favor and remove two overused words from her vocabulary—'One is "awesome" and the other is "gross,"' he said. She said, 'Sure, Dad, which two are they?'"

One guy groans, another chuckles. A woman says, "That's cool."

I am a reflection of my mother's secret poetry as well as her hidden angers.

• • • Audre Lorde

"How can she be your mother?" my friends ask. "I think you were switched at birth."

I am politically progressive, single by choice, a traveler. People tell me I am a soft-spoken and warmhearted friend.

My mother is conservative in all things. Very soon after my father died she remarried. She is married to a man who rules her decisions. She is afraid of adventure. She is loud and judgmental.

How can we be so different?

Could it be that in the singing of the lullaby at night, in the stroking of the brow during fevers, in the daily hair braiding, clothes ironing, going to church in the car, backyard picnicking, making Christmas pageant costumes, my mother channeled some of her poetry and some of her unrest to me?

And could it be that she let me speak my mind more than she ever was allowed to, and that she let me take risks even though they scared her, and that in a part of her that could never be audible, she said, "Daughter, go, soar, relate, do not be afraid."

Maybe it could be.

**My mother is a poem I'll never be able to write /
though everything I write is a poem to my mother.**

• • • Sharon Doubiago

She's been through a lot, my mother has. She nearly lost a son
to cancer, a daughter to rape and poor choices, another daughter
to irresolvable misunderstandings that led to unclosed wounds,
and now a husband to cancer. Through it all I have watched my
mother be the strong one, maintain the peace in our family, love
each one of us kids individually and truthfully. My mother is one
of the wonders of this world. She has been an entrepreneur in her
field. She started her own business, became an author, speaks to
and is adored by national audiences, runs a retreat in Mexico, and
following two trips to Africa, started a nonprofit organization.

She seems to have no limits. But think again. In my family we
have a phobia-and-anxiety gene. My mother is not exempt from
this. She fears heights, swimming, driving. How can a woman
who fears heights fly across the world? How can a woman who
has a fear of crowds speak in front of audiences in the thousands?
How can a woman who fears swimming teach her friend who
is blind to swim in Mexican waters? I don't know. My only reply
to this is, isn't she grand? I too inherited these fears. On my thirtieth birthday the two of us are going to skydive. I inherited not
only fear, but also the ability to rise above it and conquer my
dreams.

Happiness is good health and a bad memory.

• • • Ingrid Bergman

"One of the worst things I've had to go through is my daughter's heartbreak when her husband had his affair last year. Now she's taking him back. I'm still so mad at him that I don't know how I can accept him again," I tell the counselor.

She says, "I think you have to trust your daughter's decision, be glad you don't have to be judge and jury, and erase the affair from your memory. Think of the widows you know who practically canonize husbands. Once they're gone, they're perfect— men who you know were far from that. You wouldn't dream of reminding any one of them what a cad the one she married really was—would you?"

I murmur, "Of course not."

"Same thing with Linda. Give it a try. A poor memory isn't always a bad thing."

Intimacy is a difficult art.

• • • Virginia Woolf

Colorful words flowed between us. Green hope, yellow laughter, gray sorrows, vanilla anticipations. We have worked hard to get here. Years of testing, being tested, loving, raging, going away, coming back. Tonight we can enjoy the beauty of being together.

My twenty-something daughter and I are having dinner.

I say to her, "See that couple over there?"

"Yeah, why does she keep looking at us?" She smiles, recognizing the beginning of a great game that we share.

I speculate, "Because . . . she loves the man she is with. Probably her husband for twenty-eight years or so. He is a little boring. Is concerned that his steak is cold but didn't notice that she was a little sad when he didn't buy a rose from the flower seller who came to their table. But . . ."

"What?"

"But she wishes that tonight she was with her daughter. Having an intimate, laughing, loving time."

"You think so?"

"I know so."

Panic is not an effective long-term organizing strategy.

• • • Starhawk

If you grabbed a handful of feathers, threw them behind, above, and around you, the scene would slightly resemble my mother the day before one of her national presentations. Organizational, massively productive chaos. Before I dig my grave I must say that this pattern does not fall far from the tree. I too maintain my life through the procrastination power.

Do both of us finish what we need to? Affirmative. Do we do a bang-up job? We would not earn the title of perfectionist unless we did. Do we think we will not do it this way ever again? We lie and say yes but do not lift one muscle to change our ways. Are we happy? Well, our muscles are not. Our loved ones are not. Our kitchen, living room, bathroom floor, laundry are happily supporting creatures of another world.

But that all changes when our tasks are complete—a spotless house, a well-done project, no time to enjoy the success. We are holed up in our beds, taking Advil to combat the chronic fatigue that has set in for the second time this month. This pattern may have something to do with being creative but I think more to do with a well-intentioned but diseased organizing strategy. I plan to do this differently, and I realize this is part A of the plan: when I have no commitments I plan to be organized. I usually walk to the store, buy a Martha Stewart magazine and throw it on my shelf, watch cable, and crash. I am trying—oh, am I trying. What can I do? I think it is in my genes, not the magazine, my patterned panic.

Of this be sure, my dearest, whatever thy life befall, the cross that our hands fashion is the heaviest cross of all.

• • • Katherine Eleanor Conway

I wonder why he thinks I don't know. His eyes are tired, the pupils small, and he works to focus them between swallows from the bottle of water he carries. He's holed up in a nondescript apartment where he can get to drugs easily—the heroin, the nicotine, the alcohol he craves.

I hear the voice of his third-grade teacher when she retired: "I hope I live long enough to know what he becomes. He is such an exceptional child." The pediatrician saying, "You have a very special boy, and like some gifted children, he has a racing nervous system. You'll need to help him live with it."

I tried. But somewhere I've failed. I sorrow for what he might have been, born to another mother. Friends say, "You can't compete with peer pressure."

But surely, if I had made him strong, he would be the force for good among his peers. I don't hope anymore for the wasted talents I somehow didn't develop in him, and I live with the failure that casts its long shadow of lost potential on a life entrusted to me.

Laws will not eliminate prejudice from the hearts of human beings. But that is no reason to allow prejudice to continue to be enshrined in our laws to perpetuate injustice through inaction.

• • • Shirley Chisholm

I sit on our porch staring at the after-work traffic. Ordinary folk finishing their late-afternoon crunch time thoughts while attempting to merge into discombobulated lanes. I am in a zone of perplexed rage. I grew up playing Chinese jump rope on the playground, building towers out of pink blocks in Montessori school, selecting grilled cheese as my daily dietary ritual, and falling asleep in a house where I knew fundamental truths. I knew that my parents were my parents and even death could not change that. I knew that my parents were legally married, and there was no law that would prevent them from being so. I did not know that I was a lesbian until I was old enough to care.

Nothing has changed for my parents—I am still their daughter. They are now divorced but still have the right to be married again. My rights, however, have been completely stripped, just as my young years have disappeared. I have a "partner" who would love to be called my wife, legally. I have a daughter who would love to call us both parents, legally. We cast ignorance out with the dirty dishwater. Today watching the general public maintain their ordinary life, for the first or maybe the second time I am letting this get me mad. Do I care if everyone agrees with the decisions I make? No. But I care about laws built purposely to prevent me from having accountability or a defined role in the lives of my loved ones, any stability. I have decided to go to law school and I will fight as I always have to change the injustices my children and my wife—my family—are faced with.

There is no other closeness in human life like the closeness between a mother and her baby—just a heartbeat away from being the same person.

• • • Susan Cheever

I watch as she walks into the ocean, meeting each wave with outstretched palms until her feet no longer feel the sand beneath and she dives into the hollow below the crest of a wave to surface on the other side.

Her arms begin to propel her and her child within in rhythmic movement over the cradling water. She's smiling her enjoyment of this private time in sun and sea.

I imagine her little one feeling the soothing, rocking motion. I wonder if she speaks to him or her as she rolls and floats and then begins again the strong stroke of an excellent swimmer. Maybe she sings a lullaby.

After a while, she turns toward shore. When her feet once again touch the ocean floor, she rises, her dark hair and olive skin aglow with the wetness of the sea. Near me she picks up her towel. Shakes it free of sand.

I want to thank her for letting me share this time with the two of them. But instead, I ask, "Is the water warm?"

"Very nice," she says.

 August 30

Lie in the sun with the child in your flesh shining like a jewel. Dream and sing, pagan, wise, in your vitals. Stand still like a fat budding tree, like a stalk of corn athrob and aglisten in the heat. Lie like a mare panting with the dancing feet of colts against her sides. Sleep at night as the spring earth. Walk heavily as a wheat stalk at its full time bending towards the earth waiting for the reaper. Let your life swell downward so you become like a vase, a vessel. Let the unknown child knock and knock against you and rise like a dolphin within.

• • • Meridel Le Sueur

When my daughter was pregnant, I read her these words by Meridel Le Sueur. We played with and talked about its images. Her child, my first grandchild, and I understand each other's dances. We sway in the wind with the same motion. As her mother and I do, and did even before she was born.

Now, a second grandchild is expected. It is my son's. The new life grows inside my daughter-in-law.

I will not read her verses. I don't know of her life in someone else's womb. Or the rhythm of birthing stories rising in her from her women's history.

Will I connect to this unknown child as stunningly as I did to the first? I pray so.

september...

The little things / That make life sweet / Are worth their weight in gold; / They can't be bought / At any price / And neither are they sold.
• • • Estelle Waite Hoover

"Can I keep him, Pa?" I'd beg. "Puleez, he followed me home."

"No," Pa would say. "We have a dog. You'll have to find that stray a home."

Years later, I'm still bringing home strays. This year it was a shaggy mixed breed that tried to wander into an elevator in the building where I worked as I stepped out, his worn collar missing a few brass studs, his tail wagging like a fast-set pendulum. I ran one of those "pay for the ad and you have your dog back" notices.

By the final day of the ad's run, when I was ready to let the dog go only if the owners could tell me the exact number of studs remaining on his collar, a woman called, describing him down to his pendulum tail, and said his name was Benjy.

She arrived in minutes, in an aging, beat-up car, four small faces pressed against its windows. "Hi, Benjy," she said, to the convulsing heap of fur leaping at her as she came into the house. Refusing the few crumpled bills she offered, I held the door open for her and Benjy, who tore down the walk to the car erupting with childish voices crying, "Benjy! We found you, Benjy!"

Tail doing double-time, tongue slurping at laughing faces, Benjy went home.

The thing that makes you exceptional, if you are at all, is inevitably that which must also make you lonely.

⋅ ⋅ ⋅ Lorraine Hansberry

I was teased during high school. I would like to believe my mother's theory that everyone was jealous of my beauty and intelligence. I know, looking back at pictures of myself, that this was probably not so. I was an awkward child, with a plain face, mismatched clothes, and glasses. I never played sports, not because I didn't enjoy them—but I was severely intimidated and honestly pretty horrible. Most children who didn't fit in threw themselves into their studies. Not me. I was an all-around mediocre kid, until I graduated from college. To everyone's surprise, I earned a degree in marketing. Through many years of watching and not participating, I learned what people like to talk about, what their favorite and least favorite foods, clothes, music, and hairstyles were.

I am very good at what I do. I have been promoted three times in the last two years and I am happy at my job. Some days I look at myself in the mirror, seeing beyond the black-framed, square-cut glasses I wear, the popular haircut, the tailored clothes. I miss the awkward child that I used to see. Conforming means accepting other conformers and befriending them. I still spend most nights alone because I don't believe in having useless conversations. I am alone a lot. I refuse to go to the movie theatre alone, I won't eat at a table for one. I will, however, be with myself and enjoy my thoughts. If I find a companion who is as much of an individual as I am, well then, I will reserve seats for two in a movie theatre. In the meantime, I will rejoice in being alive and celebrate my individuality.

Compassion for our parents is the true sign of maturity.
· · · Anais Nin

I hurry from the nursing home into the parking lot, moving between rows of cars that tears blur into rainbows, like multi-colored ribbon stretching the length of the lot. I brush at my eyes angrily, weary of their weeping.

Inwardly, I scream at the driver whose screeching, unheeding car sped through a stop sign throwing my mother into a world of wheelchairs, lifts, and immobility. Today as I cradled her head against me, she cried enough tears to fill an ocean. I had to tell her, the woman who birthed and nurtured me, that she wouldn't be going home again.

It's all so wrong. Children cry. Mothers comfort. I don't want this—this becoming nobody's child.

If one is lucky, a solitary fantasy can totally transform a million realities.

· · · Maya Angelou

It is the shiny figurine to the left of the ones that are made of plastic. It produces a glow that wraps its arms around me and won't let me go. I am in awe. Next to my grandmother's wedding ring this may be the prettiest thing, ever!

The fifteen-minute rule is in play. I ask before we enter the store, "What will the clock say when it is time to go?" Trembling with beads of cold trickling down my shoulder blade, I agonize: Did she say the small hand will be on the eight and the big on the four, or is it the other way? Today I cannot be late, we are going to a big meeting, the one she has been worried about. She bought new lipstick, a blue scarf, matching seashell earrings.

I wonder if I could hold it if I asked. I hold my baby sister and I never drop her.

Time stops, and then I see my mother, not in the store but across the street. I am running but standing still. The people around me blur into collages of red, black, and light yellow. The door to the store opens easily, the car door does not. The baby's nose runs, she coughs. My mom quietly says, "Put on your seat belt."

I become a fortune teller of her rage, and the burning I will feel on my cheek when she belts me one. I hide in my mind, thinking of the glossy ballroom dress the angelic porcelain woman is wearing. What will the skirt look like when she spins around on the ballroom floor? Just as the figurine's dance is ending the reddened fingers of my mother leave my cheek. I realize I barely felt the sting—the figurine is magic, she protected me. I know all I have to do is think of her and it won't hurt ever again.

Biology is the least of what makes someone a mother.

• • • Oprah Winfrey

I have no children of my own. That is, I didn't give birth to any children. But I teach junior high mathematics. I would not say that I have dozens of children each year, which times twenty-three years equals hundreds of children. Because most of the children, I simply teach. I teach them well. Most understand math better when they leave my class.

But there are other children whom I think of as mine, in part at least. The child I connect with when her mother dies, or is never home, or is drunk, or sick. Or the child who has an adolescent secret that she believes her mother can't handle.

There are maybe a dozen of those children. Many of them are adults now. As their biological, or foster, or adoptive parents did, I made mistakes. But for some reason, I was the right person to be in their lives when they needed mothering.

I visit with them often. They tell me things like I saved their lives, or changed them, or just, "I love you."

Of all the things I've done, I think being a mother has been the most important.

Communication is a continual balancing act, juggling the conflicting needs for intimacy and independence. To survive in the world, we have to act in concert with others, but to survive as ourselves, rather than simply as cogs in a wheel, we have to act alone.

• • • Deborah Tannen

Packing the contents of my life into bags, plopping them in the back of my father's truck, and leaving behind the first eighteen years of my life—I am headed to college this afternoon. The first in my family to decide to go beyond high school. My parents run their own business, quite successfully. All three of my brothers followed in their footsteps. I am headed to Howard University and will major in business and communications. This decision was hard on them. I left this letter in hopes of explaining my choice:

"Dear Mom and Dad,

As I leave today I think about all of the times we have shared together. I will bring the pillowcase Grandma sewed for me, the stuffed animal Dad bought me when I was born, the birthday cards from the boys, and the first book Mom ever gave me. That book is the reason I decided to go to college. I want as much knowledge as I can get, and I know that this university will help me succeed. But please know that as I walk out that door and eventually walk down the commencement carpet I will hold my diploma for you, Mom and Dad, the ones who taught me what it means to respect, to learn, to inquire. I am doing this for you and I love you."

They might not need me—yet they might—
I'll let my heart be just in sight— . . .
• • • Emily Dickinson

Amee stands in the doorway, suitcase in hand, and wails, "Mom, it's a jungle out there." And a generations-old swinging-door scenario plays out.

Like eaglets, kids grow restless to flap their wings in freedom. Unheeding of parental pleas and warnings, they leave home to launch life from their own pads. And return with fractured dreams.

The kids of the '60s took their beads and tie-dyes and headed for the hills of San Francisco and the wilds of Woodstock with just love and revolution to see them through. We moms of the time adjusted to the empty nest, spread out hobbies and televisions into the extra bedroom or two, only to reverse it all and open doors and hearts to the returning wayward.

The twenty-first-century trend is for kids to nest in longer than their parents did. But when they leave, experience warns about that empty space: Don't hurry to take over the closets or move in the den furniture.

Don't even change the sheets.

September 7

The weariest nights, the longest days, sooner or later must perforce come to an end.

• • • Baroness Orczy

Congratulations to me, congratulations to me, congratulations to me, congratulations to meeee. In the final semester of an extended college path, I know that no one could be happier for me than me. As a nursing student I have spent three full years rotating between remote, urban, big, small, friendly, not so friendly, uplifting, depressing, challenging, always challenging hospitals. I wrote eight boxes full of research papers, care plans, and essays. I wore a uniform that should now be put to rest, missing a button, losing hems, fading blue. I had to prove my capabilities to ten instructors, hundreds of patients, nurses and doctors. My bending bookcases are lined with millions of pages of scientific discoveries, psychological theories, research techniques all of which have served as pillows. I look at the students arriving for their first day of college and my accomplishment knocks me to the ground.

I had previously attended two colleges, but I struggled with my dad's cancer, my eating disorder, living in a different part of the country, and feeling overwhelmed with the world around me. I returned to this faraway college after a long battle with anorexia to prove to myself; my father, who has survived terminal cancer for six years; my family, who always knew I could do it; and the world, which has been demanding that I make a difference. As I plan my walk down the aisle to snatch my diploma, I feel justified in saying for the first time in my life, "I am damn proud of myself." I know that this is the beginning to a longer road of lifetime education, but for now I will relish the belief that I can accomplish anything.

⑥ **September 8**

"Uncritical" support is a contradiction in terms.

• • • Joanna Russ

I was afraid to call. Nancy often says she admires me because I love unconditionally. No one else has loved her that way.

Now I must shatter the myth. I love her. But she drives me crazy, too, with her chaotic lifestyle.

She's always late. Bill collectors call so often that she doesn't answer her phone. She barges rudely into people's lives and gives them unsolicited advice.

Today, I attended a lecture by a doctor who specializes in attention deficit disorder in adults. He said if you have a friend who never balances a checkbook, collects traffic tickets, loses jobs, and tells the world it is someone else's fault, call her. Tell her to get screened for ADD.

I dial. Of course she doesn't answer. I leave a message. I tell her what the doctor said. My knees are shaking when I hang up.

I don't hear from her for several days.

"I'm off the charts!" she says from her car phone.

"What?"

"I got screened for ADD and the guy says I am off the charts! I am not crazy or stupid. Gotta go! Love ya."

I answer the phone again, a minute later.

"Me again. You have saved my life. I mean it. You have saved my life."

My insides do a flip-flop. I am so glad she loves me unconditionally too.

I often wonder if there is a parallel between good works and long life.
• • • Barbara Stuhler

Arthritic fingers strum banjos. Kids three to thirteen spin, twirl, and stomp to the beat of the Dixie band in one corner of the crepe-paper-streamed, balloon-disguised community center gym. Straw hats tip and silvered heads bow to appreciative applause.

Across the room small faces tip upward to meet the brushes of beauty-for-a-buck face-painting artists, whose aging hands tremor now and then.

The annual senior-sponsored fundraising Carnival and Ice Cream Social is in full swing.

My granddaughter hums along to "Bye Bye Blackbird" and waits to drive me home from my shift of serving up hot dogs, cutting cake, and pouring coffee.

As we leave for the crowded parking lot, Shana says, "You know, scientists are exploring the theory that the good works nuns do are what keeps them living long with sharp minds to age 100 and more. Must be something to it. Some of these old-sters working here today have got to be near ninety. They're doing whatever it takes to keep the cash coming. I'd call that good work."

"My take on the nuns is that they don't marry or have chil-dren," I say. "But, then, most of us working today have hassled the stress of marriage and kids, and we're getting pretty old. If helping out means living longer, maybe we'll get a lot older."

In the car, Shana reaches over, pats my knee, and says, "Hope so."

No one has the right to sit down and feel hopeless.
There's too much work to do.

• • • Dorothy Day

The morning sun streams through the window wall of my living room, and I welcome a clear, fall day. I press the "on" button of the television and slip my Tai Chi tape into the VCR getting set to press "play" for my daily session.

I pick up a little of Bryant Gumbel's early-morning chat with America as a special news bulletin flash interrupts, and I see a plane fly into one of the New York World Trade Center towers. I shout the news of the "accident" to my husband who's brewing coffee in the kitchen.

Bryant's voice-over says it's possibly a small private plane. But then from the left side of the screen a second aircraft moves directly toward the second tower.

I hear myself shouting, "No! No!" heart pounding, soul praying that maybe this is television's answer to radio's Orson Welles's fake attack by aliens decades ago, a cruel joke. But reality takes hold with a hollow, drained feeling in my stomach that makes me reach for a chair and freeze there as the horror enters my home.

Sorrow takes over, then anger. Then I pray that a spark of hope remains in the ashes of our failure after World War II to build a peaceful world and that we find the strength to try again.

if I cud ever write a poem as beautiful
as u, little
2
Yr
Old
brotha
Poetry would go out of bizness.

• • • Sonia Sanchez

He was so handsome. Brown eyes and hair and perfect boyish features. He had a secret language. Only I could understand it. I adored him. Was sometimes mean to him, though. I don't know what that was about.

Now I am fifty-seven and he is fifty-five. He is still handsome. We speak a language that we both understand. I still adore him. Thank goodness, I'm not mean to him anymore.

If it's natural to kill, why do men have to go into training to learn how?
• • • Joan Baez

The trademark towers crumbled on Tuesday. I watched images spray across the screen of someone's loved ones screaming, through blurred vision of terror and disbelief, "She was 5 foot 4, she has blue eyes, long dark hair, she was wearing a plaid skirt with boots that tie, she has one silver ring on that we bought when we were in Mexico." Helpful or not to expose the loss of so many, including of the ones who were probably dying or fleeing their earthly bodies at the time of the reporting. I hope sensationalism did not overtake me, everyone watching. Tragedy. There is no comparable situation for the family members—a loss of one, hell, even a possible loss paralyzes.

I knew as I watched that another tragedy was brewing: war. "We" will want retaliation of a massive kind. To say differently would be saying the deaths today were in vain, right? Saturated in sadness, I separate the situation. People died: the thought constricts my chest until I recognize the lack of air and breathe again. War is starting.

I turn to anyone I can in appeal, "How can this make sense? I know terrorism is bad, but it cannot be this simple. This is all we hear: they are evil, we are the prey, but not for long, we will out-bomb, out-man, out-terror them. We will prevail." I do not like to label myself, but in the face of one blood-filled, missing-person day, I do not think I will survive a year of the same.

Normal day, let me be aware of the treasure you are. Let me learn from you, savor you, bless you before you depart. Let me not pass you by in quest of some rare and perfect tomorrow. Let me hold you while I may, for it will not always be so. One day I shall dig my nails into the earth, or bury my face in the pillow, or stretch myself taut, or raise my hands to the sky, and want more than all the world your return.

• • • Mary Jean Irion

My husband pulls up. Puts the key in the door. Flips through his mail. Gives me a peck on the lips.

"How was your day?"

"Busy. How was yours?"

"Fine."

Then we eat dinner in front of the TV. I curl up on the couch with a quilt. He stretches out in his old beige corduroy recliner. During commercials we talk about the adult kids and the week's events.

After the news we may or may not go to bed together to each other's familiar bodies. Either way is okay.

Routine and boredom.

Or comfort and contentment.

Tonight I choose to see the latter.

The earth rests, and remembers.

. . . Helen Hoover

BuzzzzzzzzzzBzzzzzzzzBzzzzzzzzBzzzzzzzBzzzzzzzzz. From sunrise to sunset the mammoth-toothed saws tear the trees apart. Take them down.

RoooooooarRoooooarRoooooar. Huge hungry trucks come to carry them away.

My neighbors. My ancestors.

They take the mutilated limbs to places I do not want to think of, where the slicing and the cutting will continue until the great ones become a deck for parties with brats and beer or a table to put a magazine on or a funny looking moose in a souvenir shop.

And there is nothing I can do about it. Not anymore. I wrote a few letters, but it didn't help.

So now it is me and the scarred land mourning.

Neither of us will forget.

I have at last got the little room I have wanted so long, and am very happy about it. It does me good to be alone.
· · · Louisa May Alcott

The slabs of silence initiators, a.k.a. walls, in this little blue-tinged room have given me a new place to breathe. I have been married only one year and realized that I have less personal space, not a startling revelation, I realize, but scary nonetheless. I never thought I needed time alone. I never even liked time alone, until its absence. I could worry about many other things than whether I spend fifteen minutes sitting behind a closed door, but what a perfect place to do that thinking. I think my husband is able to sit in a room with me and create those walls, at times in the middle of a conversation. This must be a chromosomal gift. I, however, needed to have the process of cleaning out a corner walk-in closet, and painting the walls, imagining with every brush stroke what I will do with my time there—write letters, stare out the window, reposition my chair to face the blooming apple tree across the street. When I was a girl I played in my closet. I had many other choices, but the comfort of setting up a home within my home relaxed me. My little blue room, a safe place to run away and think within. A place where I can draw on the walls, stare at the sun too long, mumble to myself, do sit-ups in the middle of the floor with just a bra on, a place I can exhale. My little room.

Don't stop! Keep at it! Don't give up! Not for a moment!

• • • Millicent Fenwick

I tee up the ball. Cautiously. I'm on my first golf outing since a bout of tendonitis, that affliction of the shoulder joint that makes fastening a bra, or reaching back to put your arm into a coat sleeve a ten, on a scale of zero to ten of pain measurement.

"Stop if it hurts," says my chiropractor friend, Jane, who's volunteered to come out with me. I keep my head down, stiffen the left arm, and swing with a follow-through.

"How'd it feel?" Jane asks.

"Like a lot of things these days, a little painful on the upswing," I answer. There it was—an honest assessment of life after seventy— life on the upswing. Those upswing years, moving past seventy, sneak up on you. You find yourself working to keep a positive attitude, because experts say you'll live longer and enjoy it more if you do.

You begin to eat more fiber. You exercise and watch the choles- terol level. In short, you do what most people do—spend a lot of time, energy, and money postponing the inevitable. It gets to be a second career and a reason why, beyond seventy, "life on the upswing" describes living with a lot more old-fashioned honesty than "the golden years." And it gives you a choice.

You can interpret "upswing" positively—like an upturn in the stock market—and count added years an asset. If you're of a realistic bent, you can see it as a tongue-in-cheek term for what life's about as the years pile up—a little painful—like golf with tendonitis.

September 17

Reader, I married him.

• • • Charlotte Brontë, *Jane Eyre*

This is the transition so many of my friends have made. They meet, fall in love, marry, start a family. When I met him, my parents were in one of their states of mayhem and I knew for sure I never wanted to get married. It just seemed messy. As time crept along and he kept up with me, it seemed apparent that committing myself to one person might be inevitable and potentially enjoyable. He is the first man to make me dinner, write me a song, fly me to the beach, teach me to ride a bike, and best of all, help me reach the level of sexual pleasure I thought I would never know.

I am not sure what I think of having the title "wife." I am even less sure about "mother." I do know that when we sleep at night I am in peace. When I am sad he silently recognizes my need for time and a cup of tea, a favorite book, and a chest to place my head on. When I am mad he giggles at the wrinkles in my face, and when I am furious he knows to wait an hour and start the conversation again. The future battles that everyone warns me about will present themselves, I have no doubt. I hope that all of our preparation in peaceful love will build enough bunkers for us to find solitude as we rely on sensitivity, consideration, and patience. I will marry this man in a year or maybe two and I know that I am making a decision that feels as good as my mom's home-made soup in my chilled winter stomach.

Marriages used to be for the having and growing of children; now there are few marriages that can withstand the pressure of those events.

• • • Erica Jong

I went to the dentist. I hadn't been there for two years. As he is laying instruments on the tray, I notice that the well-worn gold band on his finger has been replaced by a new shiny one. With a circle of diamonds.

Later, I sit in his office as he tells me about the inevitable crowns in my future. Behind him is a photo in a contemporary pewter frame. Of him and his bride, a lovely blonde woman in her early thirties. She wears a tulle gown. He wears a tux and a smile. Next to that photo is another of them in a hospital. She holds a newborn child. He holds her hand.

The next photo, in a traditional brass frame, is of three young men about college age. What is missing is the wooden framed photo I had seen there for years. Of him and a woman, about his age, standing with their arms around each other on the top of a mountain.

I wonder how she is doing.

The birth of a child is in many ways the end of a marriage—marriage including a child has to be reinvented.

• • • Susan Cheever

We've come through the birthing together, my baby girl and I, immersing me in a joy I'd never before known.

Wires carried the news to Dad at an army camp 3,000 miles away and brought his reply. Love words spill out to the person he knows—the one I was before this miracle.

Today he enters the hospital room swallowing its length in three long strides, arms outstretched, to where I sit in the hospital-required wheelchair waiting for an aide to wheel me and my miracle toward release into a sunny, brisk April day.

"Oh, you look so good. How I've missed you," he murmurs.

Baby on the bed wails her objections to the cap, sweater, and warm blanket in a heated room. Tiny arms and legs beat at the air like spinning wheels on an upturned cart.

I hear only my baby's cries and want only to comfort my child. This new person I've become pulls free of his embrace and says, "Don't you want to see the baby?"

There are lots of great things about not being married. But one of the worst is no one believes that.

• • • Stephanie Brush

I took a new path to the shoreline tonight. It wasn't out of my way, just uncarved. Along the way I took a deep breath, looked at the fading sky, and surrendered to the movement of my feet. I noticed couples on the pier having those infamous discussions with no words, only special communication. I was not envious.

Tonight I dreamed my dreams. I am newly single and am aware of my single presence. I am thinking of him tonight but not yearning. I feel like renewing my quirks tonight. I stepped on every crack in sight. I crossed the street outside of the crosswalk. (That used to drive him crazy.) I packed my pockets full of bubble gum and chewed one piece at a time, blowing as many bubbles as I could until the flavor ran out and then started all over again. I decided where to stand based on how the wind touched my cheek. I didn't stay for long, ten minutes tops; my feet were ready to go. On my way back I purposely got lost and found my way again. My actions are pure, not calculated and not out of spite. I love gum, I love walking, I like getting lost when time is irrelevant. Tonight I was with me and I liked it. I rediscovered my favorite things and took the time to just play.

Openly questioning the way the world works and challenging the power of the powerful is not an activity customarily rewarded.

• • • Dale Spender

We work for less than minimum wage. The tips we curtsy and flirt for are supposed to compensate.

We go home stinking from the smoke and liquor the rich leave behind. Our bodies ache from our necks to our ankles.

One night the owner pulls up in his Jaguar. Comes in for dinner. His waitress has three kids. Takes two buses to work.

She smiles and takes his order. As she walks away, her arm tips a water glass. Water spills on his suit sleeve.

When he leaves, he tells the manager to fire her.

I have been trying to organize a union. That night, we sit drinking leftover coffee. "You do it," they say.

The next day I do. The day after that they fire me for being late a month ago.

I am at the restaurant emptying my locker. "You go for it. They can't fire all of us," I say.

Eyes shift to the ground. "Maybe things aren't so bad. Thanks for trying. We'll miss you."

I leave, sorry I haven't changed this corner of the world. But glad that I can carry my self-respect home along with my old aprons.

Black people are nature, they possess the secret of joy.

• • • Mirella Ricciardi

Back in the 1940s, we called it the "colored church." The priest was white, the congregation black. They loved each other.

Every Tuesday evening I attended services in the small, white-frame structure with a cross at the top of a modest steeple. On Sundays I'd bring my baby daughter with me. A tall usher with a big smile and large hands would help me get her buggy up the several concrete stairs and through the wide-open doors.

"You can leave her right here with me. You go ahead in and take a seat," he'd say.

At offering time, the same large hands would pass the silver tray down the rows of seated people. If someone put a quarter in, those hands would give ten cents back.

War and racism had no presence here. Bodies swayed to joyous music. Voices praised the Lord. Love and joy embraced me, a young, white, lonely soldier's wife. In the colored church.

What a child does not know and does not want to know of race and color and class, he learns soon enough.

• • • Beryl Markham

She opens the door in answer to my knock, and I look into the face of a slim young woman wearing jeans and a T-shirt that declares, "Kids come first."

She invites me in and closes the door against the chilly spring air. I explain, "I'm Mitchell's grandmother. He's a school friend of your son's. He lives with me so he can go to a good school, but he goes home for the weekends." I search her face. Will she understand why I came? I tell her I can't stay and that I came because her boy invited Mitchell to his birthday party.

"Oh, Matt will be so disappointed if Mitchell can't come," she says. "Is it because the party's on a Saturday?" She sounds sincere, but it's hard to tell.

I tell her Saturday's fine, but it's the first party Mitchell has been asked to since he's in that school. He's the only black child there, and I need to be sure it's all right with her. I don't say the other reason—if she's going to be appalled at the idea of a black child in her house, better I should cope with her reaction than Mitchell.

She says she's so glad he can come. It sounds like she means it.

As I leave I tell her the Lord knows I'm old to be keeping up with an eight-year-old, and I think she's brave to take on a whole bunch of them. But I'm glad, too, that Mitchell will be among 'em.

Life is a death-defying experience.

• • • Edna Buchanan

Swimming in a pool filled with water blue as fancy toilet bowl water, thick as Grandma's Jell-O molds with the floating marshmallows and canned grapes, I move to the left and my body goes right, I swim toward the top and I sink deeper. I am suffocating. My arms force the water away like a knife slicing through chilled butter, many attempts but no results. I am exhausted, my lungs tighten, my mouth gasps like a fish out of water, only I am in, I am dying, hot on the inside, cold to the touch, this is the moment.

Every day I wake up to this dream. Having congestive heart failure, at night I count breaths instead of sheep and wonder if there will be a fifth or sixth tonight. The fluid in my body is consuming me.

I have a piece of metal in my chest that the doctors say will charge me whenever my heart stops. It's very inconspicuous, but be sure not to stand near a microwave, and at the airport bypass the X ray machine. How do I explain that a low-risk surgery is more scary than dying? How do I pass on the next twenty years with my children in a few sentences? How do I tell my husband that this could be our last night together?

I don't. I tell no one. I count on no one. I will be myself, continue teaching, renew my nursing license, paint, cook, meditate, why? Life. A challenge presented to me, medical terminology, my dialect. I tango with death, it is my stage. Sometimes he dips me to the ground and I fight to rise and spin one last time. This force is not beyond me, it is me, my heart, exhausted, slowing. It is mine and I remain in charge.

I saw this thing turn, like a flower, once picked, turning petals into bright knives in your hand. And it was so much desired, so lovely, that your fingers will not loosen, and you have only disbelief that this, of all you have ever known, should have the possibility of pain.

• • • Nadine Gordimer

I am picking dead blossoms off the rose bushes. "Do you think she really doesn't know?" I hear them asking, over and over. In the ladies' room, at my son's wedding reception, at the office.

I know. A woman knows almost immediately. Evidence just digs the knives in deeper. I've seen her and my husband together. At the grocery store, at a restaurant on one of the many nights he works late.

I smell her shampoo. Hear him quote her, pretending it is someone else.

For fifteen years, I've known.

I also hold him, need him.

Remember him in our wedding bed, cutting the umbilical cord, buying take-out when I burnt our Thanksgiving turkey. The beautiful flower of our love, so desired, so fragrant will not let me release it. Even in the midst of the unbelievable pain I cherish it.

I gather up the dead rose petals from the ground. Next year's buds may have more thorns, but they will bloom.

If you leave me, can I come, too?

• • • Cynthia Heimel

Fifteen years. I can't believe it when I measure it that way. A cup of coffee. It started with coffee. In a cup like the one sitting in my kitchen sink this morning. His cup with the residue of milk and grounds. What happened next and the next are a blur of tender moments, separations, clingings, habit, history.

I know her. I know she knows. I can't imagine the pain.

He never said that he didn't love her. That he would leave her. That he would leave me.

Not when I vomited all night and he held me. Not when he dug my car out of the ditch or brought me breakfast in bed. Or came to my mother's funeral.

I fear always that she will confront me. But more that he will go. Retire to Arizona with her after the kids are gone. Have a fear of hell when he gets terribly sick. And leave me.

I could go on. But only as a half. Together we have been a whole.

Who is to say where we will find our wholeness? None of us. Not one of us.

You may trod me in the very dirt. But still, like dust, I'll rise.

. . . Maya Angelou, "Still I Rise." *And Still I Rise* (1978)

They stand at the picture window in their dining room as the small red car that had been Nora's moves up the street and disappears at the bend in the road. Though she hasn't driven it for the last few years, I know that, to Nora, selling the car is a final surrender to her growing dependence on Margaret, her life's companion.

I try not to see their tears as Margaret gently turns the woman she loves away from the window to the table where I've put out tea and scones. Nora's gnarly fingers struggle to hold the cup I hand her, and I select a scone for her from the plate, which her failing eyes can't see. Margaret gently strokes her arm and says, "We still have my car."

I go to the kitchen to get sugar cubes and glance out at Nora's small garden. The showy floral display she joyfully dug, planted, and nurtured now boasts only a few flowers, two tomatoes, and one pepper plant.

With an aching hurt for my friend, from whom age has stolen so much, I return to the dining room to find Nora sitting tall as her small frame will let her. Even the curls in her graying hair seem to have a little added bounce. She smiles at me and says, "It's just a car. And at last, I won't have to take any more of those drivers' tests."

Spiritual love is a position of standing with one hand extended into the universe and one hand extended into the world, letting ourselves be a conduit for passing energy.

• • • Christina Baldwin

A rite of passage. The question is whether I will continue going to Mass with my father. I was sixteen and the youngest of three. My siblings declined to take the hand of God, and so had my mother. I realized that my place in the church was not the same I had at home.

I attended a liberal mass, so people like to believe. We sat in a gymnasium, sang peace songs, listened to intellectual speakers, participated in social justice movements. One Sunday the main Father left for the weekend, and we the children were at play in his absence. A woman broke the bread and performed the Eucharist duties. All hell broke loose. I sincerely thought we were going to have to bend down on the gym floor and beg for forgiveness—anyone with a vagina, on your knees!

That did not happen, but what did was my detachment from Catholicism. I believe it is more than okay to be gay, female, or gay and female. I believe in a God that believes in generosity of spirit, gut-wrenching truth, mandatory equality, and not spending millions of dollars on a roof. I am not meaning to insult, just report the feelings of a young woman who grew up with progressive ideas, who every Sunday regressed to 1900.

My spiritual life is what I make of it. I attend sushi bars of religion, sampling what is congruent with me, not out of arrogance, just with respect for all. I touch the earth, commit to healing through my touch, my love, my non-prejudiced beliefs. I did not discard the beauty of spirituality, just the house in which to celebrate it.

Laugh and the world laughs with you, snore and you sleep alone.
• • • Mrs. Patrick Campbell

There they go again. My friends, telling the horror stories about their husbands' snoring. They laugh and make fun. Say that they still sleep with the old men. They just try to get to sleep first and poke them in the ribs.

I don't tell them my dirty little secret. That my snoring shakes the house. I have tried medicines, nose clamps, losing weight. But nothing helps.

My husband hasn't slept with me for over a year. Ever since my snoring got worse, he tells me. A year ago I also had a mastectomy. Which he says has nothing to do with it. I'm not so sure.

The next time the subject comes up in my circle of good friends, I think I will be brave enough to share my secret. I know they will listen, as they always do. Perhaps their support will give me the courage to tell my husband that I don't like to sleep alone.

october...

All the intelligence and talent in the world can't make a singer. The voice is a wild thing. It can't be bred in captivity.

• • • Willa Cather

I am in the middle of a bear-inhabited, mosquito-infested, birch and oak and fir tree forest. I just used the outhouse and wrote a song about it.

Tomorrow I may see a doe and write a song about love, or a lake and write a song about grace, or who knows what.

All I know is that the melody that suits my voice is clearer here than in New York City.

I / fall into noisy abstraction, / cling to sound as if it were the last protection / against what I cannot name.

• • • Paula Gunn Allen

I took a risk at the age of twenty and traveled to Africa. Sometimes I wanted to turn back, I thought I had gone too far, but so many things made me want to stay. As I flip through the journal I brought, I recall one dusk in particular. This is what I wrote about lying in my grass bed, with my eyes closed:

When I close my eyes I sense vibrations. I sense the presence of children. Many playful spirits—anticipating the mutuality of elation.

I listen to their rapid chatter and the feet that clumsily follow. Occasionally I hear adults, brief and instructive, consoling, punitive.

I hear a complex medley of whistling birds, and an echo from the watchful canine who has the entire area on house arrest. The neighborhood screams watchfulness. I am in the city tonight, not the Africa most think of—it is urban, progressed, but still poor. There are distrusting guards and attentive watch animals on every corner. I wonder, are we protected here or imposed upon? Can the children feel safe playing behind gates, while being watched by guns? It is no different at home, just not as obvious.

It's later now, the sun cools instead of heating, shadows take their places, and the air creeps in through the cotton drapes. It smells of smoking leaves and burning rubbish.

A comfortable calm prevails. Slowly as time progresses, the chirping dissipates, children's screams are contained and confined to private walls, the muffled purr of cars ceases. Slowly I am cradled to sleep. In a foreign land with sounds familiar and abstract, with smells reminiscent yet potent, people speaking differently yet with the same tone, I am comforted and I fall asleep.

New labels change nothing.

. . . Josephine Lawrence

I pick up Jamie, my kindergarten granddaughter, from school. While I buckle her into her car seat, she says, "A clown visited school today. He said, 'Hello, rug rats.' I didn't think that was very nice."

"It's not a bad thing, honey. It's a fun name for little kids," I say.

"Oh, okay," she says and settles into *The Cat in the Hat;* and I thought how early on we start accepting the labels Madison Avenue folks come up with to target their markets.

We go from rug rat to senior citizen and a lot of others in between. I didn't pay much attention to labels, but I remember turning thirty was something of a shock. But forty was still a decade away. At fifty, I had the party, got the black roses and a membership in AARP [American Association of Retired Persons]. I laughed those off, but at sixty a little uneasiness set in.

I think that's when I began reading the obituaries and subtracting my age from everyone over eighty and figuring I could possibly have another two decades to be a PAL [Person with an Active Lifestyle]. After all, I had ten years before I'd be a golden-ager.

I stop the car in my daughter's driveway. Before I get my feet on the concrete, Jamie's out of the car seat and up the sidewalk, quick like a little rug rat.

Liquor is a nice substitute for facing adult life.

• • • Dorothy B. Hughes

I have worked in bars long enough to know the power of fermented grapes and grains. Groups of picky sophisticated ladies looking to meet a prince seem to almost inevitably find a generic version of him at closing time. I find that my lack of consumption conveniently becomes the topic of conversation while socializing at the bar. I attempt to scrounge an excuse for my lack of interest in alcohol. Many factors contribute—my health, my need for control, a family with "alcohol issues"—but mainly I just have no desire.

Instead I drink coffee. My self-appointed job as a little girl after dinner was to fix my dad's cup of Sanka. I so badly wanted to share the flavor he insisted on using to wash down a home-cooked meal. I trained myself to drink it with the aid of crystallized sweetness and dairy heaven, eventually developing a coffee palate. Now I crave the bean in the morning, when studying, in the afternoon, during a movie, in the winter. This pattern seems problematic if I substitute alcohol for my drink of choice. I know that caffeine makes me more likely to converse, boogie in front of strangers, skinny-dip, giggle, and paint. That is enough for me. I mean no disrespect to those who feel I am taking a moral stance. I really think I have found my fix and if you have, too, then we should go dancing.

Someone asked someone who was about my age: "How are you?" The answer was, "Fine, if you don't ask for details."

• • • Katharine Hepburn

Cards bring words of encouragement. Flowers brighten the house. Family and friends keep the phone ringing, and "You've got mail" singing out on my computer. To the question "How are you?" I give the Hepburn quote, "Fine, if you don't ask for details."

I carry reports from doctors to the world-famous Mayo Clinic in search of a finite answer to that question that I meet at every turn. As I journey into what are for me uncharted waters, the cards, flowers, e-mails, and phone calls buoy my spirits, billow my sails, and send me riding on waves of optimistic hope—knowing that family and friends really do want to know when they ask, "How are you?"

Time is always wanting to me, and I cannot meet with a single day when I am not hurried along, driven to my wits' end by urgent work, business to attend to, or some service to render.

• • • George Sand

Men do not understand what time wanting means.

It's not that my husband doesn't do things. He works. Helps some around the house. Mows the grass.

But I know when and where the kids go to school—what kind of wine our friends like—who is a vegetarian—who is not to be invited when who is invited—when his mother's birthday is— that she doesn't like flannel pajamas—what we eat every day— whose clothes are whose—if there is peanut butter in the jar— who the vet is—what tie he should wear—what a wok is. I buy the presents and wrap them, suggest we go out, order the tickets, buy the candles and lotion for after the play, work late because the next day there is an afternoon school soccer match, say no to a dinner meeting because it is the only night to shop for the prom dress.

He does thank me for keeping things going so well. But I am wanting his time so I can have some of my own.

A woman in love never takes advice.

• • • Rosamond Marshall

"I hope you know that he's a sports fanatic," my sister-in-law-to-be tells me as we walk into the bridal shop to choose her matron-of-honor dress.

I laugh and tell her, "Of course, I know he's a sports nut. But once we're married I'll charm him out of that. I plan to be the best game in town."

"Oh, ho," she says. "Don't count on it. The sports thing can get pretty serious. My neighbor, in the spring, slips her wedding ring over the rabbit ears on their TV and says, 'See you in October.' That's the end of sex for the baseball season."

"That's ugly," I say.

"True," she says. "But, you know my friend Kate? The one I shared an apartment with before I got married? Every year, she invites Eric and me to her house for a New Year's Day afternoon dinner. And every year, Eric crabs, 'Why do you tell her we'll come? That's football day.'

"We get there, and through the meal, he strains and stretches to see the television in the next room. Last year, with the gravy boat in his hand, he stretched so far that his chair tipped. He and the gravy spilled onto the carpet.

"We've probably had our last invitation. His mother warned me, but did I listen? No. So, my advice to you, dear one, is: check out just how much of a fanatic your boy is. Be sure you know the score before you get into the game."

I want to ask thee a solemn question. Did thee ever one single time have thy Bank book balance and thy own check book balance agree exactly? Do not tell, but I never did.

• • • Hannah Whitall Smith

This is my fifth call to the toll-free checking account line. This automated system tells me what I have spent and what checks have cleared—and I believe eats my money. I have not been well respected by the population of the world that thinks planning spending is a good idea. In my earlier days I spent sporadically, irresponsibly, and emotionally. I worked a lot. I spent a lot. I have nothing to show for that time.

Today, I am on a new plane. Due to my continuous habit of attending college, I find myself digging into my pocket and reluctantly pulling out a quarter for the meter and at times feeling at ease spending five dollars on soy nut butter. I like my system, and for now I think it is working. I do not have money I could be saving, only bills that aren't accruing interest that could be paid sooner.

I am engaged to a man who likes coming home and entering his purchases into a computer program to keep an electronic list of receipts. I have habits as well. I always keep receipts until the bunch gets too large in my wallet and throw them all out. I balance my check book by calling the toll-free bank number four times a day. I have plans for my future. I want to be able to give back to my parents, to own a home, to travel, to maybe have a family. I will see a financial planner when I am done with school. For now, I think my system of spending and checking, spending and checking is a responsible one, just not a recognized one.

There's no friend like someone who has known you since you were five.

• • • Anne Stevenson

Her hair is graying, worn short with fuzzy curls. Her skin is cameo cream and her small eyes twinkle.

We visit three times a year. She always initiates it. I am busy with career, traveling, saving the world.

Her world is already saved. She stays home. Makes it lovely. Watches out for her brothers. Loves her husband. Creates ceramics and needlework. The life she always wanted—safe, organized, ordinary. Different from her unkempt childhood. She was the parent while her single mother slept or waitressed the night shift.

We share forty-five-year-old stories of playing street ball and hopscotch. She was the sincere one in our little inner-city bunch. No stealing apples or game cheating for her.

She talks of her children and coping with her mother's death.

"Now it's your turn," she always says. Listens with those eyes as I go on about my family, philosophy, and social change.

She questions. No malice, never. Just love, old love.

We hug good-bye. I open my door and think, every time, "If I am very good in this life, maybe I can come back as her." Simple goodness.

Nothing is so horrifying as the possibility of existing simply because we do not know how to die.

• • • Madame de Stael

The ashes still retain their heat, and I my fear from the stories shared in our family circle. My mother stirs the ugahli holding a wooden spoon stained scarlet from her bleeding calluses. She tells stories that send monsters to my sleep who twist and turn my body making me sweat with fright. Being a clever woman, she knows to tell her daughters of the dangers of our world where most will do what it takes to feed their family.

There are plants in the bush that contain life-ending juices. I have been told that if I ever need to escape I can suck one of these plants and go away. I have heard of girls from school who have to marry old men and birth children from nights of rape and torture. My mother tells me the older women left by these child-stealers grow crops of the escaping plant. Women here have only each other, not the law, to govern their rights. I never knew why my friend stopped coming to school. Her sister found her in her bed with her child sleeping at her breast, her heart motionless. The leaves of the escape plant are dark and spotted with thorns at the base. The drops of blood left by the pierced finger of my friend remain on the leaves. I know now why my mother tells me stories. I know I have power in a world that tells me different. I know how to die.

No person has the right to rain on your dreams.

• • • Marian Wright Edelman

I am afraid to get out of the car. Not because the lightning is striking the very ground I have to walk over to get to the house. Or because hail the size of marbles is pounding down in the torrential rains. But because of the papers in my briefcase. Just a few papers with legal words meaning nothing to me except that they are taking everything from me. Everything except Caroline, whose happiness I am about to smash.

I run into the house. Soaked with rain and sadness I grab Caroline and sob. She knows. They are not going to allow us to keep our two children. Our beautiful seven- and nine-year-old daughters who have lived with us for almost their entire lives. Foster children, they called them. Difficult-to-place foster children. Our life, love, joy, we call them. We wanted to adopt them so we could be a real family, secure in the belief we always will be. Not looking over our shoulders to see if someone is coming to get them.

But now they are coming to get them. Because we dared ask to call them our children. Not "children no one else wants so you two are better than nobody" foster kids. Our kids. It will not be so, because we are not a real family. Two loving parents cannot both be women. Not forever. It isn't . . . what's the legal word for it? I don't care. It isn't fair.

Human history is work history. The heroes of the people are work heroes.
• • • Meridel Le Sueur

I press my little granddaughter's uniform with my heavy iron filled with red charcoal. Her mother died delivering her. But she has a good home.

I love her white blouse's school smell. She reads and writes. I do not. I place the clothes on top of her new backpack and shiny shoes.

My son comes home. Smelling of sweat and a couple of beers. I don't mind the beers. They don't bring meanness. Just snoring.

I take off his shirt and pour the water I have warmed into a plastic tub for his bath.

His muscles throb through his dark skin. His hands are tough from yielding a pickax for twelve hours. Breaking up the earth to lay a walkway for fat, old North Americans and young, thin Europeans to stroll on. I don't mind them. Their life is just different from mine.

He goes to bed. I see his profile in the dark. The same profile of those who built ancient cities from stones.

And I am proud.

Fortunately analysis is not the only way to resolve inner conflicts. Life itself still remains a very effective therapist.

• • • Karen Horney

Icy metal objects thrashing themselves into my cotton-shaped behind from when I was three until I was fifteen—I realize that actions have their consequences. I learned this again when I was arrested for driving while under the influence of happiness (I thought)—suicide and attempted murder (they thought). Speaking of which, I also spent time in jail for what was supposed to be accomplished but turned out to be attempted robbery.

I think that I have spent a third of my life talking to someone who tells me my actions are not congruent with a positive self-esteem. My problem (diagnosed as impulsiveness and post-traumatic stress disorder) is that these supposed analysts of the mind do not follow my feet. If they did they might be able to tell me why I jump into windows to steal things; why when I cannot stand I want to drive; why when I am hit by my boyfriend I fall to the floor and get right back into bed with him the same night. That really is the problem, I think: I need traveling docs.

I know that I am in danger at times. I can comprehend my need for change. But truly this life holds no potential for me unless I want it to. I do believe that I am worth something, although I don't expect it from others. I do believe that I could become the nurse I wanted to be as a child, although I make no steps toward that. I know that when I leave this jail I will be a mother to my children. I have enrolled in a program that literally follows me, they come to my home, they help me parent. The only thing I want to strike my children with is my wit and love; look at where the rest got me.

Life is change; growth is optional.

• • • Karen Kaiser Clark

The movers take the last of the furniture. My husband follows the van, driving the station wagon. The cleaners have gone, leaving the house in "move-in" condition, and I'm alone. I check the window locks in the room that once housed bunk beds for two boys as memories echo.

"Mom, make him stop throwing his stuff all over the place."

"He threw his socks up here, so I threw my book down there." So long ago.

I wipe a cloth over nonexistent dust on the windowsills of the room that held the ruffle-skirted vanity table, the French provincial femininity of an only daughter. So long ago. Then into the master bedroom, the place of lovemaking, of listening for the door to close behind dating teenagers, so sleep could come.

I lock, unlock, and lock the windows, rubbing my hands lightly over newly varnished wood, saying my lone good-bye to what was, after all, just a house—sold by owner—cleared to hold the memory-building lives of a new family.

"Are you coming?" My husband asks, his voice on the phone like the sound of a distant echo.

"Yes. I'm leaving now," I answer and turn my car—and my heart—toward the townhome we've bought, prepared to let it settle there.

My life now is only mine.

• • • Toby Talbot

It was traditional. The funeral. Old church songs. Incense. Not at all like me. But it was my mother's funeral, not mine.

My mother is—was—not like me.

She valued things—the neighbors' opinions, her garden, and me—always hoping I would turn over more of myself to her.

I don't have many possessions, am not ruffled by others. I can't grow a petunia.

We talked. We fought. We often had silences that filled the gulch between her demands and my resistance.

I sit here. Wearing a classic black dress that my mother would have approved of. Looking out at my flowerless yard, I wonder why I feel so alone.

A different kind of alone than I felt during the silences.

I look at the single red funeral rose I took from her casket. Cut from its mother bush, it wilts. I understand, a little. Three days ago, she was here. Linked to me by our history and a mother's intuitive connection. She took with her parts of my life that I can't remember or understand.

We had a life together. Mine. Now I am free from having to share it with her. And I am wilting.

You seldom listen and when you do you don't hear, and when you do hear you hear wrong, and even when you hear right you change it so fast that it's never the same.

• • • Marjorie Kellogg

I detest those telephone marketing surveys. They ask first about your income. If you have enough of that to be a potential buyer, they move to the age category. When you say you fit the over-sixty-five bracket, you hear, "Thank you very much for your time," and a dial tone in your ear.

Last night I answered the phone and heard a voice say, "We'll be doing hearing tests in your neighborhood this week. Could we set up a time with you?"

"What did you say?" I asked. The voice repeated the sales line, and I asked again, louder, "What did you say?" Again, the caller repeated, louder—I could hear that he was getting a little edgy.

Then I said, "No, I don't need my carpets cleaned," and politely added, "but thank you."

There is nothing more liberating than age.

• • •   Liz Carpenter

"Geez," says Elaine, pouring her morning-break coffee, "another week after another rotten weekend. Whoever put up that Garfield 'I hate Mondays' cartoon here in the coffee room has got it right.

"Weekends should begin on Monday. Third rainy weekend in a row. Look out there today. Weather's perfect. Here we are back to our cubicles."

"My neighbor in the apartment next to mine is retired," says Tammie. "I kid her about being old, and she gives me a bad time about getting through miserable Monday, moving past Tuesday, and inching up on 'hump day,' as she calls Wednesday.

"She says, once she got past Wednesday at work, she'd hope for bad weather on Thursday and Friday so that, by the law of averages, the weekend would be good. Now that she's retired, she says, it's so sweet to know that if the weekend is bad, she always has Monday."

Diseases have no eyes. They pick with a dizzy finger anyone, just anyone.

• • • Sandra Cisneros

I have no eyes. Disease gnawed at them. The attempted cure burned them out of my sockets when I was three.

The newspaper wants me to write a story. This has happened a few times. Someone hears that I play the guitar, or parasailed, and wants to feature me as courageous.

I agreed to another story, about now being in a wheelchair, blind, partially deaf, and still "inspirationally" teaching children how to read.

Thinking I will begin the article with a quote, I go to quotation books for words about blindness. "Illness, hair, myths, animals, sensitivity" are among the hundreds of topics on the thousands of pages that I peruse. Millions of words and no one has a thing to say about blindness.

At first, I am angry. Then, I struggle with depression. I often think that I am just feeling sorry for myself. But today, I see, in a startling way, that I am not included. No one wants to come close. Distancing themselves, they debate which is worse, deafness or blindness, tell me that they admire me. And then walk away.

Who wants to know I longed to see my mother's face, to know if the sound at my window is an intruder or a lovely shadowed branch? To know I pull myself from an infinite void to get on the mobility van, hoping I remember the lyrics of the love songs I sing at their wedding, wishing it was mine?

I am blind and unseen.

To fear is one thing. To let fear grab you by the tail and swing you around is another.

. . . Katherine Paterson, *Jacob Have I Loved*

The year is 1968. For weeks Amelia, a thirteen-year-old of African American and Hispanic descent, has come to my house as part of "Teen Power," an outside-of-the-classroom learning program for inner-city kids. I called her from the list of teenagers who had signed on. Her interests, she wrote, were planning menus, cooking, and setting a "proper table." We'd plan and shop together, and became good friends.

Amelia loved it when Penny, my boxer dog, rode along when I picked her up at her house in a predominantly black area. She'd wave at neighborhood kids we passed, making sure they saw her riding away with that big dog.

"No one will mess with us," she'd say.

On Wednesday, June 5, in Los Angeles, a white man shot Robert Kennedy. In the black district, still reeling from the loss of Martin Luther King Jr. in April, people gathered in the streets, blocking traffic, threatening violence, venting frustration and grief.

Early Saturday, Amelia called. "My mother says to tell you it's all right if you're afraid to come here today. We understand," she says, disappointment weighting her words.

"Amelia, little friend, I'll be there," I say.

"Bring Penny," she says.

Fear is a slinking cat I find / Beneath the lilacs of my mind.

• • • Sophie Tunnell

I peek out. Others would call this a beautiful day. To me it is like every other day—frightening. I pull the drapes wide open. "Progress," my therapist says.

Today I make my way to the grocery store. I quiver in line with the five items I put in my cart before fear grabbed me by its claws and started my heart racing toward survival.

I don't flee the store. My therapist will be so proud. I let the claws stick in me as I practice my breathing. I imagine what the checkout girl does when she isn't at work. Fear won't be fooled by this one. It hisses at me, "You, you who used to canoe, drive cross-country, run a bank. You will never be able to do what that sixteen-year-old clerk does."

My hands sweat. All motion slows. The clerk puts the milk, crackers, red and white blurred soup cans in the bag. It takes hours. My knees are floppy. I don't think my feet have enough strength to make the double glass doors open.

One foot, one foot. The hissing stops. One foot. The claws release. I see the house. I feel despondent because I am relieved to be almost home. Water sprays my grocery bag. Fear runs away to a dry place. "I'm sorry," my neighbor says. "I didn't see you. Had to water the flowers. You've been shopping. I can't walk that far since my surgery. But someday I will regain my strength."

One eye on my front porch where fear is perched, daring me to have a longer conversation, I answer, "I am sure you will."

Opening the door, I think, "Maybe I will too." Fear curls up under a bush waiting for me to try.

◎ **October 20**

I have not ceased being fearful, but I have ceased to let fear control me. I have accepted fear as part of my life—specifically the fear of change, the fear of the unknown; and I have gone ahead despite the pounding in my heart that says: Turn back, turn back, you'll die if you venture too far.

• • •   Erica Jong

My adventures are not always exotic. For me they entail breathing, feeling, sensing, commingling, trusting, and existing with something new. Call it adventurous, call it brave, call it scary, call it insane—whatever the label, adventure is living, a new type of living, a risk worth taking and my new world. As a little girl I would worry to a fault about going to Grandma and Grandpa's for a night. I packed three of everything, which in the end meant six of everything. I had a list of numbers to call in case of an emergency—only my parents and favorite teacher were on the list.

One day, my grandfather pulled me aside and said, "You know, for a little girl, you put a lot on your shoulders. Only place what you have the strength to carry. Let me take some of those things off and carry them for you. After all, I am bigger than you." The profoundness of this statement did not sink in until I looked at my daughter when she weighed only six pounds. Everyone said how little she was. To this day I hope she and the number of things she has to carry stay that way.

Adventure is a way for me to travel light in all senses of the word. I pack only a couple of things, sometimes two of things, but only underwear and chocolate bars, and instead of cleaning my room before I leave, I clean my mind, empty the trash to make room for the new. I think of my grandfather every time I travel; it really is the only way to live.

Good manners — the longer I live the more convinced I am of it —
are priceless insurance against failure and loneliness.

• • • Elsa Maxwell

"Our ability to control some behaviors lessens as we age," said the expert on aging on public radio. "We sweep aside inhibitions that help us manage life when we're younger, like sometimes eating food we don't particularly like, just to be polite."

"Interesting, but maybe debatable," I thought at the time.

His comment came back to me with a vengeance one Sunday, when I invited eight people ranging in age from seventy to eighty-eight over to watch the football game. My granddaughter helped serve lunch on trays in the family room.

She had to return several times to the kitchen for some kind of change. The sandwich was too large for someone. Someone didn't want chips on the tray. Someone didn't want the salad or maybe the dessert.

When we finally had the food adjusted to everyone's satisfaction, she turned to me and said, "Grandma, don't ever get old."

Without music I should wish to die.

. . . Edna St. Vincent Millay

I learned to play music with the same curiosity nine-month-old babies use to learn to swim. My father threw me into the violin, as parents toss their young into the pool, only his goal was not for me to have the spirit of music. As my fingers move I feel the crassness of his hand slowly massage my inner thigh. I press as hard as I can with the tips of my fingers; I saw away at the strings and at his ability to hurt me again.

Before I had this piece of wood to craft my solitude, he would pick me up from school and tell Mom that we were going to our favorite diner to get a malt. I would overhear him chuckling as he orally massacred me, again. He explained away the act of repetitively raping his daughter by telling her that I was quite clumsy, wouldn't do well with this violin thing because I spilled my vanilla shake on myself every time he took me out. The fact that she believed the stains on my clothes and the back seat of his car were milk reinforced my permanent silence. Music replaced my family as my father replaced me with my sister. A choice I did not intend. A choice for which the ultimate responsibility remains in the lap of the man who bought those frozen treats that now make me gag. I play and play, my memories do not fade but I know that this is my way out from his hands and obscene desires and my mother's denial. I will buy my sister a guitar. I hope it will buy her some time and ultimately her life.

Writing a journal means that facing your ocean you are afraid to swim across it, so you attempt to drink it drop by drop.

• • • George Sand

I write in my journal every day.

Friends often comment on my faithfulness. Out of kindness, guilt, judgment of my obsession. I don't care.

My journal teaches me not to care so much. When I feel I am drowning, I look back at a few days of journaling. What I often find is I am forgetting to go with the current.

I am fighting the waves by worrying about what doesn't matter.

I am gasping for breath, instead of breathing in and out, when I assume others are judging me or when I judge others.

I lose my rhythm, flailing when I go so fast. I don't notice love being handed to me in a word, gesture, flower, or sunset.

My journal is my best friend. It holds the tidbits until I want to evaluate. And then it leads me to a place where I can ride life's waves, gentle and roaring.

To one who has enjoyed the full life of any scene, of any hour, what thoughts can be recorded about it seem like the commas and semicolons in the paragraph — mere stops.

• • • Margaret Fuller

Writing about living is boring, a stop in the action, in the enjoyment or the pain of whatever scene I am living. I share the plot with others when I can't make sense out of it for myself. I savor it on my own if I wish. I love being the actress strutting across the stage of my own life. I don't want to make mere stops when I can use the time to start a book club, play with my grandchildren, take reggae dancing lessons, or even fully enjoy the way the light hits the birch trees. I have no need to replay it on paper and certainly not on a computer. I might miss the entire next act recording what was, rather than living what is.

We didn't have a relationship, we had a personality clash.

• • • Alice Molloy

I assume the reason she talks with the professorial voice and has an answer for everything except why she is not a well-adjusted person is lowered self-esteem. This seems generous to most. I firmly believe in the intrinsic goodness of people. This world challenges me enough without adding the horseshoe-throwing game of taunting. For this reason I do not give her the power to affect my ability to wake up and look at myself in the mirror, put on shoes, and walk out the door. I do wonder how she belittles someone without pondering her next comment or the effect her last ones had on the people around her. My theory is that this person (who behind closed doors eats herself out of oblivion) prides herself on being intellectual and cannot face her own worst enemy. I want an equitable friendship where no one needs a bullet-proof vest. I think that I can handle making her an acquaintance instead of pushing her for an intimacy that she screams with every insult she is not comfortable having. This is an awkward and very adult decision. Sometimes I wish I were a kid.

When humor goes, there goes civilization.

• • • Erma Bombeck

"I'm a rose from an old bouquet," says Jane, a silver-haired seventy-four-year-old running for the state Senate. When she smiles, laugh lines open and fold like a lady's handheld fan.

Since her age is a sidebar campaign issue, she tells her audience, "First off, let's talk about this age thing." She leans forward on the podium, rests her chin on her fisted hand, and says, "My opponent's twenty years younger than I am. Does that make me old? How do you know when you're old?" she asks.

Hands go up. Jane straightens and points to a woman in the third row.

"When younger people get up to let you have a seat on the bus," the woman says.

"That can do it," Jane says, and points to a raised hand in the back of the room.

"When happy hour is nap time," says a fifty-something woman. The group laughs and applauds. But an elderly listener in a front-row seat activates every laugh line in the room with "When you don't buy green bananas."

Whatever is not an energy source is an energy sink.

• • • Marge Piercy

How can I tell her I don't want to go to dinner? We have been friends for years. She is intelligent, talented, not boring.

But after I spend more than fifteen minutes with her I start to get tired. When the event is over, I am exhausted. Why?

I do know why, when I admit it. It is her negativity. Nothing is ever right in her life. Even when things are. She complains about her high-paying job, her large home, her mother, her kids, her lack of time, you name it. And she believes she can't be happy, that the universe won't let her.

I've tried to tell her, sometimes not so nicely, that her victim stance gets old.

I hurt her feelings and nothing changes. So usually, I pretend she is not sucking my energy into her void.

As I get older I have less energy. I want to use it to be with people I enjoy, for myself.

Will I see her anymore? Maybe not as often.

Pain is a new room in your house.

. . . Willa Gibbs

Mother of five, daughter of two, wife of one. My responsibilities overwhelm me into the form of a freshly baked lemon meringue pie, soft and light most days, murky and tangy others; it leaves the mouth tingling and watering for more. My hands dig faster and deeper than my mind has time to process. Thousands of makeshift projects fill the house.

My husband and I used to strap packs to our muscular shoulders and hike ourselves into small canyons and large messes but come out happy that we spotted a rare flower or drenched ourselves in a sun shower. I raise farm animals, meditate, perform shiatsu, counsel friends and family members on a daily basis, write poetry my mother calls a jambalaya of incorrect phrases, sew sketches into fabric, and create pillows, clothing, and bedspreads. I sell fruits and vegetables in the summer with my children whom I raise full-time. I do it all.

I live my life in pain. I have been in several car accidents. My discs are bulging and herniated in places. With the help of a TENS unit and drugs I take by mouth, by injection, and topically, I am able to function for an hour on bad days and five on a superb day. I want to fulfill the needs of my creative gang. I hurt so badly I am beyond crying. I weep rivers that flow into the hearts of my loved ones and I am afraid I am drowning them. Today I know all I can do is go to my room, tuck myself in, and know that the work I have done loving this family is strong enough to withstand this. I will get better, but only when my body says so. I will try to be patient, for me and my family.

I discovered I always have choices and sometimes it's only a choice of attitude.

• • • Judith M. Knowlton

I didn't expect to be shopping for winter boots ever again.

When I retired I was going to follow the sun wherever it led me, anywhere warm. No more battling early morning ice, snow, and traffic.

But a move to the Sunbelt wasn't in the cards for me, for a whole lot of reasons. So I'm learning to grow where I'm planted. It's either that or turn into a miserable old lady.

I plan to look at winter days like a book of blank checks. When the weather's bad, I'll fill them in with something I don't do when it's nice outdoors.

My closets will be neat. My reading current. My bridge game better, and I'll volunteer where my skills fit. When winter's over I'm out of blank checks and into the sun.

I find some boots, good for walking. And I buy them for those days when the air is crisp, the wind is still, and the sun shines down on winter, as good as it gets for me.

She had developed a passionate longing for making other people comfortable at her own expense. . . . She succeeded in getting other people into armchairs, without their knowing she was doing it, and with nothing left for herself but something small and spiky in a corner.

• • • Phyllis Bottome

When I started the new job, she greeted me with a smile that turned me into a melted morsel of chocolate inside a freshly baked homemade cookie. In one person she combines the encouragement of my mother, the reinforcement of a proud instructor, and the sincerity of my best friend. She teaches with every movement, spewing complicated words and implementing her talk at the same time. I would want her for my nurse if I were sick. I would want her for everyone I know.

I find it amazingly complicated that a person who is unwaveringly so competent can find enough time to condemn herself and compliment others simultaneously. Her hair (gorgeous and thick) she claims is difficult and frizzy. Her recent commitment to an exercise program (phenomenal) she calls inadequate. Her expertise (unquestioned) she says is substandard (as compared to the entire world).

I want to reprogram her saying, "It is okay to admit the goodness you work hard to submerge people in and accept some for yourself." I want her to know that I love the name Lucille and think she is a wonder, a rarity, and a gift. I want her to know that by condemning herself she is not fooling any of us into thinking she is anything less than a miracle, but she is losing happiness in not knowing that others around her love her and are proud to know her. Someday I will invent the machine that can do all of that. Until then, I tell her every day how much I enjoy her and appreciate her. It is all that I can do, for now.

november...

Poor people who had escaped from poverty as I had, feared it, hated it, and fled from it all their lives.

• • • Anzia Yezierska

My uncle and aunt leave in their new 1933 Nash. I mutter, "Someday I'll burn up a pile of ten dollar bills, and watch 'em all have heart attacks," because I dread Mama's reciting the litany of successes of her six siblings and wondering aloud why she ever married Papa, who's lost his job.

I hate the social worker's periodic search of closets and shelves for anything that would label us "welfare cheaters," like a detective looking for clues to hang a murderer.

I hate the guilt about "The Wires," our practice of plugging the wires into the meter on the kitchen wall to keep it from registering electricity use. I hate having to peek out before we unlock a door, so one of us five kids can climb up on a chair and jerk the wires, if the caller is the meter reader.

With the wires ducked into a drawer, the meter needles spinning, I hate when he says, "Meter man," and we chirp, "Come on in."

She believed in excess. How can you tell whether or not you have had enough until you've had a little too much?

• • • Jessamyn West

Good scotch, rosewood furniture, designer clothes, choice meat, Door County cherries, real gold bangles.

Loud high-pitched talk, exaggerated stories, stinging words, judgments.

Classical music, cruises, bridge, international literature, good prints of the masters, *Vogue* magazine.

Poverty, single motherhood, two suddenly dead husbands, mastectomy, two-room house, two kids, peanut butter suppers, fourteen-hour days, bluffs for promotions and status, private-school tuition, high school education, fear even terror, self-doubt, hidden prolific tears.

Third husband. Rich. Catering to her excess. But how can she stop it all now? How quickly it all could go away.

Welfare as we know it cannot be fixed. Tinkering with it for decades has accomplished little of value. Bureaucracies within bureaucracies have bloomed, mutations of a polluted society. Too many contradictory interests compete at the public trough in the name of poor people.

• • • Theresa Funiciello

I came to give a talk today at a local large university. I am just not willing to kiss up to anyone. I want to cut to the chase, tell the truth because no one else can, about what the system called welfare is doing to women. I am a recovering product of the manipulation. I carried my food stamps with a clenched fist and exposed soul. I spent endless days waiting in line to ask a simple question or fill out the twentieth form to ensure my insufficient supply of food money would be sent four days late as usual. I am not complaining about the system because I expect a better way of life to be provided to me—I am furious because they claim they do provide one. I can tell during my talk to these bright-eyed, well-nourished students that my fiery intransigence is frightening.

To tell you the truth, the general public *should* be scared. A person either breaks and falls, or stands up and shouts. I am here in this room to send the message that I am an organized, rageful woman smart enough to tell the truth and make a difference at the same time. I pick my targets, plan strategically, and the results have not put an end to welfare yet, but give it time. Please do not understate the power of a mother who was starved of equal treatment, respect, and food for her children for eight years. Here I am, world—here I am, politicians—here I am, voters—don't move an inch. I will come to you.

**I am woman, hear me roar / in numbers too big to ignore /
And I know too much to go back and pretend.**

• • • Helen Reddy

Army service over, he worked two jobs and finished college.
I was housewife and mother of two with an evening job. I was
sure his degree would take him into a career that would make
him the breadwinner and me the supportive wife and stay-at-
home mom. I saw it all as an achievable goal.

But a recall into the service, a third child, and a 1950s reces-
sion pushed the goal somewhere over the rainbow into the realm
of make-believe. The day a phone company rep called to say we
were behind in paying the phone bill and on the verge of losing
service, life changed.

"My husband handles the bills; I'll check with him," I said.

"That's not a reason for nonpayment. We expect payment by
the end of the week" was the terse reply.

My face flushed and my heart raced. Visions of childhood
poverty and the bill collectors my family kept moving to escape
zoomed into my mind's eye. I juggled the family funds and paid
the phone bill. Leaving behind the goal that became let's pretend, I stepped into the dual role of wage earner and homemaker,
my eye on success.

I must say I hate money, but it's the lack of it that I hate most.

• • • Katherine Mansfield

Sometimes I feel sorry for myself because I don't have money. I have nothing against money. I just don't have it. My parents didn't have it. My husband didn't have it.

Today is the day before payday. I have exactly $1.25. I will drop that in the bus slot tomorrow to get to work.

I clean offices. People do appreciate it. Most of them. Tomorrow when I get paid, I will go to a dollar movie with friends. I eat out sometimes. Look presentable.

I figure in a few years I will live on Social Security. That's what it's there for.

Lately, with the economy slipping, I've been feeling less sorry about myself and more sorry for people who own stocks, and whatever, that are dropping. Think of having all that money and then it disappears. Into nowhere. Not a car, or furniture, or a blouse to show for it.

At least I know what I have and what it will buy.

I feel sorry for them. Those poor rich people.

Let me go, let me go.

• • • Clara Barton

I left you long ago
Years,
Days,
Minutes, seconds ago.
You left me
with a decade.
Disillusioned.
Waiting patiently I begin thinking.
I arriving here with
You arriving there without.
There,
where only those
without skill travel,
without the insight to the soul,
in the absence of love, respect,
And the other I dos.
Beyond a yearning,
Far beyond tearful anguish
I tell no one
For no one will understand.
We drifted loosened
Broke.

I say to you as I finally swim away
My dear, my confidant
You will be the only
The one
who will know
what no one does,
the lonely,
the sad,
the me
that went away.

Someone has said that it requires less mental effort to condemn than to think.

• • • Emma Goldman

I called Cindy today to see if she could come in for a few days next week. She's worked in our office before, knows all our systems. I'll gladly pay a little extra for a sub like that. But what she told me drove the thought of pay right out of my mind. She said, "I'm so glad to hear you're still there. Someone from the office called who wanted me to support an official grievance about you."

She told me more, and an ugly picture emerged. The someone is Maureen, a young woman whom I trained on the job, her first one since college. About a year past training, she began striding through the office in the most arrogant and disdainful way. I asked her about it. She told me her objections to my management style and said everyone agreed with her.

I interviewed the staff, found no support for her complaints. I even attended a seminar on handling difficult employee situations. The consulting expert said, "Either dismiss this person or wall her off so she doesn't influence other staff. She won't change."

I gave her all the time she needed to find another job. I never thought she'd try to damage me professionally. Cindy's story shook me up, but once I calmed down I realized that at least Maureen didn't succeed. Maybe someday she'll learn that managing people is the toughest job anyone could take on.

I could never be lonely without a husband.

• • • Lillian Russell

I obsess. I am untidy. I am stubborn. I blurt out my mind.
   I am highly intelligent. I am kind. I analyze. I give. I care.
   I am old. I feel no age. I am pretty. I am wrinkled.
   I want love from my husband of thirty-five years. I don't
have it. He cannot tolerate exceptions to the norm.
   I am one.
   And I am lonely.

It is the most unhappy people who most fear change.

• • • Mignon McLaughlin

The doctor on the women's talk show is saying that the change of life opens us up to who we really are. Without the fluctuations in our bodies and moods that the monthly hormonal flow brings, we can be free.

My friends use medications, herbs, creams to delay the inevitable menopause. Why is it called a pause, I wonder. It is an end. An end to cramps, tampons, mood swings. Maybe that's what we're afraid of, no more excuses when we don't want to be happy, have sex, go swimming.

Now I'm thinking maybe it is also an end to pleasing others, avoiding risks, swallowing my own music. I am not afraid of that. It might take some practice but I'll learn again how to be myself, take chances, sing out loud.

I can hardly wait to have my next hot flash. It may be warming me up for the next act. In which I am the leading lady. And I am glorious.

Him that I love, I wish to be / Free— / Even from me.

• • • Anne Morrow Lindbergh

Backup plan, gone. One marriage, two people: one a stranger, one my now acquaintance once cherished one. This is not good. My heart rumbling through my broken chest—please do not touch it, me, or anything.

I epitomized the ideal person for you and obviously you could not handle that. I was too pretty. Too out there. Waaayy too confident. Beyond your level of comprehension. We were on separate planes. Our souls, like the Indian and Atlantic . . . no . . . no . . . like salt and fresh water. It would not have worked. I would have gotten bored. We would have split for sure. I realize my potential and you, well, you just simply are not it. This is so not important.

But please, please erase this from my memory bank. I did dream about you the past three years despite our lapse in communication. I do think of you every time I pass our exit on the freeway, or when I am on the freeway, or a road, breathing, swimming, traveling, sleeping, in pain, without feeling, eating. Obsessed? No, passionately struck by a drunken cupid. Good-bye to you. Obviously all of these feelings end with your new life bond. Maybe one phone call . . . ? No. It is over. And I feel so great!

Ring, ring—"Hello? Sara, guess what I found out!"

There is no death to those who perfectly love — only disappearance, which in time may be borne.

. . . Harriet Martineau

My sister's husband has died suddenly. I fly cross-country to get to her. She meets me at the airport and we drive to her home, where neighbors bring in food, speak in muted tones, come and go quietly.

His funeral is simple and solemn. We leave the chapel on the edge of the desert city he loved. I ride along to his home in his brother's car for a luncheon he won't host, where conversation and laughter are no longer muted, where the gathering's become a social event.

I look at my sister, whose eyes are fastened on the desert sands that lie unruffled by life and death, like a lake on a calm day when a tossed stone skims and skips, briefly creates lovely circling ripples, and then disappears into the watery depths, leaving the surface unchanged.

I feel her struggle for strength in the face of loss that, for her, unlike the tranquil surface of sand or water, leaves nothing unchanged.

**The thing that destroys a person / a people / is not the knowing /
but the knowing and not / doing.**

• • • Carolyn M. Rodgers

I think if I stretched my legs enough that maybe I could, just,
almost, not quite, touch the ceiling. My back numb, my butt
seems gone; my hair resembling a cardboard box. I realize the
luxury of wasted time. Seconds that I could fill with bettering
lives, even my own, gone. One day off and I am a goner or a cat.
Fill the time, fill it fill it fill it. There is a force outside of me that
drags the energy out of my blood and into the cushions of every
chair or seating surface. I call the reassuring team. They say,
"Stay in bed; it is your body's way of telling you you need rest."
This affirmation lasts through the second soap opera and leads
me to the Kleenex box or the floor for a set of abdominal crunches.

I know that exercise induces a chemical reaction that makes
me feel happy. I know that wasted time is a sin, an unused privi-
lege. I know I am prone to depression and inactivity exacerbates
this. I know that at this point I want to live differently. The mood
shifting, I plant my slippers on the unswept frigid floor, put on
clothes, and resume the work I call my life.

I dredge some days through the experiences of the weeks,
moments that flashed like a still frame of a movie. I want to capture the life, stop the air, but I cannot breathe. I resign myself
for another moment to appreciate the time I call wasted, to plug
myself into the wall and recharge, recapture the ability to reach
out, assist, change, learn. And then I leave the confinement of
inactivity again, and yell, "I am ready, world, here I am."

Seven years I watched the next-door lady stroll her empty mate.

• • • Louise Gluck

When I was in my twenties, my husband would come home from working in the steaming heat, building roads. He lifted the kids, both of them at once, up to his shoulders, and carried them around the house. We would have a big supper and many nights make wild, passionate love.

Somehow, I thought that Alzheimer's only ate up old professors. So everyone could shake their heads and say, "What a shame it is. A man with such a fine career spending his last years without his mind."

Now my husband never leaves home without me leading him by the hand. "Early onset," the doctors say. Sometimes I have to feed him or he won't eat. I bathe his shrinking muscles. My kids come over so I can go shopping or see friends. They think that he knows them, sometimes. I don't. But why tell them?

They are having enough trouble picking themselves up, watching their father who is gone.

There will be a time you bury me / Or I bury you in the garden.

. . . Tomioka Taeko

I watch him playing with the children born from her body. The body that is, but she no longer lives in. He hides in the basement, paying particular attention to his four-year-old son, who is running the halls in an attempt to make a new world record, spinning himself until he falls to the floor, and dashing away in a dizzied state of hysteria. No words that can correct the heart of a man who is one day from burying his thirty-three-year-old wife. She died after complications during her second pregnancy. No words can express the depth at which I want to open that casket and make her come alive. No words can tell the world how it feels to be one floor down from his companion who is now lying in a wooden box in a room filled with strangers eating Bundt cake. I watch his sister carry their four-month-old daughter. I think of the life of a daughter without a mother. I hear the echo of "unfair" bounding around the room. I agree today that for this little girl, for this little boy, the loss of the person who was meant to be there to pick out their favorite foods, to remember what bedtime story helped them fall asleep, to love them and hold them as mothers do, is completely unfair. I do not mean to think of myself at an event that has nothing to do with me. I walk away remembering that I carry pieces of myself that only I have the power to share. I hope I have told enough people that they make me laugh, that I love clunky shoes, that I want to sing if I come back in a different form. I take today as a reminder that I love where and who I am, and I will continue to do the same for others.

The power of radio is not that it speaks to millions, but that it speaks intimately and privately to each one of those millions.

● ● ● Hallie Flanagan

Paul Harvey, the newscaster says, has signed another contract to continue his syndicated radio program, "The Other Side of the Story."

I tear up a little at the news, because the voice of Paul Harvey resonates through time for me with his stories of war-front action during WWII that spoke to the heart of this army wife. And at war's end, he told me the "other side of the story," his clipped, distinct style announcing that my husband's unit, the 34th infantry division, victors in the Italian campaign, was coming home.

I went wild, ran to the phone, dialed family and friends, one call after another, and without introduction shouted, "The 34th is coming home! Paul Harvey said so!"

No "other side of the story" he ever tells can top that one— or even come close.

People used to say to my friend Mary, a quadriplegic, "You still have your mind." She would say, "I still have my body."

. . . Anne Finger

You know what? You have no idea how horrible, or not horrible, it is for me to sit in this chair with wheels, wearing my various tubes and braces waiting in line with you to get tickets to the Neil Diamond concert. You do not know if you should pity me. Maybe your life is much more pitiful. You don't know if I am courageous. I could be a miserable coward.

You have no idea what it is like for me to eat, go to the bathroom, or have sex—or if I even *have* sex.

So, please talk to the person next to you or to yourself, and quit spending time talking and thinking about my horrible fate, how pitiful I am, how courageous I am, or—for heaven's sake!—about my eating, bathroom, and sex habits.

It's really none of your business. I'm just here waiting for Neil Diamond tickets, like you.

Old age is fruition, not betrayal.

Helen Hayes

Jane and I step into the checkout line at the supermarket, near the magazine display, and Jane asks, "What ever happened to those *Golden Age* magazines we used to get? Not that I miss 'em. I resented the covers. Those people supposedly in their golden years with no warts or wrinkles—gorgeous hair and teeth. So-o-o perfect," she says. "Nobody I knew looked like that."

"They've changed the names to stuff like *New Age,* targeting the baby boomers to buy the cars, condos, and cruises in the ad," I answer. "I look at it this way: the hard-sell pressure's off, and turning eighty ain't all bad. After all, the older the fiddle the finer the tune." Shaking a bag open to put groceries in, I ask, "Is that an adage or a cliché I just used?"

"Whatever. You keep believing it," Jane says, taking the bag from my hands, and adds, "Let me do that. You fiddle in your purse and pay the lady."

I prefer you to make mistakes in kindness than work miracles in unkindness.

• • • Mother Teresa

It's 6 a.m. As I wait for my bus the usual morning thoughts run through my head: Did I remember to lock the door, feed the cat, put on underwear? And where is my second quarter for the bus? Although this scenario plays out every morning I feel my panic rising. I really can't find my quarter this time, panic turning to anger. As the bus approaches, I realize that like most days I am holding the second quarter in my other hand. I board the bus, notice the regulars' faces and take my usual spot two rows back from the driver on the right. In front of me sits a man in his thirties who is talking with the new mother. I can tell he has a developmental age of about twelve.

With every person departing the bus he waves good-bye and moves one seat closer to the driver. He has a brown tattered bag. He leans gently across the aisle toward me and offers me one of the lollipops he has in his bag. He looks prepared to give one to everyone. I am frazzled this morning and politely refuse his offer. His trusting face loses its childlike smile and he returns the sweets to his bag without uttering a word. I regret my decision.

Two weeks later I step on the bus, take my usual seat, and feel a tap on my shoulder. Before I can completely turn my head around, I see in the corner of my eye a hand holding a red lollipop. I smile, accept the treat, and say, "I'll have to bring you candy; you're always giving yours away."

He replies, "No, I like to, then I always have something to share." I learned through meeting him that taking is the other end of giving, and can be as simple as eating a lollipop.

I don't know why old problems can't just go away instead of growing legs.

• • • Gayle Vann

There are certain friends you can call and say, "I know that I've complained to you about this for twenty-two years. But that doesn't mean it's gone away."

These particular friends don't especially care what "it" is.

"Have you tried to change it?"

"Yes."

"Have you tried to ignore it?"

"Yes."

"Have you chased it with a stick?"

"Yes."

"Have you prayed about it?"

"Yes."

"Cursed about it?"

"Yes."

"Have you asked it to change?"

"Yes."

"Nothing does any good?"

"No."

"Well, then there's only one thing you can do and that's try to make friends with it. Because it isn't going anywhere." Old friends and old problems, sometimes I just have to love them both even when they don't seem helpful.

Sometimes I wonder if men and women really suit each other. Perhaps they should live next door and just visit now and then.

• • • Katharine Hepburn

Jenny and Beth, new at their jobs, started on the same day. They quickly became friends, lunching and shopping together. They decide to double-date with their husbands while the Irish dancers are in town.

Both men grumble, saying pretty much the same thing: "You two practically just met. And I don't know this guy. He doesn't know me. It's a bad idea."

I tell them about a workplace friend I had who wanted to have the friendship include our spouses: "I invited her and her husband to a party at my house. My husband liked her husband just fine but he found Sally's personality overwhelming. 'She even swears,' he said.

"'She doesn't swear,' I said, indignantly. 'She may use some strong slang.'

"It didn't bother me that her language got a little colorful. I saw her every day, looking chic and smart, holding her own as a department head in a male-dominated business. I admired her.

"With another friend, I tried again. We went out to dinner. This time her husband talked a lot about Wall Street, the market, and business. My husband would rather talk sports. Both nights were bad ideas."

"I think we better put this on hold for a while," says Beth.

With a deep sigh Jenny says, "Maybe someday, somebody will make a study and find out how many women have made workplace friendships work with the men in their lives. I'd sure like to know."

November 20

All things are dark to sorrow.

• • • Augusta J. Evans

She's a gentle woman whose cheeks dimple with her easy laugh. At age forty-eight she has reclaimed her life, which she had lost to the long-buried memories of her childhood, memories that arose abruptly in the phantom figure of a little girl no one else could see.

The child appeared at her door, and then left, down the walk with the father whom she had dreaded. She wanted to save this child, and couldn't. She grieved into deep, dark depression. She knew she must be insane; the little girl wasn't real. She slashed at herself, the flow of warm blood easing her tension and calming her anxiety.

After hours and hours of therapy, she left behind the sorrow of a lost childhood in which she had created the little girl, a product of denial. It was this child, not she, who trembled when the footsteps stopped at the bedroom door.

The child is gone now, having returned just long enough to lift the shadows of doubt and fear from a woman who tells her story so that others will find the courage to tell theirs. And in the telling find healing.

Fashion can be bought. Style one must possess.

• • • Edna Woolman Chase

I am quite a fashion misfit, which on most days makes me feel stylish. Certain women, though, have an innate quality that sets them apart. For instance, there is a woman who has worked at a restaurant in town for the last thirty years of her life. Her fiery red hair has always stayed the same color, shape, and size. Her eyelash extensions try to shake your hand if you get too close. She usually wears a sleek black dress, a shimmery scarf tied around her dainty neck, and silver stiletto heels. Her favorite pastime is gambling. Over her lifetime she has won over one million dollars and lost it, twice. She was married once, has one daughter, and dates frequently.

She once told me her secret for looking good: "Stand up straight, smile, wear a pinch of perfume and a dab of blush, and always, always bring hair spray."

Although she is quite beautiful and I can only imagine what she looked like when she was my age, I do not think her charm is derived from her looks. Everyone wants to have her as a friend. She is the Hollywood star of our small town. She cannot have dinner without being recognized, cannot attend a bingo game without having a free drink waiting for her, and has never paid for a single tank of gas in her life. This lady has style, and I believe she was born with it.

The new face I turn up to you no one else on earth has ever seen.

. . . Alice Walker

We stroll around the sun-sparkling pond. Our long cotton summer skirts fluttering in the breeze. We didn't know each other before this women's retreat weekend. But we liked each other instantly.

Her life sounds perfect. Her husband is a neurologist. Her two bright children have master's degrees and successful careers. She chairs charity balls.

"I've never told anyone about this. But I trust you," she says the last hour of the last day.

"Go ahead."

"I'm leaving my husband. That will probably ruin his reputation and shame the children."

"I'm listening."

"He beats me twice a week. He has for thirty years. One of his friends treats the cuts and bruises. I'm afraid that I'm being selfish."

I wrap my arm around her and draw her close. "No, no, no, my friend. You are not selfish."

She tucks her head into my shoulder and sobs, "Thank you."

O how short a time does it take to put an eternal end to a woman's liberty.

• • • Fanny Burney

I love to attend weddings. The flowers, the cake, the dresses, the idea. Watching the actual ceremony, I begin to sweat. The woman makes her way to the altar where her soon-to-be husband awaits. She is veiled, on her father's arm, released to the custody of her fiancé and finally at the end proclaimed Mrs. husband's name. Wow. A short walk down a marble floor in a pretty dress carrying gorgeous flowers, exchanges of words, a kiss, and suddenly you walk down the same marble missing your identity.

I love the concept of marriage, but I also love my name, the identity wrapped into it, the idea that I can love someone and be an individual at the same time. I wonder how it can be that I feel so different from other women. I am planning to be married, and yet I struggle with the idea. Is there a way to be unified with another and remain an individual? Should the tradition of marriage remain untouched, and other traditions be created if you want something different? All I know is that the cessation of autonomy on your wedding day seems like worse luck than a rain shower. Rice is fine, but please do not ask me to throw the idea of myself out as I commit to loving a person.

The clichés of a culture sometimes tell the deepest truths.

• • • Faith Popcorn

"Holidays are the hardest," my friend said. The cliché was an attempt to cheer me up the night before Thanksgiving.

Today, I awake at dawn. My feet touch the cold floor and I start mourning the loss of my family's past. I can see us carving huge ruby apples to hold the candles, stirring the cranberry bread, chopping walnuts and celery, saying thanks in candlelight:

"Thanks for my family."

"For Dad's health."

"For all of us being here, together."

Today, I go for a walk in the cold air. Only kitchen lights glow. Women, like the woman I used to be, stuff birds and whip cream. My grief cries, "It will never be the same again."

Face tight with frosted tear steaks, I head for home. A small apartment. The house was too big to keep after he died.

As I twist the key in the lock, I look for shelter in my good fortune. I can make a new life.

Reluctantly, I wipe away the last tear of the day. The one that lets me live in the past.

Bitterness had become a habit between them.

• • • Edna O'Brien

My sister calls me the sponge, because if there is an emotion in the air I intensify it by 100 and internalize it. The tension between my parents was the perfect consistency for me to absorb. I watched them mull over each other as if they were planting the world's most beautiful rose garden but could only choose one variety.

This time they split for sure. This time she realized all of the manipulations, all of the insincerity, all of the alienation from all of these years. Mom and I got an apartment together. In some circumstances being twenty-four and living with your mother is a regression, but it was our turn to leapfrog and, boy, did we leap. I was happy that my parents' marriage was coming to an end, but the process of coming to it broke me. There were phone calls about what piece of furniture he was entitled to because he purchased it when they lived in Cleveland. There were letters left on our stoop requesting a meeting. There were the phone calls "just to say hello" on the day of family get-togethers where he was not allowed. There were many, many nights she spent in a rageful cleaning frenzy, her weapon Windex, her target anything in sight, including the cat.

I thought this would do it; this would be the final stage for them. No one could cut through the slime left behind the snail of an extended separation. They did, and they're back together. To this day I wonder what it will be like for me when I get married. Will I have to die halfway through only to be happy to the end? I will do everything in my power to avoid that, including leaving all of the furniture behind.

I've looked at life from both sides now . . . It's life's illusions I recall.

· · · Joni Mitchell

We meet by chance at the coffee shop on a Sunday morning. I haven't seen her since I left the bowling league years ago. Then, we were young mothers, bowling in the late league from 9 to 11 p.m. While we waited for the 7 to 9 bowlers to clear the lanes, and between our turns to bowl, we talked about life and solved the world's problems every Friday night.

Today she introduces me to her husband, Howard, who pretty much ignores us while we reminisce and laugh about how wise we thought we were when we were thirty-something, how we were doing it all exactly right in bringing up our kids. They're grown now, those children who taught us more than we ever wanted to learn.

"We found out, didn't we? Kids are a tough job," she says, "but I'd do it all over again. I wanted kids, and raising my four was the best part of life for me. And if unmarried moms were as accepted then as they are now, I wouldn't have had to get married to have them."

I glance at Howard, who's engrossed in the Sunday paper the shop provides. For him, some conversations may be better ignored than listened to.

When my mother had to get dinner for eight she'd just make enough for sixteen and only serve half.

• • • Gracie Allen

The dinner was delicious. A perfect traditional holiday: turkey, dressing, gravy, sweet potatoes, along with a new twist or two. Tofu ravioli in winter squash sauce, wild greens with balsamic vinegar. Papaya and cheese plate for dessert, alongside the good old pumpkin pie.

There were twelve of us together. That was the best part. Adult children, parents, uncle, friend sharing what was new in our lives, along with a dollop of memories.

I had set the table. The kids did all of the cooking and serving.

As my daughter-in-law and son presented the turkey to the oohs and ahhs of the crowd, my daughter leaned over and asked, "How does it feel to have your place taken over?"

"Fine. Just fine." Because it never was about the food.

What one loves in childhood stays in the heart.

• • • Mary Jo Putney

Every day that the sun shines and the winds are calm I see her.
She pulls a farm-style child's wagon with its slatted, wooden
sides that give its cargo, three curious one- or two-year-olds,
something to hold onto. Just ahead two four-year-olds ride their
trikes.

I hear them as they round the corner—the wagon full of baby
chatter and fingers that point to objects in a world so new to
them—her voice calling out to the kids on trikes to stay close.

She's an aide working in child care at the community center.
One of the two trikers is her own, who shares her mom with
the others.

Each looks to her for hugs that soothe and reassure. When
faces in the wagon change or the child on the trike is new to me,
I hope wherever the others have gone that they'll know again
the gentle touch they get from this giving woman.

Though society denies her worth and meagerly compensates
her, I believe she realizes her true reward: the seed of love she
planted that psychologists affirm will grow in the deepest of
memories when it's needed most.

My father used to say, / Superior people never make long visits.

· · · Marianne Moore

I am a clingy person. Affectionate at best. I love to love, or even to hate, as long as someone else is occupying the same space with me for an extended period of time. Growing up I would stall at my grandparents; making a tenth trip to the bathroom and this time of course I really couldn't hold it. On the way home I would pretend to fall asleep in the car and wait until someone, usually my father carried me into the house and up the stairs and tucked me into my bed. At that point I woke up, eavesdropped on my parents' past-bedtime conversation in the kitchen, and raced down the stairs to sit with them. I love being with people, but not because I hate being alone; I just need the incentive. Once by myself I establish a pattern. Most of the time I spend on the phone, thinking, reading, planning to spend more time with people, exercising, studying, inviting people over.

I cannot say that this has not caused any problems in relationships, as you might have recognized. Going shopping? I am sure I can find something to look at. Going to get the oil changed? I wouldn't mind driving by the lake. Going to work? I will help you file. At times my loved ones reach their threshold, at which point I move on and cast my love in a different direction. They will get lonely. They always do. They will call. I will answer. I always do. I may not capture the title of "superior" due to the length of my visits but I am happy and loved.

december...

Sister, dear sister, come home and help me die.

• • • Jessamyn West

"You stole my hairbrush!"

"I did not."

"Did so."

"Did not!"

"Girls, knock it off!" says Mom, and a last, faint "did so" echoes down the hallway. Aah childhood! I reflect on our times together: why does animosity grow like the weeds in Ms. Caulphin's garden across the street? We spend hours upon hours trying to pull out the roots, only to find a new bud blooming the next morning.

I am twenty-eight years old, single, a graduate of law school, and dying of a disease not deserving of a name. I have to face the fact that I will not see twenty-nine, say the doctors. I say, no big tearful funeral, just plant a flower and pull a weed in my honor.

I feel sick now; the pain medication only numbs my thoughts, dries my tears, and blurs the inevitable. Today, of all days, I want my sister. The one person who so deeply loves me that she can't admit it. The person who hates me as hard as she loves me and the only person I want to hold my hand as I enter the new realm.

She arrives in my room with a stack of blankets, a flashlight, and our favorites: two lemonades and two chocolate chip cookies. No need for a hairbrush anymore; she brought my favorite childhood picture book instead. She shelters us in a blanket fort and says, "Are you ready to hear your bedtime story, little sis?"

Loneliness persisted like incessant rain.

• • • Ann Allen Shockley

The headline, bold and black, "109 go to war," makes front-page news. One hundred nine families are disrupting their lives. Someone they care about is leaving to fight terrorism in Afghanistan, reminiscent of the '50s when President Truman called up World War II veterans for the Korean "police action."

Most vets were in their mid- to late thirties, and news hawks dubbed it "an old man's war."

My husband's notice came in an unsealed legal-size, brown envelope. It read: "The following will report to Yokohama, Japan, within twenty-two days," followed by a mimeographed list of names. He would be leaving me, a house, a dog, and two kids behind.

I found child care for the kids and went to work. But for most people, the world turned as it always had, and indifference surrounded families like mine, as though the disruption of our lives was our own fault. Comments such as "Maybe if he wasn't an officer, he'd be here now" expressed attitudes that compounded loneliness.

Fifty years later, officially undeclared war on terrorism grabs our best and flings them onto another continent. Most people will live "life as usual" as the president urges. My heart chills for families like the 109 in the headline story, for whom life becomes lonely days of fear-filled waiting.

How lovely to think that no one need wait a moment, we can start now, start slowly changing the world.

• • • Anne Frank

I started in the Birthing Center last month. This is a new environment—I worked in oncology before. The change will allow me to work days instead of nights and maybe take a little stress off my shoulders. This is new to me; I am not as familiar with the clientele or the ways of the floor. I have many mother hens, other nurses and staff, who support and guide me. They are veterans to this place. They know where to find the hidden objects that no one else can find, the rules of conduct that are not found in any policy book, how to care and love each patient as your own.

At times I see them watching me. They have told me that I am idealistic. I am assured that is meant with the best intentions. I believe them. I do know that I try hard to meet the needs of the people I take care of and I am fresh, a greenie. I attended a college that taught me to be analytical, to question, to support, to put your feelings to the side, and by all means to protect your patient. I am lovingly challenged by this group of watchers. I know certain questions raise disputes, and that decisions I make are susceptible to a ruling committee decision. I honestly thank them for that. I appreciate that together we are clarifying why we are here. I do not know everything, which means I know nothing about everything. Every day I bring my naïve thoughts, my romantic ideas to work, and I know little by little we are constructively dancing to create a better place to birth children. I thank the wise and encourage the dreamers.

Mankind will endure when the world appreciates the logic of diversity.

• • • Indira Gandhi

The wedding was perfect, of course. The bride radiant, the groom rich, the vows perfect. Of course.

I go through the reception line to greet the parents. Our daughters went to school together. We've exchanged holiday cards. Kept in touch through mutual friends. "Congratulations," I say to the mother of the bride. "She certainly is a beautiful bride."

"Thank you. And how is your daughter? She was always so cute."

"She's in Chicago. Doing fine."

We blow bubbles at the newlyweds as they leave the church. I follow one to the sky. She's in Chicago. I think. Last time I heard. I have no idea how she's doing.

I release another bubble. "She was always so cute." That's what they all say. Cute when we went to Korea to get her. A trophy piece of diversity in our white suburb. Invited to birthday parties, "My little Korean friend," they called her. They came to her parties. Giving her white Barbies and books filled with white children. She took ballet lessons. "I didn't know Koreans did ballet," today's mother of the bride said then. "What a porcelain doll she is."

Another bubble soars. Then came the slams, about her eyes, hair, and skin. They always took me by surprise. The movies of Asian women as whores. The "I can take you to the movies but not home to my parents" line. Then drugs. Therapy. Tears, tears, tears.

I'm alone now. I blow one more bubble. Was it the taunts, the Barbies, the movies? Or was it my naïveté, believing it was logical to love a child and it would somehow all be okay?

Faced with unmeasurables, people steer their way by magic.

- - - Denise Scott Brown

I defy many statistics. I am thirty-three and twice divorced. I am 5 feet 5 inches and weigh 290 pounds. I lived in the projects as a child and now, well, actually, that one stayed the same. I drive a car that died fourteen years ago, along with my first child, Ray. Day is my nightmare. I work nights not because I have to, but because it is congruent with my elusive lifestyle.

Growing up I hated nothing more than the ridicule of children in my neighborhood. I would grab my lunch pail from my mother's sandpaper hands and push open the buckling screen door, which released a tired squeak, sounding an alarm. They knew when I was near. They waited for me and exhaled the pent-up anger they had stored since the night before when their mothers told them to use their inside voices during dinner. I wore mismatched plaids; my hair was blood orange; I had freckles the size of marbles; and I was not a light foot by nature, but I pretended I was invisible on the walk to school.

I have spent my life disappearing, aided by temporary magic: pills, drinks, and food. The difference between what I felt as a child and what I feel now as an adult is that today I am the bully that comes running as I walk out the door. No insult will outdo what I tell myself every day. I wear my cape, disappear into the night, this is my magic, this is where I hide, this is where I am safe.

One writes in order to feel.

. . . Muriel Rukeyser

I want to be a good writer. A really good writer. I wonder why that is. And then a day like today comes. The anxiety and busyness that usually cloud my psyche, inexplicably go on a holiday. And I can reach into myself. Into who I am. I am intrigued by the person I find and a bit afraid of her. I wonder if she is insightful or a little crazy. Either way, I do feel the world profoundly. I want to understand those feelings. I know no other way to do that, except to wrap words around them. It takes a good writer, a really good writer, to do that.

In memory each of us is an artist; each of us creates.

• • • Patricia Hampl

My granddaughter's friend showed me a memoir his grand-mother had written, a slim book titled *Bailing Twine & Burlap Sacks.* In it, she tells stories from her life on a Pennsylvania farm in the early 1940s.

She writes about thawing out the milking machine to make it work on cold winter mornings. She doesn't mention the frigid grayness of those winter dawns, but describes the beauty of white frost on the hay in the loft and in the cracks of barn walls.

She writes about simple pleasures such as her garden's spring awakenings and about regrets like the friendliness of a neighbor that she never quite returned. She sprinkles in vignettes about the many uses of bailing twine and burlap sack, twisted around a broken pump handle to make it work, holding the driver's door closed on a rusted-out Chevy, or stuffed with hay in barn wall cracks to keep out the cold, subtly teaching a lesson in survival.

She chooses not to write explicitly about the difficulties of farm life following the Great Depression but instead records, with the artistry of a poet, how she coped with the freezing mornings by looking for beauty, and with the lack of money to make repairs on buildings and equipment by appreciating what she had to work with.

She creates a memoir that shares with her family the hard-ships and joys of her time, without comparisons—"You never had it as hard as I did" or the "I walked three miles to school in snowstorms" tales—a model for those of us who hope to leave our written stories behind.

Life since thou hast left it, has been misery to me.

• • • Cleopatra, as quoted by Mrs. Jameson in *Memoirs of Celebrated Female Sovereigns*, 1831

It was yesterday that we were swinging from trees, eating peanut butter and banana sandwiches after swimming in the river. Even though she was eight years younger, I never felt the difference. When my parents said, "We are expecting a baby," I thought, "Whose?" My startlement soon changed to excitement and then an amazing love when I finally held her in my arms. She looked like a prune but was as sweet as fresh strawberries.

I remember the last day that I saw her. We packed a lunch, wore our bathing suits underneath our clothes, and headed out. I was the responsible one. I was to watch her and I did, I always had, I thought I was. She must have slipped on a rock. I had just plunged under the water and by the time my head reached the surface again, my little sister was gone. I don't tell my mom and dad but I am pretty sure someone took her and she is alive today. I can feel her yelling for me at night.

I have decided to become a police officer. I will find her, I know I will. I promised her that I would never love someone the way I loved her. I promised her that I would not have children until I found the one I lost. I felt like her mother and I let her die. I was only fourteen, but she was only six. I quilted her hair ribbons into my coverlet and I know now when I tuck myself into bed that at least part of her is there with me, safe and warm. I don't know how to move on without Jessica. My mom tells me that I was good to her and she knew I wouldn't purposely let anything happen, and I remember that when I sleep, I just have to keep remembering that again and again.

⊚ **December 8**

The stars are more than reflected on the water, they are doubled and tripled in brilliance as the wind stirs, as if combing them through its black hair.

• • • Marjorie Holmes

Her heart is filling with water—drowning her energy and her money. That is why she is not going on our annual winter trip to a tropical place. A place where her black hair, small features, and demure nature attract others and she shines. A place where at night, when the others are playing cards, afraid to be in the dark, she and I walk along the beach, looking at the stars. We don't say much. We just share their mystery.

Not this year. Too many bills. Not enough oxygen.

As I kiss her good-bye, she gives me an envelope, which I hastily put in my purse.

A few nights later, I am walking the beach alone. I reach into my purse to get a tissue to remove the speck that is making me cry.

I find her note. Written on plain paper in her simple hand it says, "Tonight, when I look at the stars, I will be thinking of you."

For the homeless always wither like flowers.

. . . Nelly Sachs

A gust of wind swirls in with her as she enters the free store where I volunteer on Saturdays. It's cold, and she's wearing half-laced Adidas, no stockings, and a short-sleeved jersey dress.

Nervously, she finger-combs her short, dark hair and glances watchfully at the dented, older car she's parked on the street with all her possessions and her baby in it. She asks me if the store helps with money as well as clothing. I tell her the store has no money.

She says she couldn't pay the rent, so she's lost her apartment. She offers her car registration as security for a $100 loan so she can drive to another state where her sister expects her.

I suggest a church that might lend funds. She says they give money for only one tank of gas. That's not enough. I ask about her baby. Her face softens into a small smile, and she says she has food certificates for him and warm clothes, and his father is going with them.

I suggest a shelter that may have emergency space until she can get money. "I don't want my baby in a shelter," she says. And adding, "Thanks," she leaves. The car pulls away from the curb; mother, father, and baby, seeking refuge, travel on.

May a star guide their way.

Her handshake ought not to be used except as a tourniquet.

• • • Margaret Halsey

Coming to this school meant leaving home for a year. My parents sent me away because I had bad behavior and even worse grades. They told me that if I did not finish school I might as well throw myself in the river with a rock attached to my ankle, a thought they should not have planted in my mind two days prior to shipping me off. As I got off the bus that first day, the sky literally turned black, the squirrels darted to the pines, and tumbleweeds took over the streets.

I saw her making her way, tree-trunk legs stuffed within knee-high leather boots, her claw hands holding a horsetail whip, and her protruding neck the size of a triple-decker meatball submarine. She was cuddly as a puppy, warm like my mom's pie—considering that my mom doesn't bake, and I am allergic to dogs. The only thing I hated more than school was the teachers, and she seemed to drool at the thought of my distaste. Her name was Bunny. I called her Peter, a more fitting rabbit's name.

Over the 365 days, one hour, and twelve minutes, I learned to fear her more than school. I avoided her by running to the library or the chemistry lab or the track or the math center. I found refuge in my thoughts. I ate well. I exercised. I knew the enemy of my life without education was Bunny. It felt cruel. It felt wrong. It was probably both of those things, but I graduated. I will never name anyone Bunny or Peter, but at least I can spell some other options.

To be alone is different, to be different is to be alone.

• • • Suzanne Gordon

I hide it pretty well. The way I look at the world. It's more sad than cynical. I don't revel in patriotism or believe it is okay to have a thousand dollar watch when people are starving. I do think racism and sexism still abound. That we are pawns of corporations who convince us we cannot be happy if we don't buy their stuff.

I try to live in both worlds. I eat at restaurants but order vegetarian. I will drink a $4 cup of coffee, if the beans come from farmers in Guatemala. I buy used clothes. But they are stylish. I go to protests. Then meet friends for a movie, perhaps a somewhat sexist one, and drinks.

As I grow older, I am spending more time alone with my thoughts and working on things that matter to me.

A sixties rebel who never grew up. That's what people think. Feel a little sorry for me that I am intense.

I did grow up—just differently than they did.

You can be wise from goodness and good from wisdom.
∙ ∙ ∙ Marie von Ebner-Eschenbach

I admire women over sixty-five. The ones wrapped in bright and subdued hues of wisdom and goodness. The woman who works part-time at the bakery. Or gives a lecture on writing. Or bounces a baby on her lap. Or rolls her chair through a nursing home.

They let things be. Are silently patient with the young fired-up ones who are so sure of themselves. Speak of their pasts, not constantly, but judiciously, and tenderly. Wear sleeveless dresses and shorts, even around young women who are all tight and smooth. Teach what is obvious to them without making others feel stupid. Laugh easily because there is so little that is truly serious. Are good to animals, children, men, and those older than they are.

When did they get this way? It wasn't overnight, I know. I am thinking that I should start practicing.

She was about as subtle as a see-through blouse.

• • • Helen Van Slyke

I walked past my old house today. I had to drive thirty miles, after flying more than 400 miles, but, yeah, I just nonchalantly walked past my old house today. I had birthdays one through eighteen there. I learned how to read, ride a bike, kiss, swim, drive, and ice-skate while living in this house. As I am snooping through the back yard, where various parts of my old childhood pets are scattered, I see a familiar face staring at me through the slots of the fence.

I remember the eyes. Eunice hated children. She was the one who put up the fence to keep us out. The older I get the more I revel in the humor of people who are bold enough to block out neighbor children with a ten-foot fence. For a second when I saw her peeking through the fence I reverted to my ten-year-old self. I remember how once I wanted to pick a flower for my mom. Eunice had gorgeous flowers. My brother kept guard as I crawled through the grass. I swear she must have been watching through her hand-stitched lace curtains because right before my scissors came in contact with the stem of the flower she had me by the ear lobe.

I was trespassing again this afternoon, and I hoped she wouldn't call the police. I could tell she was going to say something, and then I saw her aged fingers slip something through the fence. I reached my hand out and she passed me a perfect white rose and said, "I know you always liked these." She is a woman who would scream from the mountaintop when she was mad, and yet her sincerity was easy to miss—but not today, twenty years later, not today.

⊚ **December 14**

I shall die very young . . . maybe seventy, maybe eighty, maybe ninety. But I shall be very young.

• • • Jeanne Moreau

I have spent four quarters of life up to now. I'm 101. In my seventies I had many bad illnesses, which are now behind me. But usually, in your seventies you're expected to have retired to a house in Florida where you begin to have a little arthritis (they used to call it lumbago), and ask everybody to stop mumbling because you can't understand them.

Eighty's better. People are surprised you're still alive and that you can walk and talk sensibly. They want to carry your baggage and help you up the steps. They forgive you anything.

If you forget your name or anyone else's, your own telephone number, or how many grandchildren you have, or promise to be three places at the same time, you need only explain that you're eighty. So, I'd say life begins at eighty.

In my nineties I flew alone to California to visit family members each year. I even stepped into the cockpit a few times to visit with the pilots. Did I enjoy myself? You bet. And I await more adventures. I'll have to wait and see what's next in line for me.

Grandma . . . had a great deal to do with the education of her granddaughters. In general she not so much trained as just shed herself upon us.

• • • Bertha, *Grandma Called It Carnal*

Snip, big snip. Tussle hair. The young woman cutting my hair is taking chances. Hurrah! Usually I ask for a "now" cut. The young hairdresser nods, eyes my sagging chin, and gives me a safe cut. I leave looking like I'm wearing a helmet.

We start chatting. "I just don't get it," she says, waving her scissors. "Why do we have everything and some people don't have food?"

"Why do you wonder about such things?" I ask. "Most people don't."

"Oh, I don't know. Well, I think it's because my great-grand-mother watched National Geographic videos. The animals didn't interest me as much as the poor children I saw."

"Did she talk to you about the children?"

"No, she just liked the videos."

"Is she still alive?"

"Yes, but she had a stroke. She outlived three husbands. She square-danced until the stroke. 'Eat your dessert first so you really enjoy it,' she always said."

"Did she travel?"

"Not much. She had adventures where she was."

"I see where you get your spirit," I say.

"Oh, yeah. When I leave the nursing home, I still feel like the kid skipping away from her house with pockets full of cook-ies. She keeps you lively. There—finished. What do you think of your hair?"

"I love it. Thanks. And thank your great-grandmother, too."

When one loves in a certain way, even betrayals become unimportant.

• • • Colette

He's married to her best friend. At the Christmas party, he says, "You know, Ellie's a wonderful person, but I fantasize about you." She laughs and chalks up the remark to too much merry in his Christmas drink.

At the summer picnic, he puts his arm around her and asks where she got her beautiful tan. She says, "Ellie and I take the kids to the beach most afternoons. I guess the tan is one of the rewards," and slips free.

At his birthday party, he sits next to her and takes her hand in his while Ellie's busy setting out snacks. "Looks like Ellie could use some help," she says and moves away. She's guessing that he likes to test out his charms with these flirtations that go nowhere. At the end of the evening, he stands, his arm around his wife, saying his good-byes. She passes him to hug Ellie, who whispers, "Thanks for being you."

Years pass. Weeks after his death, Ellie brings her friend a book of poems with a flower pressed on a page where the verse reads:

I am with little well content,
and a little from thee sent
Is enough, with true intent,
to be steadfast, a friend.

"He would want you to have this," she says.

I'm not upset about my divorce. I'm only upset that I'm not a widow.

• • • Roseanne Barr

I summon everyone to call him the leech. I was not even fully, head-over-heels, knock-me-over in love with him. He did have healthy sperm; we did parent a child together.

Our divorce was like tequila shots without the liquor—salt and lime. If I analyze myself, which I shouldn't have to because nothing was my fault, I would say that at times I give him too much of my energy. I attempt to avoid him. There is no reason to have him in my life. He has never tossed a penny in the direction of his child or even attempted a visit. I still believe that no one deserves to be stalked, cheated on, emotionally sterilized. Not even me.

Now that it has been five years, I can admit that I did not marry my intellectual equal. A smart cookie like me should not get involved with a marshmallow. No substance, short-lasting sweetness, and cavity causing. The largest cavity is the absence of a father for my daughter and the hole in my self-esteem. I try every day not to give the silent power back to him. I try to live through the shame and anger and somehow teach my daughter that she is worth more than the moon.

A poverty that is universal may be cheerfully borne; it is an individual poverty that is painful and humiliating.
• • • Amelia E. Barr

The kids that will sing in the all-city high school Christmas choral program gather in the civic auditorium in the heart of the city. Those who go to public schools climb the stairs to fill the balcony.

When we are all in our places, the private-school singers, in their natty private-school uniforms, walk in cadence onto the main floor below—girls in pleated skirts and spotless white saddle shoes, boys in military dress from the military schools, the non-military boys in dark trousers, white shirts, dark ties, and blazers with pocket emblems.

I stand in the second-tier balcony in my county welfare issue clothes: practical, styleless oxfords, skirt, and blouse and at age thirteen decide that when I have kids, they'll march on the main floor.

And they did.

I need no takers / To leave me half empty / I'd rather be alone / Half full.

· · · Nikki Grimes

I soared down the grocery store aisles. I know saying, "I soared," sounds like an exaggeration. My husband accuses me of exaggerating.

"You *never* articulate the facts. You *always* exaggerate." Quite an exaggerator himself, don't you think?

Anyway, I know that my soul *flew* up and down those aisles. Why? Because I was shopping for my supper and supplies for my new apartment. I chose groceries without worrying if he would be pleased or if he had it for lunch.

As I turned the key to my new home, I realized that I felt ownership. Strange that in thirty-one years, I hadn't noticed feeling as if I were an intruder in the place I lived. Maybe that's part of why I turned from optimism to depression, slowly, unknowingly.

Well, that's over. He kept the car, the house, and the Christmas decorations. But I kept me.

I pour a half a glass of cranberry juice (chasing away the voice that would say, "That stuff is sour!"). I lift the glass. I see that it is more than half full—way more.

"Delicious," I say, savoring the sweetness.

Like many young women, I grew up believing that (1) physical ability wasn't very important, and (2) I didn't have any.

• • • Janice Kaplan

At twelve, the only thing in life I hated more than being alone was shellacking onto my body the rubber cement plaster-of-paris contraption called gym shorts that my fifth-grade phys. ed. instructor required. I had the hips of a thirty-year-old never tempted by exercise. There is no originality in the feeling of embarrassment and torment during grade school.

I ritualistically spent twenty minutes in the mirror the evening before horrid Tuesdays. I glared at my body as I practiced the sport assigned during the hour period. I asked my older sister to sew a replica pair of shorts so I could look at myself from all the angles my classmates might, just to verify my concerns of escaped bits of loose flesh. The shorts were hunter orange. I dreamed that, as deer seem oblivious, maybe my so-called peers were color-blind. This seemed possible due to their inability to see sadness, horror, desperate desire for acceptance, in the baggy eyes of a prepubescent girl who spent the previous night rotating between frenzied sit-ups and tearful breakdowns.

Monday night. The well-intentioned yet morbidly ineffective talks with my mother that never ended in any form of "yes, honey, you will never have to go ever again, you poor thing" left me enough time to create a sick day list of plausible symptoms.

Fifth grade ended, and now when I face a situation like the act of plastering on a pair of hideous shorts, I remember my sister, my mother, and the world of women who know why my gift to this universe is larger than my hips ever were.

People are only disappointing when one makes a wrong diagnosis.

• • • Charlotte Mew

We travel together to an international conference, she in her twenties, single; I in my fifties, married. We share a hotel room. On arrival we circle the schedule's must-attend events and take in the get-acquainted party.

We sidle through the crowded room to get a glass of wine. I'm noticing the name tags of people I should meet. She's working the room, not seeking the people she should talk to, but those who look interesting enough to make talk worthwhile.

She attends some sessions. I attend others. The evenings are our own. She spends hers with a young Australian man she's met.

The last night, after the usual excursion to a host city restaurant, I sleep until the wake-up call comes. Her bed remains undisturbed. I hope she shared the Australian's room, the least frightening thought I can come up with.

We meet at breakfast, pack together, gather our luggage, and leave. In the office, she talks about her trip to female co-workers in the hushed tones of girl talk and checks through the mail daily for about a month, when her eagerness finally wanes into disappointment, taking with it her joy.

From a generation away, I wish life's lessons were not so painful to learn.

What fresh hell is this?
• • • Dorothy Parker

I fled before I had my period. I held the invisible hand of my slain father as I cut through the tall grasses desperate to find a place where men do not carry guns, rape my sisters, eat our only food, burn the garden my mother was tending. I am desperate to scream of the horrors faced by my family. The only thing propelling my small feet through the leech-infested mud is the knowledge that people will welcome me as my family welcomed the fleeing boy I now call my brother. I kept a journal, from charcoal on bark and even sketched the faces of the men that penetrated my sister.

I find my way not without struggle but not without power either. I find many clean faces round with freedom. They are ghosts—they hear but cannot create change. I think they are afraid. That must be the reason they ignore my letters. They hold me as I cry and then invite me to restaurants where the only face matching mine is washing dishes and is invisible too.

I feel my mother and father here; they did not know that people lived like this. They told me that everyone farmed, everyone used kerosene to cook if they were fortunate; they told me everyone had bleeding blisters from the work they do; they told me that I would learn and go to school because we were blessed. They were wrong. I am alone in the universe that ignores me. I do my best to fit in by eating these rich foods, drinking the gold of crushed grapes, riding on wheels instead of walking with bare feet. I think that I will not stay long in this place. I think I will return to the war, to the place where I will surely be killed, but the only place I could live.

I'm the child of an alcoholic. I know about promises.

. . . Sandra Scoppettone, *I'll Be Leaving You Always*

I see two children and a man looking at the few trees left along the fence of the sales lot late Christmas Eve, and I'm back again waiting for Papa. The street lights are on when his old Chevy pulls up in front of the house. We kids grab our hats and coats and tumble over each other getting into the car.

At the tree lot, the man is stacking the few firs that didn't sell. In his boozy voice, Papa says, "Wait a minute now. I promised my kids a nice tree."

"It's pretty late. Not much left," the man says.

"How about these?" Papa asks, throwing one after another off the stack, stumbling backward as he holds up a tall, skinny specimen. "How about this one? Needs a filling out, but I can fix that. How much?

"Take it. Merry Christmas," the man says and helps tie the tree on the car. I whisper to my brother, "He'll saw it down, drill holes, and stick the branches in. Just like last year."

Christmas sleep comes to the rasps of a saw and whir of a drill and Mama serving notice: "This is the last time you get by with this. Don't promise what you won't do."

It's compassion that makes gods of us.

. . . Dorothy Gilman, *The Tightrope Walker*

I can only imagine him standing on the front steps, looking in at the idyllic scene in my living room—a tree aglow from floor to ceiling, children stepping over wrappings and boxes, searching out yet unopened gifts.

And I can only imagine him mustering his courage to move to the front door. I hear his first soft rap, but I decide it's part of the music on the stereo. When I hear it again, I open the door.

I hadn't seen or heard from my father in months, not since my parents separated again, in the pattern of together and not together I'd known all my life. Usually they managed "together" for Christmas. But this year my mother sits in my living room unwrapping gifts from children and grandchildren. My father stands at my door, nervously fingering the hat in his hand.

"Come in," I say and feel my mother's tense reaction from across the room. The kids shout, "Hi, Grandpa!" as though they expected him. Strange, but I can't feel anger at him as I know my mother expects me to. I see a man who loves family enough to risk their scorn and rejection to share Christmas with them.

I reach out to take his coat, clear paper and ribbon from a chair, and tell him to sit down and join us.

Nervous hands as if the fingers were dripping from them like icicles.

• • •   Fannie Hurst

My doctors tell me that the cloud will never lift, and similar
to a thunderstorm moving in the sky at dusk, it will only become
progressively darker. The checklist of things I attempt to spot
includes my hands, the picture of my baby niece on my night-
stand, the tree outside the window, and the color of the sky. I
realize that this list will disappear along with my sight in three
or four months, and at that time I will replace it with tangible
objects. I decide that learning Braille will be easier while I retain
the ability to see the dots. Hopefully my uncoordinated self will
picture the pattern. The average age of students in Braille 101
is six. I am thirty-three as of yesterday.

I wonder who I will become when the darkness prevails. I
sold my diamond engagement ring and replaced it with a beaded
loop. I let my hair grow long so it brushes my shoulders. I bought
silk and natural wool instead of polyester. I picked out black out-
fits in multiple sizes so they will match even when I am old and
probably larger. I copied the CDs that exhilarate me, depress me,
and soothe me into slumber. I want to memorize the faces of my
family, so I replaced all the art work with blown-up versions of
my favorite family events.

Some of my friends think I am obsessing. I invite the skeptics
to hold my rattling hand as I trace the paper in my Braille class
and tell me that planning my new world is insane. I am scared.
I am learning. I am faced with a challenge that I have to meet as
my heart still beats and my eyes go to sleep.

**Know the difference between success and fame. Success is
Mother Teresa. Fame is Madonna.**

• • • Erma Bombeck

"You've made such an impact. We want you to speak at the
national conference."

I feel like I am falling out of bed during a dream. "Let someone from the community speak. I don't do that kind of thing."

More pleading from the heads of organizations, professors,
colleagues. "But you bring so much insight, experience, research,
and vision."

I shake my head. "No."

I am back in my childhood neighborhood. I hoped I would
finish high school before I got married. I did. Then I did the
motherhood thing through the usual marital struggles, strep
throats, making food and love stretch our meager budget.

I finished college last year at forty-eight. Over the years I
worked in my community. Ran programs for unwed mothers
and child care centers. Once in a while I spoke up for our Latino
families at a school board meeting. Mostly, I was invisible and
comfortable.

Now I have a degree and a university wanted to have a diverse
staff so they hired me. To their amazement, and to mine, a little,
I am really competent. People respect me. And they are pushing. I
do not like to be on stage. I am an introvert, shy, humble, inclusive.

"I don't want to be famous. I just want healing and justice,"
I tell my daughter.

"Healing hurts, Mom," she says. "In your case it may mean
feeling the pain of ripping off the mask that keeps you invisible."

Maybe.

December 27 ◉

**What would happen if one woman told the truth about her life?
The world would split open.**

• • • Muriel Rukeyser

Split open,
spilling,
streams of truths,
that we women keep inside,
hide, embarrassed that we
are real
imperfect
deep
beyond common sense into intuition
incomprehensible truths
misunderstood
unless
we
step out of the shadows of
self-doubt
destruction
obedience
Subservience
image
fear
and hear
generations generations generations
circling
telling each other

 December 28

the truth
of our lives
the only lives we have
our own
should not be lost
wasted
die untold
we hold each other together
with the truth
and we are not

so

alone.

The charity that begins at home cannot rest there but draws one inexorably over the threshold and off the porch and down the street and so out and out and out into the world which becomes the home wherein charity begins until it becomes possible, in theory at least, to love the whole of creation with the same patience, affection, and amusement one first practiced, in between the pouts and the tantrums, with parents, siblings, spouse, and children.

• • • Nancy Mairs

To all young mothers
Who stay at home with their children
And spread love by giving time to volunteer work:
Keep the above quotation to read to those who ask,
"Why isn't it enough for you just to be home with your family?
Why are you involved with all of that volunteer stuff?"
Keep it to read to yourself on those days when you wonder
if you are stagnating at home.
It seems not.
Where else can you practice the patience, affection,
    and amusement
that make you so good
at loving the whole of creation?
I, an older mother, watch you caring for your children,
    giving to your family, setting aside your careers, and
    making a difference for people less fortunate than you.
I, an older mother, am pretty certain that you will be glad
    that you stayed home and gave your children the security
    they deserve at the same time that you taught them to share.
All is possible because you practice charity at home and
    over your thresholds.

 December 29

I can see everything from here: where I've been and what I've left behind; where I'm going and who I wish to be. I've named my fears and overcome a few, swallowed my regrets, focused on what to cherish and what to change, and tried to accept the things I cannot help.

• • • Letty Cottin Pogrebin

If I am very lucky, I have ten, twenty, thirty, with a miracle, forty years to live.

Or I may have today.

In either case I hope that each day I get closer to the top of the mountain where I can see the landscape of myself and my life spread out before me. And that I will like what I see.

**If my boundary stops here / I have daughters to draw new maps
on the world / they will draw the lines of my face / they will draw
with my gestures my voice / they will speak my words thinking they
have invented them / they will invent them / they will invent me /
I will be planted again and again / I will wake in the eyes of their
children's children / they will speak my words.**
• • • Ruth Whitman

As we end this book, we encourage you, mothers, daughters, grandmothers, aunts, sisters, great-grandmothers, women community leaders, friends, elder wise women, young wise women, all wise women to continue what women from always and everywhere have done.

Tell your stories to each other.

Tell the truth of your lives as the women in this book do.

And our descendents will know, for generations to come, how strong today's women are, that we have complex lives of pain, joy, integrity, fear, and love.

Wherever on the globe we live, whatever age we have accumulated, we sit bravely together, without boundaries. Through our shared words, gestures, plantings, drawings, voices, we will survive. And we will sing!

Peace.

Book Club Discussion Questions

The first seven questions refer to the book's general content. Questions eight through eleven explore the book's intergenerational aspects. You may choose to discuss one set of questions, both sets, or a combination of the two.

1. What do you think the quote that opens this book, "What would happen if one woman told the truth about her life? / The world would be split open" (Muriel Rukeyser) means?

2. What do you think is the value in women telling their stories to the world?

3. There are 366 stories in this book. Which one did you enjoy the most? Why?

4. Which story disturbed you the most? Why?

5. Are there any stories that reflect feelings or experiences you have had but have not revealed to others? What has kept you from sharing them?

6. Think about these lyrics to Ann Reed's song: "All the tales that tumble on through time. There's room enough in this world for mine." Which woman alive or dead do you think has the greatest story of all time? What similarities does your story have to hers?

7. Ann Reed also says, "I'm gonna tell my story. I'm gonna bring my life to light. Give it wings: let it all take flight." If there were no impediments, where would the story of your life take you?

8. How is the writing style of each author unique? What generational differences have affected the writing styles

of the three authors? In what ways are the writing styles of all three authors similar?

9. What common themes run through the writing of each generation? Why do you think those themes are central to all three generations? Are there topics which are unique to each generation? Why do you think this is so?

10. What are the differences and similarities with which each generation speaks of the following topics? (Choose several or all):
   a. The mother-daughter relationship
   b. Other family relationships
   c. Romantic relationships
   d. Work—domestic and career
   e. Self-esteem
   f. The wider world
   g. Health and illness
   h. Change
   i. Grief
   j. Happiness
   k. Marriage and divorce
   l. Friendship
   m. Conflict
   n. Views of women's roles
   o. Parenting

11. Imagine what it would be like to write a book with your mother, daughter, or grandmother. Talk about it.

This Year I Sing

• • • words and music by Ann Reed

The sun comes up
I stand, I breathe
No one will hear me if I will not speak
The legend of my life
Is locked inside

All the tales
That tumble on through time
There's room enough in this world for mine
This will be the last time
That I hide

This year I sing
I'm gonna tell my story
I'm gonna bring my life to light
Give it wings; let it all take flight
This year I sing

Joy and pain
Delight and fear
Walking the labyrinth that brought me here
Inching through the shadows
'Til it's clear

Voices from
Inside my bones
I hear them echoing
"You're not alone
Remember, oh remember
As you go"

Revealing what I've hidden inside
Means I'm leaving this invisible life

All the tales
That tumble on through time
There's room enough in this world for mine
This will be the last time
That I hide
This year I sing

This Year I Sing: My Story

This Year I Sing: My Story

About the Authors

Jean Steiner, Mary Steiner Whelan, and Shawn Whelan are a grandmother, mother, and daughter team from the Minneapolis/St. Paul area.

Jean Steiner has been involved in the fields of education, writing, and public relations. She was public information officer for the Minnesota House of Representatives for fifteen years. She worked as a college instructor and consultant. Jean has received many national awards for her professional work. A mother of three, grandmother, and great-grandmother, she continues to do freelance work and to write.

Mary Steiner Whelan's experience includes teaching, management, and editing. She is the owner of a-ha! communications and does speaking and training on educational, women's, and contemporary African issues. Mary is the author of *But They Spit, Scratch, and Swear! The Do's and Don'ts of Behavior Guidance with School-Age Children.* She is the mother of three and a grandmother.

Shawn Whelan recently graduated with her BSN from Alverno College in Milwaukee. She will be pursuing her nursing career in Minneapolis. She has worked at Columbia Birthing Center and St. Luke's Oncology in Milwaukee. Shawn helped establish and worked in health camps in Kenya and Uganda. She has a sister, a brother, and a niece.

Mary and Shawn are co-founders of Give Us Wings, a non-profit organization that works with Kenyan and Ugandan women, children, and men to overcome poverty. All three generations volunteer for the organization. Mary volunteers as director, Shawn as a board member, and Jean as a steering committee member.

Jean and Mary are co-authors of the popular book *For the Love of Children: Daily Affirmations for People Who Care for Children,* published by Redleaf Press.

The authors are available for keynotes, book readings, and workshops. Please contact them at a-ha! communications at 651-642-5116 or at steinerwhelan@aol.com.

About Ann Reed

Ann Reed is a singer, songwriter, composer, arranger, storyteller, playwright and screenwriter wanna-be, do-gooder, nice person, lifetime Girl Scout, friend to all park rangers.

Ann has captured every major Minnesota music award.

She has performed at world-renowned folk festivals including Bumbershoot and the Winnipeg Folk Festival. She's also gathered a wall full of plaques and trophies from Billboard Magazine and the National Association of Independent Recording Distributors, as well as from numerous nonprofit groups.

Ann donates 25 percent of her time to support nonprofit organizations that primarily benefit women and children.

Contact: www.AnnReed.com to purchase her CDs or for personal appearances.

About the Designer

Cathy Spengler is a freelance designer with a love of book design. After honing her skills during ten years at a Minneapolis corporate design firm, she established her own business in 1997. She has since pursued projects closer to her heart, including books, which allow her to employ a love of typography and clear communication.

About the Illustrator

Morgan Brooke has been an illustrator of children's and adult books for more than twenty years. Most of her work features bright colors, interesting patterns, and imaginative characters. Morgan especially enjoys working with authors to develop the strongest synergy between a book's words and visuals. Morgan lives in Minneapolis. E-mail her at: morgan@bitstream.net.

Index

Abuse January 26, February 10, April 26, July 19, July 23, August 20,
  September 4, October 23, November 21, November 23
Activism March 8, April 9, April 17, May 23, July 18
Achievement June 1, August 7, September 8, December 19,
  December 27
Affairs September 26, September 27
Aging January 2, January 27, February 5, February 17, March 9,
  March 23, April 22, September 17, October 22, October 27
Alcohol January 30, February 26, July 23, July 24, October 4
Anger May 29, July 16
Attitude October 30

Blindness October 18, December 26
Body image February 28, March 16, April 4, May 2, June 15, July 8,
  August 5, November 22, December 5, December 27
Brothers April 28

Cancer March 13, March 22, July 16
Change May 26, June 21, July 9, August 3, August 11, September 28,
  October 3, October 14, November 17
Children January 14, February 3, February 20, February 29,
  October 11
Comfort zone March 21, March 30, April 13, May 7, May 21, July 27,
  August 10, September 14, September 18
Community March 12, April 11, July 6
Conflict March 20, June 5, October 26, October 28
Coping June 12, October 10
Creativity March 4, April 27, July 30, July 31

Daughters May 8, June 4, June 7, June 8, June 9, August 14, August 26
Dark side January 28
Death, Dying March 17, April 2, June 13, June 16
Diversity January 7, January 31, July 3
Divorce/Separation January 17, January 18, March 14, August 25, September 19, November 26, December 18
Dreams March 1

Equality June 14, June 17, June 28
Exercise November 12
Expectations July 14

Fantasies June 22, November 10, December 17
Fathers February 2, June 11
Fear August 19, October 21, November 2
Feminism January 19, July 5
Finances October 8, November 5
Forgiveness May 22
Friendship February 1, February 11, April 6, April 14, April 15, June 3, June 20, August 21, October 9, November 19

Gender roles April 20, April 25, June 2, July 11
Gossip January 24
Grandparents/ing May 25, June 10, August 3, August 4, August 6, August 31, December 16
Grief/Loss January 22, February 13, March 19, April 21, August 13, September 3, November 6, November 11, November 14
Guilt April 24, May 3

Healing June 25
Health January 5, February 16, April 7, April 19, July 7, November 9
Holidays November 25, November 28, December 24, December 25
Humor February 8, May 6, June 26, June 27, July 29

Illness May 15, September 25, November 13, December 9
Incest July 15, July 28
Inclusiveness April 30, July 3, September 23, September 24,
    October 19, November 16, December 4
Independent women January 1, February 4, February 22, May 10,
    September 6, September 21, December 20
Individuality June 29, July 4, September 2
Intimacy January 6, February 27

Kindness February 7, March 10, March 11, November 18

Laughter March 27, May 16
Lies January 8
Loneliness November 8
Love February 14, February 15, February 21, July 1, October 7

Marriage March 15, March 26, May 4, June 6, July 14, August 1,
    August 2, November 27
Meditation January 4, March 25
Memories March 2, April 8, May 14, July 1, November 15,
    December 14
Mental illness May 15, June 30, October 13, October 20

Mindfulness May 15, June 30, October 13, October 20
Mothers May 9, August 23, August 24, October 15
Motherhood January 3, January 25, March 28, May 1, July 13, July 30,
   August 16, August 17, August 18, September 7, September 20

Nature April 16, September 15, October 1

Pain October 29
Pets January 13, March 5, April 5, September 1
Play July 2
Poverty January 2, February 23, March 18, March 24, March 29,
   May 31, June 23, June 24, July 17, November 1, November 3,
   November 4, December 10
Pregnancy February 9, August 30

Rape April 10
Reading January 12, April 12, June 18
Recovery July 8, July 19
Relationships January 16, March 7, April 29, May 5, May 12,
   November 30
Religion January 10, September 29
Risk August 12, September 9, September 22, October 2

Self-esteem April 23, May 19, May 27, October 31
Self-help January 29
Service March 3, September 10, December 29
Simplicity February 18, February 24, February 25, May 17,
   July 4, July 20

Sisterhood July 12
Sisters May 11, December 1
Solitude March 6, September 16
Sons April 18, August 28
Spirituality April 9, July 21
Stress May 28, August 8, August 9, August 27, October 6
Support September 30, October 5

Teachers September 5, November 29, December 11
Technology February 19, May 24, August 8
Tragedy September 11, September 13, December 2, December 8,
    December 23
Truth December 28, December 31

Weddings January 9, November 24
Wisdom December 13, December 22, December 30, May 18, May 30
Words January 15, February 9, February 12, August 15, August 22,
    December 3
Work January 11, July 3, October 12, October 17, November 7,
    November 20
Writing January 9, November 24

To Order Steiner-Whelan Books

Quantity	Title	Amount
_____	*This Year I Sing* By: Jean Steiner, Mary Steiner Whelan, Shawn Whelan $15.00	_____
_____	*But They Spit, Scratch, and Swear! The Do's and Don'ts of Behavior Guidance with School-Age Children* By: Mary Steiner Whelan $27.00	_____
_____	*For the Love of Children: Daily Affirmations for People Who Care for Children* By: Jean Steiner and Mary Steiner Whelan $10.00	_____

Subtotal _____

MN Residents Add 6.5% tax _____

Shipping and Handling _____

TOTAL _____

Your Address:

Name _____

Address _____

City/State/Zip _____

Phone _____ E-mail _____

Shipping Address *(if different from yours)*:

Name _____

Address _____

City/State/Zip _____

Shipping and Handling:
If your subtotal is up to $24, add $2.95; if $25–$49, add $3.95; if $50–$75, add $5.95; if above $76, add $7.95

Quantity discounts available.

Photocopy this form and send it with your check or money order to:
Mary Steiner Whelan, a-ha! communications,
3141 Dupont Ave. S., Minneapolis, MN 55408
Phone: 651-642-5116   E-mail: steinerwhelan@aol.com